D1608976

Termination in Psychotherapy

Termination in Psychotherapy

A PSYCHODYNAMIC MODEL OF PROCESSES AND OUTCOMES

Anthony S. Joyce
William E. Piper
John S. Ogrodniczuk
Robert H. Klein

AMERICAN PSYCHOLOGICAL ASSOCIATION
WASHINGTON, DC

Published by
American Psychological Association
750 First Street, NE
Washington, DC 20002
www.apa.org

To order
APA Order Department
P.O. Box 92984
Washington, DC 20090-2984
Tel: (800) 374-2721; Direct: (202) 336-5510
Fax: (202) 336-5502; TDD/TTY: (202) 336-6123
Online: www.apa.org/books/
E-mail: order@apa.org

In the U.K., Europe, Africa, and the Middle East, copies may be ordered from
American Psychological Association
3 Henrietta Street
Covent Garden, London
WC2E 8LU England

Typeset in Goudy by Stephen McDougal, Mechanicsville, MD

Printer: Maple–Vail Press, Binghamton, NY
Cover Designer: Berg Design, Albany, NY
Technical/Production Editor: Devon Bourexis

The opinions and statements published are the responsibility of the authors, and such opinions and statements do not necessarily represent the policies of the American Psychological Association.

Library of Congress Cataloging-in-Publication Data

Termination in psychotherapy : a psychodynamic model of processes and outcomes / by Anthony S. Joyce . . . [et al.]. — 1st ed.
    p. cm.
Includes bibliographical references and indexes.
ISBN-13: 978-1-59147-730-3
ISBN-10: 1-59147-730-1
1. Psychotherapy—Termination. 2. Psychotherapist and patient. I. Joyce, Anthony S.
II. American Psychological Association.
    [DNLM: 1. Psychotherapy—methods. 2. Professional-Patient Relations.
3. Treatment Outcome. WM 420 T319 2006]

RC489.T45T47 2006
616.89'14—dc22
                                           2006018642

British Library Cataloguing-in-Publication Data
A CIP record is available from the British Library.

Printed in the United States of America
First Edition

In memory of my parents Nora Evelyn and John Thomas. Though the actual endings recede into the past, your absence is felt each day.
—*Anthony S. Joyce*

To all of the patients in our research studies who endured the challenges of both psychotherapy and research to provide us with the insights needed to write this book.
—*William E. Piper*

To Jennifer, Mikayla, and Ethan—your unconditional love reminds me of what is most important in life.
—*John S. Ogrodniczuk*

To Serena and Sasha
—*Robert H. Klein*

CONTENTS

PREFACE

Our interest in writing a book on the termination of psychotherapy was stimulated by our clinical experiences and research collaborations. As clinicians, we have each occasionally experienced uncertainty about the "correct" way to go about concluding a psychotherapy case. This uncertainty may have been associated with the timing of the termination; that is, is this patient indeed ready to end therapy at this particular time? Alternatively, the uncertainty may have been associated with the termination process; that is, have all the pertinent issues been addressed sufficiently with this patient such that the ending of therapy will leave no loose ends? Beyond the patient's feelings in regard to the end of therapy, have I as the therapist been honest about addressing my own feelings and conflicts about the termination of this therapy? Furthermore, we have sometimes experienced lingering concerns after the conclusion of therapy, implying that additional work around the termination was needed. Seeking guidance on these issues from the literature has not always proven satisfactory. Relying on the process of supervision by a more experienced colleague frequently led to terminations that felt only more or less successful. As clinicians, we felt a thorough examination of the subject of termination would prove instructive for our own practice as well as for the clinical work of colleagues.

Our research collaborations provided another impetus for this book. For three of us (Joyce, Piper, and Ogrodniczuk), short-term, time-limited forms of dynamically oriented psychotherapy have represented a focus for our research in both individual (e.g., Piper, Joyce, McCallum, Azim, & Ogrodniczuk, 2002) and group formats (e.g., Piper, McCallum, & Azim, 1992; Piper, Rosie, Azim, & Joyce, 1993) for over 20 years. Applications of time-limited approaches to treating specific patient problems and disorders have also represented a fertile ground for us, reflected by our contributions to clinical theory (e.g., Klein & Schermer, 2000; Piper et al., 1992). In the time-limited approaches to treatment, the date of termination is known from the outset, and the ending is addressed throughout the course of therapy. A requirement of contemporary psychotherapy treatment development and research is the elaboration of therapy manuals to specify the nature of the treatment provided to patients and to increase the probability of empirical replication or implementation in other clinical settings. In terms of developing therapy manuals or guidebooks for these time-limited forms of treatment, then, we were aware of the need to convey the importance of considering the termination throughout therapy and, particularly, in the closing phases of the treatment.

In our reviews of the literature for the purpose of developing therapy manuals, we were again struck by the relative scarcity of systematic examinations of termination phenomena. The volumes by Kramer (1990) and Kupers (1988) represent exceptional and important work in this regard. Both Kramer and Kupers emphasized clinical issues associated with the termination in the context of individual psychotherapy. Both authors took a psychodynamic perspective on termination. In fact, the psychoanalytic or psychodynamic perspective is predominant in the literature on termination; relatively speaking, the cognitive–behavioral and interpersonal therapy perspectives are not particularly well represented. We felt that a more comprehensive approach was possible by incorporating the findings of empirical research and providing indications for addressing the termination across different modalities (e.g., group therapy) and durations of psychotherapy. Although our own orientation is psychodynamic, the approaches to termination formulated from other orientations (i.e., cognitive–behavioral, interpersonal) are also examined in this book and represented in the model we present.

The psychotherapy research literature indicates that therapy manuals that strictly prescribe the therapist's behavior at different stages of therapy or with different patients can increase the probability of negative effects. That is, strong adherence to manuals that compromise the therapist's flexibility and creativity can adversely influence the therapy process and outcome (e.g., Henry, Strupp, Butler, Schact, & Binder, 1993). Similarly, a therapist's rigid or overzealous use of interventions that are key to a particular therapy approach can facilitate the emergence of vicious cycles of unproductive interaction during sessions (e.g., Piper, Azim, Joyce, & McCallum, 1991). To avoid these negative effects, we deliberately developed our therapy manuals to serve as general guidelines for the therapists who participated in our clinical trial studies of time-limited outpatient therapies. We also encouraged the therapists to retain their individual styles and to be as flexible and creative as needed. The general guidelines put forward in our manuals were supplemented by examination of actual cases presented in the seminars that were held for the duration of each research investigation.

We approached the issue of the termination of therapy in the manuals in a similar way, that is, in terms of general guidelines that each therapist could implement in his or her own way, given the particulars of the case in question. A number of these general guidelines were carried over into the termination phase model depicted in Figure 3.1 (see chap. 3) and explicated in this book.

A more specific impetus for writing a book on the termination of psychotherapy came out of our experiences with a necessary reorganization in our mental health service during the early 1990s. Because of fiscal constraints, the outpatient clinic was required to shift emphasis from long-term, open-ended therapy groups to closed groups conducted in a short-term format. We decided to convert three open-ended, long-term groups to time-limited groups, with a termination date 1 year hence. The six clinicians involved with these groups met regularly for supervision purposes, beginning prior to the announcement about the change and continuing on through the final sessions in each group. The therapy groups involved three distinct male–female cotherapist dyads. Two of us (Joyce and Piper) served as the male therapists in two of the cotherapist dyads; as the senior clinician, Piper also served as the leader of our peer supervision group. Over the year or so that we met, we articulated the experience of the termination from the clinician perspective and became more clear about the demands that the termination process can pose for the patients as the therapy sessions wind down toward a conclusion. For example, the therapists' guilt associated with announcing an end date for the group served as an initial impediment to examining the patients' reactions to the announcement. Furthermore, although some patients used the shortened time frame to accelerate their work in therapy, other patients were relieved to "escape" having to work on certain issues. These contrasting responses called for quite different strategies on the part of the therapists, often within the same sessions.

We were also struck by the regularity of the patterns in the process of the different therapy groups. These patterns were clearly associated with the termination and transcended characteristics of the distinct membership and cotherapist system within each group. For example, each group invariably had the same affective trajectory, moving from shock, to anger, through sadness, into an exploration of the ambivalent feelings associated with the impending loss, and culminating with a deeper sense of connection to the other members and the work that had been shared. In a similar fashion, perceptions of the therapists in each group evolved through the roles of fellow victim (i.e., of powerful administrators), insensitive abuser, and idealized healer to a more realistic depiction reflecting a greater sense of equity between group members and leaders. We published our experiences and ideas regarding these group phenomena (Joyce, Duncan, Duncan, Kipnes, & Piper, 1996).

Following this experience, we remained intrigued by two ideas: first, that the termination of psychotherapy could be described in terms of general principles capable of adaptation by the therapist to the context of a particular case, and, second, that the termination phase might comprise reliable and recognizable patterns (i.e., themes, affective experiences, and interactions) in the therapy process. These ideas provided the foundation for the current volume. As clinician–researchers, we additionally thought it would be critical to survey the literature and incorporate into our presentation the empirical findings in regard to the termination of psychotherapy. Our aim in deciding to write this book was, thus, twofold: first, to provide a comprehensive description of the termination phase that was psychodynamically based but flexible enough to apply to different therapy modalities and orientations, and, second, to identify areas regarding the termination of psychotherapy that deserved further empirical scrutiny.

We do not consider this volume to be a complete and static statement in regard to the termination of psychotherapy. Our hope is that the general model we present will serve as a useful framework for clinicians and researchers to think about the termination phase, the process that unfolds between patient and therapist during this phase, and the requisite tasks associated with bringing different therapy approaches to a close. We also expect that others will offer critiques of the model and further extend its development in areas that lie outside our expertise (e.g., family therapy). In short, the model we present in this book reflects an initial synthesis of the termination in psychotherapy, informed by both clinical experience and empirical study, that we are optimistic will undergo further evolution and refinement by the reader.

Termination in Psychotherapy

1

INTRODUCTION AND OVERVIEW

Dr. A[1] and his patient, Sue, had worked well together over the course of the 3-year psychotherapy. Sue had shown consistent progress in coming to terms with the traumatic experiences that had marked her early years and in developing an understanding of how those experiences had influenced her choice of and behavior in current relationships. In her weekly therapy sessions, Sue worked hard to reflect on her experience and make use of Dr. A's focus on recurring emotional themes in their therapeutic relationship. She highly valued the work she had done in her therapy with Dr. A. In turn, Dr. A had found himself looking forward to each session and pleased with the quality of engagement he had enjoyed with the patient. These personal evaluations had not, however, been communicated within the relationship. When Dr. A announced that the next therapy session would be their last together—on the basis of his view that Sue's goals for treatment had indeed been realized—he was unprepared for the feelings of shock, hurt, and anger that characterized her response. He became increasingly mystified when Sue did not attend what was to be their final therapy session or return his telephone calls regarding this uncharacteristic absence. Months later, Dr. A discovered that

---

[1]Some unique features of this case have been altered, masked, or deleted to conceal the identity of the participants. The essential features of the case are preserved to accurately reflect the therapy process.

Sue had initiated psychotherapy with a colleague, presenting with many of the same symptoms and concerns that had been central to the work they had done together. The abrupt and difficult ending of this treatment, and the apparent unraveling of the patient's gains, could be attributed to insufficient time and attention being paid to an appropriate termination of the psychotherapy.

Across clinicians, the termination is accorded varying degrees of emphasis as a critical phase in the psychotherapy endeavor. This is, in part, a function of the therapist's theoretical orientation: Therapists favoring an interpersonal or psychodynamic approach, for example, may place more emphasis on the final phase of treatment than those working from a cognitive–behavioral orientation. The variation in emphasis is also a function of the therapy focus for a given patient: The termination is less often addressed in treatments that highlight skills development, relative to treatments that place the examination of relational functioning or character in the foreground. Notwithstanding these variations, it is undoubtedly true that issues associated with termination are more or less evident in any psychotherapy. Whether the issues are manifest and dealt with directly by patient and therapist or remain latent and outside of the patient's awareness, they will likely be present at the close of every therapy relationship. An understanding of the potential impact of the termination should be part of the knowledge base of every competent therapist.

Clinical writings following Freud's development of psychoanalytic technique suggested that the termination represented a profound loss for the patient, with all of the attendant emotional upheaval that that experience might entail. The impact of the termination of therapy on the therapist, or vice versa, was rarely considered. The image of the termination process that emerges from the early clinical literature is one fraught with obstacles, volatile in terms of its effect on the overall outcome of treatment, and potentially perilous for patient and therapist alike. A more realistic appraisal of the termination of psychotherapy has emerged in the literature over the past 2 decades. This has been due to the greater popularity of briefer forms of therapy, in particular, and the movement toward integration of common therapeutic principles and eclecticism, in general. Certain broad principles in regard to the termination of therapy have been clarified:

- For the patient, the termination of psychotherapy can stimulate a resurgence of the issues and conflicts that were addressed in the treatment. The termination can also stimulate unresolved issues associated with loss and separation. This latter point is apparently as true for the therapist as it is the patient.
- If the termination can be managed appropriately and adequately by the therapist, it can reinforce the changes achieved by the patient; if not dealt with appropriately, a poor termination can undo the accomplishments of the therapy.

- The termination phase can serve as an opportunity for resolution of the issues in the patient–therapist relationship (e.g., understanding of transferential perceptions, dealing with anger or frustration about the ending, highlighting and internalizing the positive aspects of the collaboration).
- The termination phase can also provide an opportunity for a realistic appraisal of the tools available to the patient to maintain healthy functioning, following the end of therapy.

It is ironic that given the critical importance assigned to the ending of therapy by many authors, the actual proportion of the psychotherapy literature devoted to the demands and processes of the termination phase is small. Once again, the available literature varies by theoretical orientation. The majority is written from the psychoanalytic or psychodynamic perspective; by contrast, the proportion of the cognitive–behavioral or interpersonal therapy literature devoted to the ending of therapy is slight.

Some authors have suggested that the paucity of literature on this topic reflects defensiveness on the part of clinicians; that is, little attention is given to the phenomenon because of clinicians' own conflicts associated with the ending of therapy and the therapy relationship. It is generally accepted that stimulation of the therapist's own issues in regard to loss and separation is likely during the termination and that this has the potential of giving rise to detrimental effects on the overall outcome (see Martin & Schurtman, 1985; Viorst, 1982). For the latter reason, consultation and supervision, although important throughout therapy, are particularly important during the termination phase.

In this book, we describe and explicate a model of the termination phase that is applicable across distinct theoretical orientations of psychotherapy and modalities of treatment. The model is developed in the context of a general treatment, that is, moderate to longer term dynamically oriented individual psychotherapy. We have relied on psychodynamic concepts to develop the model largely because of the aforementioned preponderance of this perspective on the termination in the available literature. At the same time, we believe that the psychodynamic orientation, because it encompasses the full range of affective, cognitive, and behavioral responses of both patient and therapist to the end of therapy, can provide for a more comprehensive understanding of the termination process. The complete model may not of course generalize exactly to those approaches to therapy that are not psychodynamic in orientation. Nonetheless, we believe that the model outlines themes and tasks that are common across all therapy terminations. These themes and tasks may not always be manifest in the observable transaction between patient and therapist yet still have a profound influence on the process in the closing sessions. Consequently, our position is that the therapist should always consider the themes and tasks highlighted by the model presented in this book, whatever his or her orientation, as the end of therapy draws near.

Our initial presentation of the model is framed in terms of individual, dynamically oriented psychotherapy of moderate or longer duration. In the exposition, we also attend to variations associated with different approaches, that is, briefer forms of dynamically oriented therapy, supportive therapy of varying duration, and group therapy. As our expertise does not extend to those approaches, the discussion does not consider the termination in couples or family therapy. Our expectation is that readers with expertise in these forms of treatment would offer useful extensions to the model outlined in this volume.

Following our presentation of the termination phase model and discussion of the outcomes and clinical tasks associated with this phase of therapy, the focus shifts to factors associated with variations from the general model. We consider differences in approach to the termination across the predominant therapy orientations (e.g., interpersonal, cognitive–behavioral, supportive, experiential), variations in the termination associated with structural factors of the therapy (e.g., therapy duration, group composition), and variations associated with patient characteristics (e.g., interpersonal maturity, diagnostic category). The presentation concludes with discussions of unilaterally determined terminations, whether initiated by the patient or the therapist.

Despite the brevity of the literature, there have been a number of excellent examinations of the termination in the past 40 years. These include articles on theory and practice (Blum, 1989; Dewald, 1982; Garcia-Lawson & Lane, 1997; Quintana, 1993; Shane & Shane, 1984), compendiums of expert panels and clinician surveys (Firestein, 1982; Klein, 1996; panels of the *Journal of the American Psychoanalytic Association*: Firestein, 1969; Pfeffer, 1963; Robbins, 1975), and complete books devoted to the topic (Edelson, 1963; Kramer, 1990; Kupers, 1988). For the most part, these works have addressed specific aspects of the termination of therapy (e.g., the criteria for termination), have been primarily theoretical while neglecting clinical recommendations, or have focused on practical issues of drawing therapy to an end at the expense of a theoretical grounding. We have drawn freely from this literature to synthesize a conceptual model of the termination phase and to examine the processes and outcomes specific to the termination phase. Throughout the presentation, we have endeavored to incorporate material from both the clinical and empirical literatures on termination.

Our intent in this volume is twofold. First, we outline a comprehensive representation of what the termination phase is about; that is, the outcomes that are particular to this phase and distinct from the outcomes of treatment. Second, we develop an experience-near understanding of the therapy process that emerges during the termination phase, with attention to the tasks associated with each termination outcome and other practical considerations (e.g., examination of transference and countertransference). The termination outcomes and associated processes are represented in the termination phase model presented in chapter 3. This model of the termination has served to organize our thinking about the "how" of bringing psychotherapy to a close. We believe the model can also suggest areas for fruitful empirical study. Above all, we hope that our depiction of the tasks and activities of the termination process prove useful to practicing clinicians.

In chapter 2, we first consider the fundamental principles in regard to termination that can be drawn from the psychoanalytic literature and the literature on brief therapy approaches. On the basis of these principles, we define the outcomes of the termination phase; that is, the objectives to be realized within the ending phase of treatment. These are differentiated from the criteria for termination; that is, those indications on the part of the patient that a transition into the termination phase is appropriate and should be addressed. The termination phase model considers that three outcomes are specific to the ending of therapy: (a) reviewing and recapitulating the therapy gains and process, (b) resolving issues in the patient–therapist relationship, and (c) establishing preparedness for the maintenance of healthy functioning (Kramer, 1990).

Consideration is then given in chapter 3 to the processes that are associated with the termination phase. These follow directly from each of the three termination outcomes described in chapter 2. Therapist tasks associated with the evaluation of each termination outcome are discussed. In a dynamic or interpersonal therapy, we regard the second termination outcome, resolution of issues in the therapy relationship, as the most important of the three outcomes and likely the most demanding for the therapy participants. The discussion of this termination outcome encompasses the participants' experiences of separation and loss, patient transference, and therapist countertransference. Figure 3.1, depicting the termination phase model provided in chapter 3, concisely summarizes the therapist's tasks associated with determining the appropriateness of termination, making the transition to the termination phase and bringing the therapy to a close.

Attention is given to variations in the model associated with the practice of brief, supportive, or group therapy. These are rather general distinctions, however, therefore in chapter 4 variations associated with four common therapy orientations are considered in more detail. The approaches considered include cognitive–behavioral therapy, interpersonal therapy, supportive therapy, and experiential therapy. Variations associated with the structure of therapy—time limited versus open ended, individual versus group therapy, and group composition—are considered in more depth in chapter 5.

Chapter 6 addresses the profound variations in the process and outcomes of termination that are associated with patient characteristics. The patient variables considered range from attitudinal and personality traits, through aspects of interpersonal style (quality of object relations and attachment), to important diagnostic variables. This chapter includes an extended discussion of the termination of therapy with patients characterized by borderline personality disorder.

The decision to engage in a termination phase is ideally a mutual one by patient and therapist, who then jointly implement the processes associated with termination and progress toward attainment of the termination outcomes. It is unfortunate that this scenario is less frequent than terminations brought about unilaterally by the patient or therapist. Terminations initiated by the patient—generally categorized as *premature terminations*—are addressed in chapter 7. Terminations initiated by the therapist—generally categorized as *forced terminations*—are addressed in chapter 8. In chapter 9, we conclude our discussion by revisiting important themes that characterized the discussion, reiterating recommendations for clinical practice, and presenting suggestions in regard to possible directions for research on the termination phase.

Our intent in this volume is to describe a model of the termination phase that is applicable across different therapy approaches and modalities. We certainly do not regard the model advanced in chapters 2 and 3 and used as a framework for discussion in subsequent chapters as complete or as not requiring revision. We anticipate and expect critique and evolution of the model by others. If the model proves useful to clinicians of different theoretical orientations, as well as suggesting approaches to the empirical study of the termination phase, we will have accomplished our aims for this book.

2

IDENTIFYING FUNDAMENTAL PRINCIPLES AND DEFINING THE OUTCOMES OF TERMINATION

A view of termination that applies to most approaches and modalities of psychotherapy practice—a pantheoretical model of therapy termination similar to Bordin's (1979) model of the working alliance—could be particularly useful for the field. As Zinkin (1994) pointed out, "The fact is that there simply is no agreed way of doing it (ending therapy), nor when it is right to end" (p. 16).

In this chapter, we first identify principles suggested by the literature that appear critical to understanding the phenomena of therapy termination. We then go on to highlight the outcomes that are expressly associated with the termination of therapy, regardless of the context and focus of the particular treatment. We suggest that these outcomes are conceptually distinct from the patient's and the clinician's objectives for psychotherapy and distinguishable from the indicators proposed as evidence that the time for termination of therapy has arrived (i.e., the termination criteria).

To be relevant across therapy approaches and modalities, the model of termination naturally has to be somewhat general. Open-ended, dynamically oriented individual psychotherapy served as a general frame for development of the model presented herein, essentially because the termination naturally emerges as a culmination of the ongoing process, rather than being defined by the structure of the treatment (e.g., time-limited individual therapy). A clearer picture of the termination can be developed by using the frame of open-ended dynamic therapy. Particular factors associated with the treatment (e.g., duration, relationship emphasis) or patient (e.g., pathology, history of loss) that may influence the degree of importance placed on the termination in the larger treatment context are highlighted to address the ending in other forms of psychotherapy. These two features—a general approach to psychotherapy and a set of relevant factors that distinguish variations from the general approach—provide sufficient flexibility for our model of termination to be relevant to clinicians from all points on the spectrum of therapy practice.

The chapter begins with a review of the seminal contributions to the understanding of termination by early and contemporary psychoanalytic theorists. Early contributions were by Freud and the "traditional" analysts that followed him. These contributions helped to lay a foundation of fundamental principles in regard to the termination of therapy. Later contributions were by practitioners who were adapting analytic principles to short-term, time-limited formats. The short-term therapy adaptations called attention to a number of factors that can influence the degree of importance assigned to the termination phase. Additional influential factors are identified in a discussion of the general approach to treatment—open-ended individual psychotherapy—as differentiated from psychoanalysis, brief individual therapy, supportive therapy, and group therapy approaches. The fundamental principles and statements in regard to influential factors serve as building blocks for the model of termination developed in the chapter, and they are therefore highlighted in italics as they appear in the discussion.

Following this exposition, three specific outcomes of termination are defined and then contrasted with the outcomes of therapy and the criteria for termination, that is, those indications that a transition to the termination phase of therapy is pending and appropriate. The nature of this transition— from a working therapy process to a process of ending therapy—is examined. The treatment and patient factors that may influence the degree of importance assigned to the termination are then considered. The review of these factors provides for a conceptual extension to therapies that are not primarily dynamically oriented, moving along a spectrum from those emphasizing relational issues and focus (interpersonal, supportive) to those emphasizing a pragmatic orientation, structure, and skills development (behavioral, cognitive). The chapter concludes with a consideration of contrasting metaphoric conceptions of the termination phase—termination-as-loss and termination-as-transformation—to further clarify our perspective on the phenomenon.

Overall, our aim in this chapter is to provide a clear conceptualization of the termination and how an appropriately implemented termination phase can function to consolidate the achievements of the overall psychotherapy endeavor. Glover (1955) saw the termination in relation to the therapy in the same way as a touchstone is used to test the purity of gold samples. The chapter considers the factors important prior to, during, and at the conclusion of the termination phase. This will set the stage for a discussion of the process of terminating therapy in chapter 3.

PSYCHOANALYTIC CONTRIBUTIONS

It was noted earlier that the preponderance of the literature on termination has been contributed by clinical theorists working from a psychoanalytic or psychodynamic perspective. We provide an overview of the psychoanalytic perspective on termination in this section.

Freud struggled to understand the issue of termination throughout the course of developing the psychoanalytic approach. He initially asserted that the termination was straightforward and predictable. In his own clinical work, however, Freud had clear difficulties bringing treatment to a close, his own countertransference feelings frequently interfering with the ending. By the close of his career, Freud was pessimistic that a termination of psychoanalysis was even possible. A fuller development of theory about termination was left to analytic practitioners following in Freud's footsteps.

Sigmund Freud

As is the case with many psychotherapy concepts, the original contributions to an understanding of termination were by Sigmund Freud. Throughout his development of the psychoanalytic method, Freud struggled to formulate a definitive view of termination and adequately address the phenomenon in his clinical practice (Kupers, 1988). In his first statement on the subject, part of his essay on beginning the treatment, Freud (1913/1964b) likened termination to the endgame in chess. He asserted that the analyst would clearly know the final moves beforehand, could implement them in "an exhaustive systematic presentation" (p. 123), and would, thus, be able to facilitate a successful completion of the therapy (Blum, 1989; Golland, 1997). However, the criteria for termination, the characteristics of the termination process, and the analyst's management of the termination phase were not addressed in this early work. It was nonetheless clear from his initial statement that Freud believed that *the termination of therapy involves certain understandable elements*. He was also convinced that a termination phase could be clearly demarcated in the course of treatment; that is, *the termination phase can be distinguished from the earlier working phase of therapy*.

More than 20 years later, Freud (1937/1964a) revisited the concept in his well-known essay on the interminability of psychoanalysis. In this work, he expressed his pessimism that a lasting curative outcome was possible at the end of analytic treatment. Once again, Freud did not deal directly or extensively with termination as a phase of treatment or with the techniques used to initiate and proceed through such a phase. Instead, he dealt primarily with the inherent limitations of the analytic technique, the patient, and the analyst. By this point in his development of psychoanalysis, Freud had come to appreciate that the objective of therapy is change and not necessarily cure. He had advanced as a basic tenet that moderate goals in analysis—and by implication psychotherapy—are essential (Kramer, 1990). Later analytic writers who advanced progressively more idealistic goals as the required criteria for termination (see the following section) apparently ignored this recommendation.

In line with his view that the objective of psychoanalysis is change in the patient, Freud addressed the phenomenon of termination solely as a pragmatic issue. He argued that the analyst should set the date for discontinuation of contact on the basis of perceptions that (a) the analysand is no longer suffering from symptoms, (b) the symptoms are not likely to reappear, and (c) no further change in the analysand would take place if the analysis were to be continued. These judgments would be evaluated against the criterion that the "best possible psychological condition for the functioning ego" had been secured by the analytic treatment (Freud, 1937/1964a, p. 250). Thus, Freud suggested that *the possibility of termination emerges naturally once the patient has achieved (a) relief from distress, (b) mastery of the problems that gave rise to the symptoms, and (c) the capacity to function independently of the therapy and therapist.* He also emphasized that it was critical to address the analysand's feelings and fantasies about the ending to prevent subsequent acting out and undermining of a successful outcome. Freud was, thus, asserting that *appropriate attention to termination can consolidate a successful outcome, while insufficient consideration of the ending may serve to accentuate the limitations of the treatment.*

In other writings, Freud was more explicit that resolution of the transference neurosis was the single most important criterion for successful termination of psychoanalysis. In other words, the transition into the termination phase should encompass a shift in the patient's view of the therapist and the therapeutic relationship, that is, one that is less characterized by distortion and more accurately representative of the therapist as a real person. In his own practice, however, it was evident that Freud failed to give enough time or attention to the issues surrounding termination. In a telling fashion, he endorsed the use of a ritual to mark the ending; that is, "a gift from the patient could contribute, as a symbolic act, to lessening his feeling of gratitude and his consequent dependence on the physician" (Gardiner, 1971, p. 150). "Indeed, he seemed incapable of helping his analysands with their actual feelings about the separation and loss" (Kupers, 1988, p. 18) because his own countertransference feelings interfered with the ending of treatment.

Thus, although Freud was aware of the potential for an emotional impact of the ending on the analysand and the importance of addressing this impact, he was much less likely to acknowledge how the analyst's own difficulties with separation and loss could interact with bringing the treatment to an end. The transparency of Freud's documentation in regard to his own cases underscores two important assumptions regarding termination: First, the *termination can stimulate issues associated with separation and loss, and this can be true for patient and therapist.* Second, *termination requires that the therapist be responsive to the patient's idiosyncratic reactions to the ending, as well as being attentive to countertransference issues that may arise.* The patient's emotional response to the transition represented by the termination strongly determines how much attention should be given to the ending. The therapist's emotional response to the transition also needs to be considered through self-analysis or in supervision, with more clarity of awareness being required as the importance of the termination phase for a particular therapy case increases.

Other Psychoanalytic Contributions

A member of the early psychoanalytic circle with Freud, Ferenczi (1927/ 1955) described the sense of timelessness that is experienced by the analytic participants, in parallel with the timelessness of the unconscious phenomena being explored. At the end of treatment, Ferenczi saw the participants engaging in a "time-bound departure" from the analytic encounter and "re-entering their respective social worlds" (Kupers, 1988, p. 29). Thus, *the termination requires a shift in focus on the part of the therapy participants. The termination may be represented as a point on the calendar but actually serves as a transition between the work of therapy and going on in life without therapy.* In terms of recognizing when termination is due, Ferenczi wryly suggested that "the proper ending of analysis is when neither the physician nor the patient puts an end to it, but when it dies from exhaustion" (1927/1955, p. 85). He did suggest, as a criterion for termination, that the analysand be fully capable of free association. In Ferenczi's view, then, the patient should end treatment with the capacity to make independent use of the tools of therapy.

The Freud and Ferenczi papers served as the only statements on the ending of therapy until a 1950 symposium on termination was published in the *International Journal of Psycho-Analysis.* A well-defined termination phase became consensually accepted as critical to successful analytic treatment. At the same time, this phase was not regarded as distinctly different from the therapy process that had preceded it. Golland (1997) described the perspective that emerged from this 1950 symposium:

> Terminations would evolve, naturally, from properly conducted analyses; the phase would proceed from a mutually agreed-upon date and would

include regression, reactivation of symptom complexes and a mourning process; the technique would be a continuation of transference and resistance analysis, especially regarding reactions to the fact of impending termination, with the only essential difference being the analyst's agreement to the actual date of ending. (p. 259)

However, a survey of practice conducted 5 years after publication of the symposium findings (Glover, 1955) indicated that there was considerable variation in how analysts technically approached the termination of treatment. Nonetheless, Glover insisted that "unless the terminal phase has been passed through, it is very doubtful whether any case has been psychoanalyzed" (1955, p. 140). His view of a tripartite analysis—an opening phase initiating the process, a middle phase of the major analytic work, and a terminal phase with its own criteria and characteristics—was not widely accepted until the 1970s.

The view that termination would emerge naturally and required only a consistency of technique was also not supported in two later practice reviews by Firestein (1974, 1982). A plethora of criteria for termination were identified in these reviews, many linked more to abstract psychoanalytic theory than to the realities of clinical practice. There was also little unanimity demonstrated in regard to technique during the termination phase. Firestein (1982) concluded that the conditions for termination were as idiosyncratic as the specific symptoms, character problems, and life situation of a given analysand. Controversy also continued to surround using symptomatic improvement as the sole criterion for termination or whether analysts should maintain or modify their technique during the termination phase. What could be agreed on was that treatment endings did not readily fit endgame rules: "Termination phase issues and technique are as complex as issues and technique in the overall psychoanalytic enterprise, and . . . terminations always fall short of any ideal" (Golland, 1997, p. 261). A clear principle that emerged between the earliest works on the subject and the period just prior to the development of the brief therapies was that *termination must be tailored to the specific patient and treatment, and warrants some degree of attention in all treatments.*

CONTRIBUTIONS OF THE BRIEF THERAPISTS

Progress in analytic theory and practice resulted in a tendency for psychoanalyses to become longer and consequently for the termination to assume greater importance. The variety and depth of psychopathology considered amenable to analytic treatment also increased, in line with the progressively greater emphasis placed on preoedipal issues, early object relations, and more primitive defense mechanisms. These shifts in theory, inspired by the treatment of more severely disturbed patients, were applied to more functional analysands, leading to more in-depth and again longer treatments: "As analyses grow longer, probe deeper, and aim to alter more firmly fixed psychic structure, termination becomes a more critical phase of treatment and there is a larger potential for negative repercussions of poorly navigated terminations" (Kupers, 1988, p. 42). This principle would also be applicable to long-term psychotherapy as distinct from psychoanalysis. It would also apply to patients with more severe psychopathology, whatever the type of intervention—purely supportive therapy, psychoeducational interventions, or therapy involving more expressive interventions and objectives reflecting characterological change. In general, then, *longer treatments tend to focus on character or more profound psychopathology; duration of therapy and degree of pathology tend to heighten the critical nature of the termination.*

In counterpoint to these developments was the emergence of short-term, time-limited forms of individual psychotherapy. The impetus for development of these approaches was threefold: First, there was interest in adapting traditional psychodynamic techniques to briefer treatment formats (e.g., Malan, 1976; Mann, 1973). Second, increased patient demand for services and reduced economic support meant the time for briefer treatments had arrived (Bauer & Kobos, 1987). Third, brief therapies were particularly amenable to research investigation, with a number of approaches emerging in that context (Luborsky, 1984; Malan, 1979; Strupp & Binder, 1984). A number of brief therapy approaches appeared in the last 3 decades of the 20th century. There was substantial variation in these approaches in regard to the emphasis placed on the termination and on the importance of working through themes of mourning and loss during the termination phase.

Termination is a central focus in certain brief approaches, notably the time-limited therapy of Mann (1973; Mann & Goldman, 1982). A 12-session time limit is made explicit at the outset of treatment and, consequently, the inevitability of separation and ending—in therapy, in other relationships, and in life—becomes a major focus throughout the treatment. In the last third of therapy, Mann (1973) recommended an explicit and "relentless" focus on the termination. He asserted that the patient will respond to the impending separation with "the same feelings that characterized earliest separation and loss as well as later ones" (p. 362). Strupp and Binder (1984) also emphasized the significance of the therapy relationship and its termination in their time-limited dynamic psychotherapy. From their perspective, the termination represents a significant challenge for the therapist and, if handled poorly, might result in a vitiation of gains made in treatment: "Depending on the management of this issue, therapy may turn out to be a success or a failure" (p. 259). Other brief therapists (e.g., Dewald, 1980; Glick, 1987) regard termination as a central focus only when the therapy must be interrupted prematurely, that is, any terminations that are "forced" by the therapist, because of, for example, a therapist move. In certain approaches, then, *an explicit time limit determined at the beginning of treatment is associated with greater emphasis being placed on the termination throughout therapy.* In like fashion, *the more overtly the termination is decided upon solely by the therapist, the more emphasis may need to be placed on the termination to address the patient's feelings of rejection.*

In contrast, the termination is a minimal focus in the brief therapies of Sifneos (1972, 1979) and Davanloo (1978, 1979). Sifneos's stringent selection criteria meant he would not accept into treatment those patients experiencing "dyadic conflicts stemming from early childhood dependency" (Sifneos, 1972, p. 363). Instead, his focus on conflicts associated with oedipal issues (e.g., competitiveness) allowed Sifneos to devote relatively little attention to termination. He also avoided presetting a definite date for termination, deciding on the ending when progress had been mutually acknowledged. The importance of loss and abandonment is minimized by Sifneos's emphasis on competence and an orientation to the future. In his anecdotal reports of short-term anxiety-provoking psychotherapy, Sifneos (1979) reported an absence of the ambivalence and anger associated with endings in analysis or long-term therapy. Like Sifneos, Davanloo (1979) also paid attention to stringent patient selection criteria and discouraged dependence and a regressive transference during the process of therapy. Davanloo agreed that with a focus on oedipal conflicts, termination is typically not a problem. If loss is central to the patient's experience, however, then Davanloo suggested a process of working through over 1 to 5 sessions. These theorists suggest that *the less the patient's functioning involves structural deficits and dependence on the therapist, the less the emphasis required to manage the termination.*

Relative to his brief therapy contemporaries, Malan (1979) occupied a middle ground position in regard to termination. He recommended fixing an end date from the start and devoting the last quarter of therapy to working on the separation. At the same time, he contended that the termination is not necessarily a critical component of therapy, given that "patients who are not overly dependent take what they need from therapy and leave replenished without undue pain over separation" (Noy-Sharav, 1998, p. 70). Wolberg (1980) also recommended a flexible approach, with treatment length being determined by the patient's ego strength. He differentiates between patients who have endured serious losses during critical developmental stages and thus require a special period of time to work through and prepare for termination, and those patients for whom loss is not critical. *Serious loss,* in this context, refers to the absence of an important caregiver during a central period of psychosocial development. In contrast, Bauer and Kobos (1987) viewed termination as an opportunity for exploring and coping with past separations and losses, but not necessarily a traumatic event in itself.

On the basis of these contributions, it appears that *a history of serious object loss, particularly during critical developmental periods, increases the importance of the termination.* Patients with a history of significant or traumatic losses may respond to the ending of therapy with intense affect, and attention to these responses during the termination can have a great deal of therapeutic impact. Naturally, this consideration may also be as pertinent for the therapist as it is for the patient. The therapist's history of loss can influence the development of countertransference reactions that may interfere with an appropriate ending of therapy. Examples of countertransference responses to the termination of therapy are considered in chapter 3. Awareness of these issues and being open to a discussion of their bearing on the termination during therapy supervision or with colleagues can be critical to a successful conclusion of the treatment.

Research on termination has largely been restricted to the brief individual therapy context. Malan (1963, 1976) suggested that the success of therapy was correlated with the patient being able to work through grief and anger about termination. However, in a number of these successful cases it was evident that the termination had simply not been a concern for the patient. Stewart (1972) studied 20 cases of 6-month dynamically oriented therapy, used with patients selected for ego strength and a capacity to develop a therapeutic alliance. Neither the method of termination nor the patient's attitude toward it and the outcome, or the degree of personal involvement the patient felt in regard to the therapy and its outcome, were correlated with the success of the treatment. Stewart suggested that given the variation in the relationships involving the patient, his or her complaints, and the therapist, "one cannot make any generalizations" about the impact of termination (p. 434). Similarly, other research on termination in brief therapy suggests that the frequency and intensity of negative patient reactions are not reflective of termination as an inherent crisis over loss. Most patients have predominantly positive reactions to termination, in direct contrast to the view that termination invariably represents a crisis (Fortune, 1987; Marx & Gelso, 1987; Quintana & Holahan, 1992). In these studies, only a small minority of patients experienced any kind of urgent feelings in regard to the end of therapy. When it did occur, the crisis appeared to focus on a disappointing or negative outcome rather than specifically on loss of the therapy or therapist. This research suggests an assumption of general caution: *The more negative or disappointing the therapy outcome, the more emphasis may need to be placed during the termination to addressing the patient's dissatisfaction.*

As noted earlier, however, certain brief therapy approaches do make the ending and the separation of patient and therapist key issues in the treatment. Miller et al. (1983) looked at the number of sessions during which termination was discussed, in cases of the time-limited therapy approach of Mann (1973). The average was 1.3 sessions; in many cases, the topic was discussed only in passing. Miller et al. suggested that either Mann overestimated in his claim that the final third of the 12-session therapy is necessary for working through the termination or that his thesis is correct and the therapists in the study colluded with the patients to avoid or postpone a discussion of termination (i.e., an effect of countertransference). The latter conclusion reinforces the lessons learned from Freud's difficulties with the ending of analysis; that is, in any therapy where the termination represents a critical phase of the relationship, patient transference and therapist countertransference are likely to exert an influence on the quality of the ending. This influence may be manifestly evident or latent and require identification and explication. Authors emphasizing the importance of termination generally agree that patient transference and therapist countertransference must be addressed in equal measure to achieve a satisfactory termination.

DEMARCATING A GENERAL PSYCHOTHERAPY FOR THE MODEL OF TERMINATION

We noted earlier that moderate to longer term, open-ended, dynamically oriented psychotherapy was used as a general frame for the development of our model of the termination. In this section, we present our rationale for the selection of this modality and approach as the frame. We accomplish this by using a method of comparison and contrast with other therapy approaches, namely psychoanalysis, brief therapy, supportive therapy, and group therapy. The discussion also serves to identify additional fundamental principles in regard to the termination of psychotherapy.

Psychoanalysis Relative to Brief Therapy

Since the original works on the subject by Freud (1937/1964a, 1913/ 1964b), the majority of the literature on termination has addressed the ending of psychoanalysis proper (Palombo, 1982). In the past 3 decades, more attention has been given to the termination in short-term, time-limited forms of psychotherapy (e.g., Donoghue, 1994; MacKenzie, 1996; Pinkerton & Rockwell, 1990; Quintana, 1993), in accord with the dominance of these approaches in current clinical practice. These two forms of therapy— psychoanalysis and short-term, time-limited therapy—represent contrasting extremes on a number of variables (Ticho, 1972). The most obvious contrast concerns duration: Psychoanalysis is an open-ended therapy, commonly lasting up to 3 years or more, whereas brief therapies are by definition closed ended and commonly restricted to 12 to 30 sessions. In turn, duration is a function of the ambitiousness or extensiveness of treatment goals. Psychoanalysis aims at a thorough exploration of historical experience, characterological and relational functioning, and defensive style. The analytic emphases on free association and use of the couch tend to foster a deeper regression in the patient than commonly seen in face-to-face forms of psychotherapy. In contrast, the brief therapies as a rule address circumscribed problems and seek to initiate a process of learning that the patient can use to deal with future life crises. The degree of patient regression fostered during brief therapy is limited and generally a function of the importance of a transference focus to the approach.

The two therapy approaches can also be contrasted in terms of clinical technique. The psychoanalyst strives to remain neutral and avoids becoming a model for the patient, whereas the psychotherapist is more active, deliberately functions as a model, and is more likely to engage in efforts to educate the patient. Additionally, the analyst's technique is often restricted to the provision of interpretation, whereas the therapist may be just as likely to give advice and offer support as make use of an interpretive strategy.

Reflecting the intensive nature of the treatment, termination in psychoanalysis is to be considered only after the patient's core problems and transference neurosis have been completely resolved. "In psychotherapy neither the patients seen, nor the techniques used, lend themselves to such an outcome in the vast majority of cases" (Palombo, 1982, p. 16). As noted, the analytic relationship tends to be prolonged and characterized by an intensive and intimate examination of psychological functioning. Ending this relationship can stimulate the emergence of issues associated with separation and individuation, and the termination can involve a high degree of emotional upheaval. In brief forms of individual therapy, the date of termination is frequently decided on at the outset of treatment or after a comparatively short interval, and remains fixed, independent of the degree of success in meeting the goals of therapy. Research has indicated that brief therapy patients are much less likely to experience the termination as painful; the restrictiveness of the format often means the therapeutic relationship is relatively less intimate and can be relinquished more easily (Miller et al., 1983; Pinkerton & Rockwell, 1990).

A consideration of the process and outcome of termination from the perspective of either of these therapy approaches would be unlikely to generalize well across the spectrum of psychotherapeutic treatments. Open-ended individual psychotherapy can be regarded as falling between psychoanalysis, on the one hand, and brief therapy approaches, on the other. In terms of duration, open-ended therapies commonly require 1 to 2 years of patient involvement, thus exceeding the number of sessions offered in brief formats but demanding fewer hours than a full-scale psychoanalysis. Furthermore, the goals of open-ended therapy tend to be more ambitious and extensive than the focused brief approaches (e.g., examining early experience and the effects of same on current interpersonal relationships) but less exhaustive than the complete character restructuring sought in psychoanalysis. Finally, therapist technique in open-ended treatments may involve the analytic strategies of neutrality and interpretation, but it can also include other interventions familiar to brief therapy practitioners. It is most important to note that the clinician would be more likely to consistently use the therapeutic relationship relative to a brief therapy counterpart, but without seeking to facilitate the development of a transference neurosis as seen in psychoanalysis. In open-ended therapy, moreover, "the therapist's task is to find a point somewhere between a premature termination, where the results of therapy quickly unravel, and an excessively long and dependent therapeutic relationship" (Kupers, 1988, p. 2). In a sense, then, open-ended individual therapy offers an average expectable environment for emergence of a termination phase that is regarded as important and critical to completion of the treatment. Considering the termination from this perspective is thus likely to offer the greatest clarity; specifying variations in the direction of brief therapy or analysis would also tend to be easier from this midpoint than from either extreme.

Supportive Psychotherapy

Supportive psychotherapy, whether a short-term problem-solving treatment or a long-term "holding" therapy, generally relies on the quality of the patient–therapist relationship for its effectiveness. (For a discussion of the differentiation between interpretive or expressive psychotherapies and those characterized by a supportive strategy, see Klein, 1979, and Piper et al., 2002.) In supportive psychotherapy, that is, the specific effects of interventions are less of a concern than the bolstering provided the patient by the therapist's warmth, interest, encouragement, and guidance. For many chronic patients, an open-ended supportive therapy frequently offers a form of benevolent parenting and can often serve as a buffer against decompensation or suicidal behavior. Some supportive therapies may be implemented with a time limit but with the presumption that the therapy is one installment in a serial course of care. Termination in these instances might be better conceptualized as an interruption, rather than a separation, because there is agreement that the therapeutic relationship will be on hiatus until the patient feels a need for further contact. Nonetheless, because of the importance of the patient–therapist relationship, the termination in supportive therapy can often be a critically important period in the patient's treatment.

Therapies Emphasizing Skills Development

The forms of therapy that emphasize structure, therapist directiveness, and skills acquisition can also be distinguished from the approaches outlined in this chapter. The most familiar examples are the time-limited forms of cognitive or cognitive–behavioral therapy. As a general rule, these approaches do not focus on relational issues manifest in the patient–therapist interaction as a means of facilitating patient change. Consequently, the termination of treatment is not regarded as necessarily critical to treatment success or difficult for the patient. Indeed, the protocols for these treatments frequently include "booster" sessions some months following the conclusion of the therapy proper. Thus, *the more the treatment is structured and oriented to skills acquisition, the less emphasis may need to be placed on the termination.* However, it is the case that recent approaches to cognitive–behavioral treatment (e.g., Safran & Segal, 1990) encourage greater attention to the quality of the patient–therapist relationship and interpretative understanding of the patient's relational issues (see Crits-Christoph & Connolly Gibbons, 2002). The greater the degree the therapeutic relationship or alliance is attended to and utilized in this type of therapy, the more importance the termination of the relationship begins to assume. The distinction between the therapy approaches using a cognitive–behavioral or skills development orientation and more relationally based approaches begins to blur when the common factor of the alliance is given equivalent emphasis. In turn, the more this factor is used as a basis for the therapy approach, the more likely the termination will be of critical importance. In other words, in a general sense, *the more the therapeutic alliance is addressed and utilized in the therapy, the more emphasis may need to be placed on the termination.*

Group Psychotherapy

The termination in group therapy, whether in the time-limited or open-ended format or in the context of inpatient or outpatient treatment, can be regarded as isomorphic to the termination in individual therapies, with at least three modifications. A first modification concerns the departing patient's relationship with cotherapists, a common treatment strategy in the group format. At the time of termination, the patient may need to address issues (transferential or not) with each therapist and with the therapists as a couple (or subgroup within the larger group). A second modification concerns the departing patient's relationships with those peer members who will be remaining in the group. Frequently, the other members have served directly or indirectly as catalysts for change in the individual patient and have thus had a therapeutic impact equivalent to or greater than that of the therapists or group leaders. In the group format, then, the termination would also include an acknowledgment of these contributions. Similarly, just as the ending of therapy may highlight unresolved issues between patient and therapist, termination in group therapy may also highlight issues in the relationships with fellow members that require efforts at working through and closure. A third modification concerns the departing patient's relationship with the group as a whole. The group may become an important internalized object for the patient, representing a safe refuge, a forum for profound personal development, and a strong sense of belonging among other critical experiences. Furthermore, particularly in inpatient settings, the patient can also have a variety of responses to the contextual factors (e.g., ward environment, hospital values) that shape and color that member's involvement in the group (Klein, Hunter, & Brown, 1986; Klein & Kugel, 1981). These connections to the whole group and institutional transferences are also elements of the patient's therapeutic relationship that require examination at the time of termination.

Summary

In summary, open-ended individual therapy represents a standard frame for examination of the termination. This is primarily due to the emergence of termination as a naturally occurring development in this form of treatment. Addressing a longer duration, increased ambitiousness of treatment goals, or a narrower range of technique leads the consideration of the termination more in the direction of analysis. In contrast, addressing a predetermined time limit, a circumscribed treatment goal, and a greater range of technique leads the consideration of the termination more in the direction of brief therapy. Supportive therapies of varying duration all rely on the quality of the patient–therapist relationship for effectiveness, and the termination of these therapies—temporarily or absolutely—frequently requires a high degree of attention and care. The emphasis on structure and skills acquisition, relative to an emphasis on relational issues and the alliance, serves to distinguish brief therapies of contrasting orientations (e.g., cognitive–behavioral vs. psychodynamic) and determine the lesser or greater degree of attention that is necessarily given to the termination. Finally, addressing therapeutic impacts and unresolved issues in the relationships with group leaders and fellow members, as well as the patient's ties to the entire group and its larger environment, allows for the consideration of the termination in group therapy approaches.

THE TERMINATION OF PSYCHOTHERAPY: FUNDAMENTAL PRINCIPLES

The previous review of the literature highlighted a number of fundamental principles in regard to the termination of psychotherapy. Exhibit 2.1 presents the set of eight principles that emerged from the review. In this section, we offer further discussion of each of these principles, with reference to the development of a general perspective on the end of therapy and its specific processes and outcomes.

Freud suggested that, first, *the termination of therapy involves certain understandable elements.* These elements emerge in a given therapy to a greater or lesser degree as a function of patient factors, the nature of the treatment approach, and the importance and quality of the therapeutic relationship. A second basic principle is that *the termination phase can be distinguished from the earlier working phase of therapy.* This demarcation marks the required shift in focus from the objectives of treatment to the outcomes of termination. The various criteria for termination proposed over the years can be reformulated

EXHIBIT 2.1
Fundamental Principles in Regard to Termination

1. The termination of therapy involves certain understandable elements.
2. The termination phase can be distinguished from the earlier working phase of therapy.
3. The possibility of termination emerges naturally once the patient has achieved (a) relief from distress, (b) mastery of the problems that gave rise to the symptoms, and (c) the capacity to function independently of the therapy and therapist.
4. Appropriate attention to the termination can consolidate a successful therapy outcome, whereas insufficient consideration of the ending may serve to accentuate the limitations of the treatment.
5. Termination stimulates issues associated with separation and loss, and this can be true for patient and therapist.
6. Termination requires that the therapist be responsive to the patient's idiosyncratic reactions to the ending, as well as being attentive to countertransference issues that may arise.
7. The termination requires a shift in focus on the part of the therapy participants. The termination may be represented as a point on the calendar but actually serves as a transition between the process of therapy and going on in life without therapy.
8. Termination must be tailored to the specific patient and treatment and warrants some degree of attention in all treatments.

as indicators of this demarcation; the emergence of these indicators occurs during a pretermination phase as the working phase of therapy winds down. The termination criteria are discussed later in this chapter in the "Criteria for Termination Versus Termination Outcomes" section. The second principle therefore marks the termination as a unique period in the course of therapy, both in terms of specific outcomes and as a distinct phase in the course of treatment.

In his paper on the interminability of psychoanalysis, Freud (1937/1964a) provided one of the more concise definitions of treatment success and, by implication, of when it is appropriate to consider the termination of treatment. A third fundamental principle follows from Freud's view that *the possibility of termination emerges naturally once the patient has achieved (a) relief from distress, (b) mastery of the problems that gave rise to the symptoms, and (c) the capacity to function independently of the therapy and therapist.* The various criteria for termination of psychoanalysis advanced since the time of Freud's paper have essentially reflected one of these achievements: symptom improvement, increased ego strength or capacity for coping, and personal autonomy. This fundamental principle is clearly most applicable to open-ended therapies with broader treatment objectives. At a certain point in the working phase of therapy, it becomes evident that the patient has achieved success in dealing with the symptoms that initiated the contact and has developed some capacity to prevent the recurrence of the symptoms. Certainly, a sense of urgency that may have marked the beginning of therapy will have long since been dissipated by this point. In addition, the natural emergence of the possibility of ending the therapy may be marked by one or more of the criteria for termination (see the "Criteria for Termination Versus Termination Outcomes" section).

The main point is that in a reasonably successful open-ended therapy, the move into a termination phase and process will in most instances represent a natural evolution—it becomes clear that the work has for the most part been accomplished and the time to conclude the relationship has arrived. For psychoanalysts, achievement in these areas would ideally be absolute or at least sufficient to prevent the emergence of symptoms in the future. For psychotherapies where the objectives are less ambitious or extensive, briefer treatments where the end date has been negotiated from the outset, or where the approach is structured and emphasizes skills acquisition, the relative degree of achievement shown by the patient in these areas would still be evaluated. In the context of a time-limited psychotherapy, evaluations of achievement and success may be constrained to the circumscribed problem focus. In certain instances of brief therapy, whether oriented to psychodynamic insight or structured skills development, the rapid emergence in the patient of relief, mastery, and a capacity to function independently might be used in mutually deciding to end the therapy earlier than planned. Considering the qualifications associated with treatment focus and duration, indications that the patient has attained symptom relief, improved adaptation, and increased independence generally suggest that the time for termination of the therapy has been reached.

An important theme in the literature is that the termination can make or break a therapy. For example, Palombo (1982) stated that "the termination phase plays an essential part in the consolidation of the treatment process" (p. 16; see also Maholick & Turner, 1979; Martin & Schurtman, 1985; Mozgai, 1985; Quintana & Holahan, 1992; Reid, 1980). In this view, the manner in which the termination is managed can solidify gains made during therapy and prepare the patient for continued adaptation and growth after therapy (Garcia-Lawson & Lane, 1997). More specifically, the fourth fundamental principle asserts that *appropriate attention to termination can consolidate a successful outcome whereas insufficient consideration of the ending may serve to accentuate limitations of the treatment.*

In the context of brief therapy, studies have demonstrated positive relationships between an active focus on termination issues and favorable outcome (Malan, 1963; Quintana & Holahan, 1992). Evidence also suggests that an omission of attention to the termination may negatively influence the patient's experience of therapy as a whole. This is especially likely with unsuccessful cases, where therapists have been shown to limit their discussion of patients' feelings about ending, to spend less time reviewing the course of therapy, and to make fewer attempts to bring closure to the therapeutic relationship (Quintana & Holahan, 1992). Therefore, allowing time for the work necessary to examine the feelings and reactions to the termination can help to underscore what the patient has learned from therapy and help to evaluate his or her capacity to apply this learning to future stressful situations. If the therapy was concerned with interpersonal health, dealing with the termination can provide a concrete experience of a more mature separation and a healthier response to loss. Conversely, if the termination is given short shrift, the patient may not have the opportunity to deal successfully with the feelings and reactions that emerge at the ending of therapy. Furthermore, a perception that the therapist has failed to address issues of some importance as therapy concludes can serve to establish or reinstate a view of others as untrustworthy, possibly undermining gains accomplished to that point in treatment. "If early developmental pain is reexperienced and reinforced, the termination can have devastating effects on the entire treatment process and outcome" (Kramer, 1990, p. 3).

Two fundamental principles directly address the emotional valence the termination can have for therapy participants. The fifth fundamental principle states that *the termination can stimulate issues associated with separation and loss, and this can be true for patient and therapist*. The ending of treatment involves both the ending of a relationship and the ending of a collaborative process. At one extreme, the parties may conclude their involvement in a businesslike fashion without any emotional arousal. At another extreme, the ending of the therapy process and severing of the therapy relationship may be marked by intense feelings of loss, gratitude, or anger. The more issues of separation and loss are stimulated by the termination of therapy, the more painful the termination process is likely to be. Where on the spectrum the experience of the participants may fall is jointly dependent on the nature of the treatment (e.g., the degree of here-and-now relational focus) and the participants' prior histories of separation and loss. The sixth fundamental principle is related to this latter point: *Termination requires that the therapist be responsive to the patient's idiosyncratic reactions to the ending, and attentive to countertransference issues that may arise*. Clearly, a history of profound object loss will intensify the patient's response to the termination, even if the treatment and therapeutic relationship were unlikely to necessitate attention to the ending (e.g., a brief and strictly cognitive therapy where a student–teacher relationship was fostered between patient and therapist). Conversely, if a history of significant loss applies to the therapist, countertransference responses to the ending may increase the difficulty of the termination, even if the patient is relatively healthy and the treatment was successful. Dealing appropriately with the termination requires that the therapist monitor the interaction for indications of strong reactions to the ending—whether the patient's or his or her own—and explicitly address these if they emerge.

The termination represents a turning point in treatment, as the patient shifts from the actual work in the therapy process to contemplating moving into a life without therapy. In other words, "there is an explicit transition from the past to the future" (Lamb, 1985, p. 608). Therapy reaches a point where the possibility of an ending can be considered and the criteria for termination have been approximated, that is, during a pretermination phase. During this time, the parties negotiate an agreement on the date for their last session. The establishment of the ending date ushers in the termination phase proper (Blum, 1989). Thus, identifying that the time has come to conclude treatment and establishing a concrete date to mark the conclusion results in the therapy moving into a transitional stage. That is, the seventh fundamental principle suggests that *the termination requires a shift in focus on the part of the therapy participants. The termination may be represented as a point on the calendar but actually serves as a transition between the process of therapy and going on in life without therapy.*

During this transitional period, the focus is on the termination outcomes and the patient's feelings and reactions to letting go of the therapist and therapy. The eighth and final fundamental principle asserts that *the termination must be tailored to the specific patient and treatment, and warrants some degree of attention in all treatments.* This principle implies that there is no one standard or endgame for termination that applies consistently across all psychotherapy cases or approaches. The importance of termination will vary considerably across different cases that receive a similar therapy and across different approaches to therapy. In like fashion, the experience of the termination will vary considerably across cases and treatments.

Although these fundamental principles do apply in all instances, the weight placed on the termination and the difficulties experienced negotiating the ending of therapy can vary from minimal to considerable. Specific factors associated with the treatment and patient determine the emphasis given to the termination and the nature of the participants' experience at the end of therapy. These factors are discussed later in this chapter.

THE OUTCOMES OF TERMINATION

Termination outcomes are specific to the final phase of the patient–therapist involvement, that is, the ending of therapy. They emerge as a focus following the pretermination phase when the criteria for termination emerge and are acknowledged. This occurs specifically following the transition from the working phase of psychotherapy and prior to the setting of the date for the actual conclusion of treatment. Essentially, the focus during the termination phase is on a review of the treatment and its successes and limitations, the ending of the therapeutic relationship, and planning for life after therapy. Therefore, the concerns during this transitional period are whether the patient can (a) reflect on and acknowledge the effects of the treatment, (b) appreciate the importance of the therapeutic relationship, and (c) look ahead to applying the lessons of therapy to problems in the future. These concerns translate into the three outcomes that are directly associated with the termination phase: (a) reinforcement and consolidation of the therapy process and the gains made in treatment, (b) resolution of issues in the therapy relationship, and (c) preparedness for maintaining healthy functioning outside of treatment (Kramer, 1990). Barnett, MacGlashan, and Clarke (2000) have defined these outcomes of termination more concisely as assessment, resolution, and generalization.

The first termination outcome, *reinforcement/consolidation of the therapy process and gains made in treatment*, requires a review and recapitulation of what transpired between patient and therapist from the beginning of therapy, the accomplishments secured by the patient, and those objectives as yet unmet. With regard to this outcome, then, termination is "a time for self-assessment, for looking at what has been achieved, at where one now stands, who one now is, what one still needs to work on and how to arrange day-to-day life so as to consolidate gains" (Peternel, 1991, p. 163). The review draws attention to the steps the patient has taken toward health as well as encouraging acknowledgment and acceptance of those areas where steps have not been taken. In a sense, the patient and therapist develop an updated view on the patient's functioning and the accomplishments attained within the therapeutic relationship to incorporate those changes associated with the therapy endeavor. In doing so, an appraisal of the stability and durability of the therapeutic accomplishments can occur (Gold, 1996).

This review can afford the patient with an integrated perspective on the gains made over the course of treatment; additionally, areas of functioning that still require work can be identified and possibly addressed in the time remaining. The investment of time and energy in this review process will commonly be a function of the extensiveness and intensity of the treatment, that is, the breadth of the psychotherapeutic exploration and the degree of personal investment and intimacy associated with it. It is certainly the case that no treatment or termination will attain an ideal outcome (Golland, 1997). However, for those cases where the outcome of treatment or therapy is less than expected or disappointing, greater attention needs to be given to this particular outcome of termination.

The second outcome of termination concerns the *resolution of issues in the therapeutic relationship*. The termination phase is not just the period of therapy when loose ends in the relationship are tied up—it also provides a unique opportunity to work on the unconscious relational meaning of this ending and separation for the patient (G. Frank, 1999). These issues may be associated with aspects of the transference (Dewald, 1982; Garcia-Lawson & Lane, 1997; P. Levinson, McMurray, Podell, & Weiner, 1978) and fantasies in regard to the termination (Shechter, 1993) or with the real loss of the therapy enterprise and the therapy relationship (Kupers, 1988). In the frame of the general open-ended psychotherapy and similar approaches,

> the ability to sustain loss and retain a cohesive sense of one's self is an important part of the process of therapy. It (the termination) involves

an acknowledgment of the real losses as well as a careful working through of fantasies and transference distortions evoked by the experience of separation. (Caligor, Fieldsteel, & Brok, 1993, p. 184)

Of course, the importance of this outcome will vary considerably as a function of the therapy approach, that is, the degree of focus on relational issues, particularly those associated with the therapeutic relationship itself, and the characteristics of the patient or the patient's difficulty. The more the treatment reflects the characteristics of the general psychotherapy, the more this outcome will involve attention to aspects of mourning associated with the ending (Golland, 1997).

Furthermore, the actual degree of resolution achieved in regard to the issues in the therapy relationship will also vary, both within and across approaches to treatment. This variation will be a function of the quality of the working collaboration between patient and therapist. It may also be associated with how much a particular issue intersects with long-standing difficulties that challenge either patient or therapist. As is the case throughout a dynamically oriented therapy, but perhaps with greater force at the time of termination, the therapist must attend to aspects of the transference and his or her countertransference, that is, the "unspoken promises, expectations, transferences, and resistances on the part of both persons in the therapeutic relationship" (Schafer, 1973, p. 138). Quintana (1993) and Barnett et al. (2000) have emphasized that the therapist can help the patient resolve transference feelings by promoting the real relationship between them as the conclusion of therapy nears. To this end, the therapist might engage in increasing amounts of appropriate self-disclosure, actively structure the relationship to be more egalitarian, and respond to patients' inquiries directly and with less interpretation. This strategy is more congruent with the brief therapy approaches and perhaps moderate-length interpersonal or dynamic treatments; in analytic therapies or psychoanalysis, the usual recommendation is that the therapist maintain the same stance used throughout treatment during the termination phase (Firestein, 1982).

The third outcome of termination concerns the patient's *preparedness for maintaining healthy functioning outside of treatment*. To varying degrees, again as a function of the treatment approach, the extensiveness of the treatment goals, and so on, this outcome reflects some internalization of the therapeutic process and the therapist's function (Kramer, 1990). Structural components of the internalization process refer to images of patient and therapist (e.g., a distressed self and an interested and nonjudgmental therapist). Functional components refer to the provisions of the therapist in the treatment process, such as empathy, support, the challenging of irrational beliefs, or the analytic function. Research has shown that patients internalize functional aspects of the therapy experience (Quintana & Meara, 1990) and that this process is associated with positive therapy outcome. For those therapies aimed at bolstering the patient's capacity for coping, this outcome may be limited to the demonstration of having learned specific skills. In a brief therapy addressing a circumscribed problem, the outcome may reflect an internalization of the process of resolution achieved with the therapist, such that a similar process can be used when encountering related or different problems in the future. For therapies that focus on the patient's relational style and its early origins, the patient would be expected to more fully incorporate the style of exploration and insight development achieved with the therapist and put this to use to deal adaptively with relationships. In a full psychoanalysis, the expectation would be that the patient has internalized the analyst as a benign internal object and has become able to independently engage in the therapy process as required, that is, the self-analytic function (Firestein, 1978; Grinberg, 1980; Novick, 1982; Ticho, 1972).

The point is that, during termination, this outcome requires that the patient's internalizations of the therapy process and relationship are emphasized as resources to confront future crises (Quintana, 1993). In other words, it can be shown that through the course of therapy, the patient has developed tools that allow for an independent continuation of the therapeutic process. Edelson (1963) addressed this outcome of termination as follows:

> The problem of termination is not how to get therapy stopped, or when to stop it, but how to terminate so that *what has been happening keeps going on inside the patient* [italics added]. It is a problem of facilitating achievement by the patient of the ability to hang on to the therapist (or the experience of the relationship with the therapist) in his physical absence in the form of a realistic intrapsychic representation. (p. 23)

Achieving this termination outcome involves demonstrating that the patient has developed a capacity to function as his or her own therapist. This demonstration would be commensurate with the therapy approach; that is, the patient has mastered certain coping skills, can more appropriately deal with relational conflict, or has developed greater self-awareness and empathy in all relationships. Demonstrating the achievement of this termination outcome will serve to reinforce the patient's sense of self-reliance and confidence (Barnett et al., 2000). Kupers (1988) argued that achieving this outcome of termination also serves to underscore the patient's commitment to return for another course of therapy if and when the need arises.

Termination outcomes can be distinguished from the more general classes of outcome associated with the treatment and with the therapy. *Treatment outcomes* reflect the degree of change brought about in the patient's clinical condition; that is, these outcomes reflect the clinical goals of the treatment. The concern is whether the patient has shown movement from dysfunction to adequate function on the clinical dimensions of interest, for example, symptoms of depression. Treatment outcomes are generally evaluated from the treatment provider's point of view; for example, "Did treatment bring about a change in the patient's diagnosis?" By contrast, *therapy outcomes* reflect the degree of change regarding the patient's individual and idiosyncratic objectives; that is, these outcomes reflect the unique objectives of the patient's personal psychotherapy. The concern is whether the patient can report the satisfactory accomplishment of the goals he or she outlined at the beginning of therapy. Therapy outcomes are generally evaluated from the patient's point of view; for example, "Was therapy effective in helping me address the underlying reasons for chronically unsatisfying intimate relationships?" Thus, treatment and therapy outcomes consider the overall success of the patient–clinician involvement as a whole from the contrasting perspectives of the participants. In most cases, there is a considerable overlap not only between the objectives the clinician holds for the treatment and the objectives the patient holds for his or her therapy but also between the outcomes of treatment and therapy. At the same time, however, each perspective may emphasize changes that the other does not. For example, the clinician may hope to see a decrease in the patient's overdependence on others that is not recognized by the patient; conversely, the patient may seek changes in a particular relationship that the clinician does not regard as central to the patient's primary difficulties.

The central points to be emphasized here are that, first, the outcomes of termination refer to the patient's and therapist's success in addressing the three tasks that are specific and critical to this phase, and, second, that these outcomes are distinguishable from the outcome achieved by the patient as a function of the therapy as a whole. The phase-specific tasks associated with the termination are examined in more detail in chapter 3. While the termination outcomes are distinguishable from the overall outcomes of the treatment, this is not to say that the attainments are considered in isolation. Successful fulfillment of the termination outcomes can frequently have a reinforcing effect on the gains realized in the entire treatment. Conversely, insufficient attention to any or all of the termination outcomes can result in an undermining or unraveling of treatment gains and leave the participants demoralized by the time of the last session.

CRITERIA FOR TERMINATION VERSUS TERMINATION OUTCOMES

Defining the criteria for termination has preoccupied clinical theorists since Freud's first statements on the phenomenon. Pedder (1988) recounted the repeated reviews of termination criteria that have marked the history of psychoanalysis: first in 1949 and collected in a 1950 volume of the *International Journal of Psycho-Analysis*; the reviews by Firestein (1974, 1978); three panels (Firestein, 1969; Pfeffer, 1963; Robbins, 1975) reported in the *Journal of the American Psychoanalytic Association*; and in a collection of papers in the 1982 volume of *Psychoanalytic Inquiry*. Each succeeding review was characterized by a longer list of criteria, often of a metapsychological nature, and invariably representing an idealized depiction of therapy success (Gold, 1996). For example, in 1950 Balint emphasized three criteria for termination: greater tolerance of the instinctual aims, improved object relationships, and more cohesive structure of the ego. By 1978, Firestein had identified 10 generally accepted criteria for termination of psychoanalysis in the literature:

- symptoms have been traced to their genetic conflicts;
- all symptoms have been eliminated, mitigated, or made tolerable;
- object relations have been freed from transference distortions and improved;
- ego strength has increased as a function of decreased conflict;
- the ability to distinguish fantasy from reality has sharpened;
- acting out has been eliminated;
- the capacity to tolerate some anxiety has improved;
- the ability to tolerate delay of gratification has increased;
- the capacity to experience pleasure without guilt or other in-hibiting factors has improved; and
- the ability to work has improved.

From the perspective of the ego psychologists, the criteria for termination addressed increased ego autonomy, the acquisition of adaptive defenses, improved interpersonal relations, and an increased sense of self or identity (Blanck & Blanck, 1988).

As is evident from the Firestein (1978) or Blanck and Blanck (1988) listings, one problem with the various proposed criteria is their independence from the particular objectives of the therapy. That is, attainment of these criteria (or partial attainment; see Shane & Shane, 1984) indicates that the time for termination of the therapy has arrived, but this may be distinct from whether the patient's, the therapist's, or both participants' objectives for treatment have actually been realized. In part, this is a function of the abstract focus of the criteria on intrapsychic functioning and their primary association with a full psychoanalytic treatment. A second problem is the idealized nature of the criteria—examples of clear attainment of all the criteria, even in successful psychoanalyses, are very few. A more practical focus, that is, criteria that reflect the particular objectives of the patient's therapy, may offer greater clarity and usefulness across approaches. A third problem is the use of the term *criteria* itself, implying that the patient's functioning must be evaluated by an external authority to determine when the patient's graduation from therapy is permissible. A more patient-centered view would consider possible indicators that therapy has reached a point where concluding the clinical contact can be entertained as a possibility.

In the context of general psychotherapy, then, termination criteria can be defined as those indicators that demarcate the shift from the working therapy process to a termination phase. The emergence of these indicators presage the move into a demarcated termination phase; the period of focus on these indicators constitutes a pretermination phase. Acknowledgment that *the shared goals of therapy have been reasonably fulfilled* constitutes a first indicator that the termination is a possibility. In Palombo's (1982) view, "termination is the process that begins with the achievement of the goals mutually agreed upon by both patient and therapist" (p. 24). These negotiated goals represent the overlap of the therapist's treatment objectives and the patient's targets for therapy. Thus, a reasonable amount of progress should have been made toward achieving the predetermined goals of therapy and both parties should be able to agree that this has occurred (Weiner, 1975). The criterion is not absolute—"reasonably fulfilled" suggests that the patient should be able to express satisfaction with the degree of goal accomplishment realized through therapy.

A second indicator is *a change in the patient–therapist relationship* reflecting a decrease in transference distortions and an increase in the quality of the real relationship. This may be reflected by greater spontaneity in the therapeutic dialogue, patient references to a changed perception of the therapist, and patient behaviors that reflect an improved ability to appreciate the therapist as a real person (Ferenczi, 1927/1955; Kramer, 1990). There may be an augmentation in the quality of the therapeutic alliance (Hurn, 1971). In a dynamically oriented therapy, this change may suggest the initiation of a resolution of the patient's transference to the therapist.

A third indicator is *an observable shift in the patient's concerns towards the future and extratherapeutic circumstances and relationships.* The patient may be explicit about the imminent approach of the end of therapy or this may be implicit in a growing number of references to adaptive future activities, plans, and projects (Quintar, 2001). These references may also be marked by increasing confidence in the ability to independently continue the work of therapy in the absence of the therapist. Fieldsteel (1996) summarized this simplified view of termination criteria as follows:

> When the patient has been able to use the insights and understandings developed in the therapy to respond differently to situations that previously were painful or disruptive, when there is a consolidation of the sense of self, when both positive and negative transferences . . . have been identified and modified, and when the goals set by both patient and therapist have been met, then termination is to be considered. (p. 28)

The indicators of termination just described can be directly linked to the proposed outcomes of termination. Thus, references to attainment of the predetermined goals of therapy can set in motion a process of review, reinforcement, and consolidation of the treatment process and the actual gains made. An experience of a shift in the patient–therapist relationship can initiate a focus on remaining issues between the parties and feelings in regard to the eventual ending of the contact. This dialogue can have the effect of further dissipating transference-based distortions in the patient's perception of the therapist. Finally, the emergence of a perspective on the future and extratherapeutic concerns can mark the start of an evaluation of the patient's readiness to go on without therapy and the degree to which a self-analytic function has been internalized.

Identifying that the indicators of termination have emerged and making this development explicit and concrete ushers in the termination phase proper. The move into the termination phase can be formalized by a discussion of the plan for the ending and the actual setting of the termination date (Lamb, 1985). Often the therapist's proposal of a possible date for the ending will prompt an iterative return to consideration of the criteria for termination. This can be regarded as the patient's effort to feel comfortable with the idea of being ready to terminate therapy. The interaction in regard to the date for ending often resembles a form of negotiation. Frequently, however, if the therapist is clear that countertransference concerns are not acting as an influence on the process, then this negotiation reflects the patient's own ambivalence about moving into the termination phase. Once an end date has been established with mutual agreement, the process of termination is engaged and the termination outcomes assume priority for patient and therapist.

TREATMENT AND PATIENT FACTORS THAT INFLUENCE THE IMPORTANCE OF TERMINATION

In the earlier discussion of brief therapy models and the general approach to psychotherapy used as a basis for the model of termination, we alluded to various factors that influence the degree of importance assigned to the termination in the larger treatment context. These influences can serve to relegate the termination to a minor status or increase its importance so that the phase is critical to the success of the therapy. In this section, we consider in more detail the set of eight factors with potential to influence the importance of the termination. These factors reflect characteristics of the specific therapy case, the treatment approach implemented with the patient, and the personalities of the individual patient and therapist. Exhibit 2.2 lists the factors according to this categorization.

Factors Associated With the Specific Therapy Case

The first factor associated with the specific therapy case is the duration of treatment. Longer treatments tend to focus on character or more profound psychopathology, and the duration and degree of pathology tend to heighten the critical nature of the termination. Longer treatments—open-ended indi-

EXHIBIT 2.2
Treatment and Patient Factors Influencing the Importance of Termination

Factors Associated With the Specific Therapy Case

1. Longer treatments tend to focus on character or more profound psychopathology; duration and degree of pathology tend to heighten the critical nature of the termination.
2. The more overtly the termination is decided upon solely by the therapist, the more emphasis may need to be placed on dealing with the termination to address the patient's feelings of rejection.
3. The more negative or disappointing the therapy outcome, the more emphasis may need to be placed on the termination to address the patient's dissatisfaction.

Factors Associated With the Treatment Approach

1. In briefer therapies, an explicit time limit determined at the beginning of treatment is associated with more emphasis on the termination throughout therapy.
2. The more the treatment is structured and oriented to skills acquisition, the less emphasis may need to be placed on the termination.
3. The more the therapeutic alliance is addressed and used in the therapy, the more emphasis may need to be placed on the termination.

Factors Associated With the Patient or Therapist

1. The less the patient's functioning involves structural deficits and dependence on the therapist, the less the emphasis required on the termination.
2. A history of serious object loss, particularly during critical developmental periods, increases the importance of the termination.

---

vidual or group therapy and psychoanalysis—typically center around fundamental aspects of personality or character or more profound or long-standing psychopathology. They also frequently involve a more extensive exploration and confrontation of the patient's character pathology, object relations, and defensive functioning, meaning that patient and therapist are engaged in a more complicated and arduous therapeutic journey together. Concluding this journey requires that greater emphasis be given to the termination. Duration of treatment and more severe patient pathology, in general, are directly associated with a heightening of the critical nature of the termination because of the degree and period of the patient–therapist involvement.

The second factor concerns the degree of therapist influence on the decision to terminate. The more overtly the termination is decided upon solely by the therapist, the more emphasis may need to be placed on the termination to address the patient's feelings of rejection. That is, in forced terminations, more emphasis may need to be placed on dealing with the patient's response to the ending. Therapist-initiated terminations can dramatically raise the likelihood that the patient will experience the ending as a rejection or abandonment, stimulating issues of separation and loss associated with similar early experiences. Even without an emotional response to the perception of rejection or abandonment, the patient's experience of powerlessness associated with not having input into the decision to end therapy may require airing and review.

The third factor to consider is the quality of the benefits realized in treatment. The more negative or disappointing the therapy outcome, the more emphasis may need to be placed on the termination to address the patient's dissatisfaction. When the patient regards the outcome of therapy as disappointing or less than expected, there is a greater likelihood that the patient's response to the termination will be negative. In this circumstance, attention to the termination is critical to work through the patient's disillusionment and dissatisfaction and help develop an appreciation of what may actually have been accomplished.

Factors Associated With the Treatment Approach

There are three factors associated with the treatment approach. First, in briefer therapies, an explicit time limit determined at the beginning of treatment is associated with more emphasis on the termination throughout therapy. In the previous section, it was noted that longer therapies tend to require greater attention to the termination. A contrasting principle, that is, that the termination is less important in brief therapies, is specifically true only for those short-term approaches that do not place explicit emphasis on a time limit from the outset of treatment. These approaches tend to be either more structured and oriented to skills acquisition or involve a reliance on strict patient selection criteria to reduce the emphasis needed on termination. Examples would include time-limited cognitive–behavioral treatment or the psychodynamic approaches of Sifneos (1979) and Davanloo (1978, 1979). By contrast, the termination is emphasized throughout therapy in the brief approaches of Mann (1973) and Strupp and Binder (1984), approaches which rely on setting a date for the conclusion of treatment at the outset of the patient–therapist contact.

Second, the more the treatment is structured and oriented to skills acquisition, the less emphasis may need to be placed on the termination. These treatments tend to focus on teaching the patient particular skills to use in his or her daily life. By way of examples, the emphasis in these therapies may be on increasing the patient's ability to appraise situations realistically, expanding the patient's repertoire of coping responses in the face of stressful events, or improving the quality of interpersonal interactions. A focus on the patient–therapist relationship is rarely a feature of these approaches. In similar fashion, strains in the relationship are not commented on; instead, the therapist will make use of support and praise to deal with these difficulties. Consequently, issues and feelings around the termination of therapy are rarely addressed; indeed, the ending of treatment is more often approached as a graduation.

Third, and by way of contrast, the more the therapeutic relationship or alliance is addressed and utilized in the therapy, the more emphasis may need to be placed on the termination. These latter two factors associated with the treatment approach in most instances occupy the far extremes of a single dimension, that is, the contrast between therapies that emphasize a relational focus and process to develop insight into the patient's intrapsychic and interpersonal functioning versus those pragmatically oriented therapies emphasizing the development of particular cognitive or behavioral skills. In general, the greater the emphasis on the relational aspects of the patient's pathology, particularly the degree to which the therapeutic relationship or alliance is addressed and used in the therapy, the greater the emphasis that may need to be placed on the termination. This principle includes those therapies that place understanding of the transference (and countertransference) in the foreground, for example, open-ended dynamic psychotherapy. It would also encompass those therapies that exclusively focus on the patient's relational style without making explicit use of transference interpretation or highlighting relational patterns in the therapeutic relationship, for example, short-term interpersonal therapy. With the more skills-oriented approaches, attention to the patient–therapist relationship as representative of functioning in other interpersonal domains is usually not emphasized, although this has been changing with a shift toward greater eclecticism (Safran & Segal, 1990). With regard to the importance assigned to the termination, the central issue is the degree to which the patient–therapist relationship figured into the therapy process and must therefore figure into the negotiation of an ending of that process.

Factors Associated With the Patient or Therapist

Finally, there are two factors associated with the patient or therapist that can influence the degree of importance assigned to the termination. First, the less the patient's functioning involves structural deficits and dependence on the therapist, the less the emphasis required on the termination. The patient's pathology often determines the approach to therapy and its duration, largely reflecting the degree to which the therapist fulfills certain functions for the patient that are lacking because of structural deficits. Consequently, therapy with the more immature or primitive patient often involves the development of an intense dependence on the therapist. The relinquishment of this dependence occurs as patients begin to assume more responsibility for their own functioning, a process that can require an extended period of time. Once again, the depth and duration of involvement between patient and therapist, as well as the patient's anxieties about leaving the safety and security of the relationship where the therapist has functioned in a self-object role, tend to heighten the importance of the termination.

Second, a history of serious object loss, particularly during critical developmental periods, increases the importance of the termination. It is not unusual for patients who present with severe deficits to also report a history of critical or traumatic loss experiences. Termination of therapy for these patients invariably requires a substantial investment of attention and duration.

This principle applies equally strongly to the therapist as it does to the patient, that is, the termination of a therapy that has represented a significant investment for the therapist can resonate with previous experiences of significant loss. These consequences of the current therapy termination may or may not be available to the therapist's awareness, underscoring the value of receiving supervision while engaging in the ending of a therapy. Although the issues of loss brought to therapy by the patient are more explicitly linked to difficulties experienced during termination, the therapist's anxieties about the separation may translate into an abrupt conclusion of the termination process (i.e., avoiding the goodbye) or an inappropriate extension of the ending (i.e., because of perfectionistic fantasies; Ticho, 1972). In other words, the therapist's issues with loss can covertly interfere with the ending by way of countertransference effects unless the therapist has attained a degree of self-awareness or has access to an effective supervisory process.

TERMINATION AS LOSS AND TERMINATION AS TRANSFORMATION

It is commonly held that the termination of therapy can be a source of stress for both patient and therapist and certainly represents a complex period in the therapy, whatever the emotional valence attached to the ending (Schafer, 2002). There is less agreement about whether the termination is invariably a period of crisis for the parties, that is, whether painful issues associated with loss, separation, and mourning tend to predominate over experiences of accomplishment, gratitude, and positive change. From an analytic perspective, Ruderman (1999) emphasized the view that termination is a crisis of loss:

> For patient and analyst alike, termination is often the most intense, painful, and tumultuous phase of analytic treatment. The termination phase can reactivate, or it can activate, for the first time, memories of intrusion and loss from the patient's earliest developmental phases. For both patient and analyst, vulnerabilities, resistances, reactivations of early traumas, and separation and abandonment phenomena become integral to this part of the psychoanalytic journey. In addition, symptoms that had significantly waned or disappeared as the analysis progressed often reappear during the ending phase of treatment. (p. 185)

From this viewpoint, then, termination is invariably a tumultuous, painful, and difficult crisis for the therapy participants.

This termination-as-loss metaphor has represented the prevailing view in the therapy literature. Proponents of this view do not imply that crisis will occur as a function of certain patient factors (e.g., degree of pathology or history of loss) or is due to the aspects of the particular case (e.g., the quality of the treatment outcome) per se, but because crisis is believed to be an inherent aspect of the termination (Quintana, 1993). This bias, thus, tends to ignore the multiple influences discussed previously, that is, the variation in patient responses to termination as a function of psychodynamics, the nature of the problem, and the quality of therapeutic relationship (Wolberg, 1980). As noted earlier, research on patient reactions to the termination of brief therapy suggests that negative reactions occur so infrequently or tend to be so mild in nature as to argue against the idea that the termination is inherently a crisis over loss. Indeed, most patients are reported to have predominantly positive reactions to termination (Fortune, 1987; Marx & Gelso, 1987; Quintana & Holahan, 1992). It is obvious that similar research on patient responses to the termination of moderate to long-term psychotherapies is required to clarify whether the findings of positive reactions are restricted to the brief therapy approaches. In response to these findings, however, clinical theorists have recently placed more emphasis on the termination as an opportunity for patient development that is not otherwise available at any other time in therapy (Barnett et al., 2000; Maholick & Turner, 1979; Quintana, 1993).

The impending loss of the therapist is thought to promote personality development by facilitating internalization of the therapy process or the functions of the therapist. In this view, termination is a critical transition that, if appropriately addressed, can promote transformations in the therapeutic relationship and in how patients view themselves, their therapists, and their therapies (Quintana, 1993, p. 429). A consideration of the factors likely to increase the importance of the termination as represented in a given therapy case can help determine the likelihood that the termination-as-loss experience will be salient for the patient, the therapist, or for both participants. At the same time, attention to the outcomes of termination can demonstrate to the patient that change has indeed occurred over the course of therapy, can be maintained in the absence of contact, and can actually be continued through the patient's ongoing use of the capacities and skills developed during treatment. In other words, an effective termination means that unmet expectations and problematic feelings have been dealt with, and positive changes acknowledged both as accomplishments and as a foundation for further personal development. "While the termination leads to mourning and disappointment, the patient often experiences this phase as a new beginning" (Ticho, 1972, p. 325). For a given therapy, then, the termination has the potential to be both an experience of loss and a potent opportunity for transformation. Chapter 3 considers those aspects of the process of termination that should be addressed at the ending of psychotherapy to increase the likelihood of a positive transformation.

CONCLUSION

This chapter has laid a general groundwork for understanding of the termination in psychotherapy. Fundamental principles in regard to the ending of therapy were derived from review of the literatures on psychoanalysis and the brief therapy approaches that began to emerge in the 1970s. Additional principles were derived from a comparative discussion of the general psychotherapy, moderate-to-longer term dynamically oriented therapy used as a frame for the development of the model of termination; and psychoanalysis, brief therapy, supportive therapy, and group therapy. The identified principles, summarily listed in Exhibits 2.1 and 2.2, address both general parameters of therapy termination and the specific factors associated with the patient or treatment approach that influence the degree of importance to be placed on the termination phase.

It should be clear from the discussion that there is no single way to conceptualize the termination—this kind of uniformity myth would only be possible if there was a single method of psychotherapy available to practitioners and if all patients were similar in all essential respects. Instead, what emerges is a general view of the termination as a sequence of interdependent phases. In terms of the general psychotherapy, the termination begins to emerge naturally as the working phase winds down, that is, when further examination of the patient's issues or problems proves less likely to yield additional benefit. At this point, the model suggests that attention to the termination criteria by patient and therapist becomes appropriate; we referred to the period when this occurs as a pretermination phase. In simple terms, the termination criteria have been met when (a) the shared goals of therapy have been reasonably fulfilled, (b) a change toward greater equity is evident in the patient–therapist relationship, and (c) there has been a shift in the patient's concerns toward the future and extratherapeutic circumstances and relationships. Agreement that the criteria have been adequately fulfilled leads to a negotiation in regard to the end date for the therapy; once this date has been established, the termination phase has been initiated. Thus, the pretermination phase represents a transition between the working phase of therapy and the termination phase. In turn, the termination phase represents the transition between the time spent engaged in the therapeutic process and a life without therapy.

Factors associated with the therapy approach and characteristics of the patient were noted as influencing the degree of importance assigned to the closing phase of treatment and, consequently, the degree of fit the model described here might have for a given therapy case. We return to a more detailed discussion of these treatment factors in chapters 4 and 5 and of the patient characteristics in chapter 6. Prior to those discussions, chapter 3 fleshes out the termination phase model introduced here, and an examination of the specific tasks and elements of the process associated with the termination phase is undertaken.

3

THE PROCESS OF TERMINATION

The primary focus in this chapter is on the process of those terminations that arise "as a natural organic outcome of the treatment process itself" (Loewald, 1988, p. 155) in open-ended, psychodynamically oriented therapy. The discussion applies to open-ended therapies in both individual and group formats. These terminations can be contrasted with endings associated with preestablished time limits in brief therapy approaches, terminations characterized as temporary interruptions in the ongoing supportive treatment of more chronic patients, or endings due to extraneous factors. Implications for practice based on the general psychotherapy are generalized to these other therapy approaches in the manner discussed in chapter 2.

This chapter is divided into three major sections. The sections follow the late phases of an open-ended therapy. The first section considers issues associated with the ending of the working phase, with a focus on the therapist's preparation for termination. The second section addresses the pretermination phase, the relatively brief period associated with emergence of the termination criteria. The third section considers the termination phase proper. The text of the discussion implies that the boundaries between these phases are distinct. In practice, however, the boundaries will not be as readily evident unless made explicit by the patient or therapist. The exception is the setting of the actual date of the last session that marks the move from the pretermination phase to the termination phase proper.

The discussion in chapter 2 included a description of the three outcomes associated with the termination of therapy. In this chapter, each outcome is addressed as an endpoint of the process of the termination phase. The affective themes and therapist tasks associated with the process of working toward each of the termination outcomes are discussed. The discussion also includes an examination of the issues that characterize the closing and final sessions of therapy.

Figure 3.1 depicts the termination phase model introduced in general terms in chapter 2. This model provides the framework for the discussion in this chapter. It summarizes the tasks of the therapist associated with determining the appropriateness of the termination, evaluating the termination criteria, and implementing and conducting the termination phase itself. The tasks of the latter phase are organized in terms of the three outcomes of the termination. The concluding section offers a summary of the clinical principles identified in the discussion that are relevant to the process of bringing an open-ended psychotherapy to a successful termination.

ENDING OF THE LATE WORKING PHASE

In open-ended therapy, the conclusion of the working phase and the move toward the termination phase are marked by indications that the patient has attained the objectives of the treatment and the emergence of the termination criteria. For the therapist, this transition necessitates a consideration of the entire course of treatment. The therapist's review is oriented toward preparing for the termination of therapy, centered on a "best guess" prognosis regarding the likely problems to be encountered in the termination process.

The quality of the impending termination process will have been foreshadowed by how the patient's earlier achievements of greater inner freedom and individuality were experienced in terms of distance in the ongoing therapy relationship (Loewald, 1988). If the patient has been comfortable with the growth in autonomy and the therapy relationship has actually developed a greater intimacy, then the likelihood is that the termination phase will be fairly smooth. However, if the patient has experienced anxiety with each step toward greater autonomy, and the therapy relationship has been upset by issues associated with dependency (e.g., at the times of therapist vacations), then the termination phase is likely to be characterized by more turmoil and affect.

Every therapy relationship involves some degree of patient dependence on the therapist. This dependence might be limited to the patient's need to acquire skills or obtain support for maintenance of function. Alternatively, it may extend to resolution of intrapsychic or interpersonal conflict or to development of a more resilient personality structure. Consequently, regardless

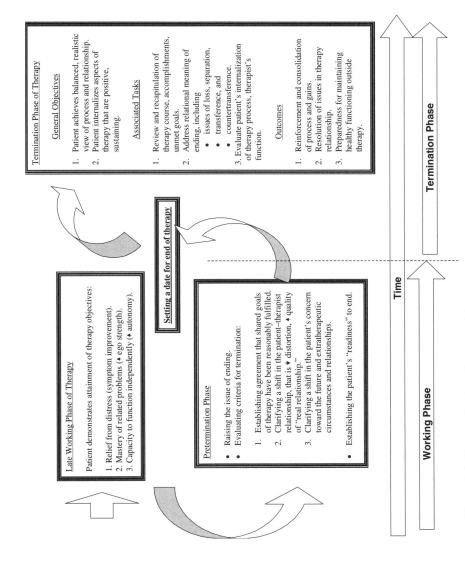

Late Working Phase of Therapy

Patient demonstrates attainment of therapy objectives:

1. Relief from distress (symptom improvement).
2. Mastery of related problems (▲ ego strength).
3. Capacity to function independently (▲ autonomy).

Setting a date for end of therapy

Pretermination Phase

- Raising the issue of ending.
- Evaluating criteria for termination:

1. Establishing agreement that shared goals of therapy have been reasonably fulfilled.
2. Clarifying a shift in the patient–therapist relationship, that is ▼ distortion, ▲ quality of "real relationship."
3. Clarifying a shift in the patient's concern toward the future and extratherapeutic circumstances and relationships.

- Establishing the patient's "readiness" to end.

Termination Phase of Therapy

General Objectives

1. Patient achieves balanced, realistic view of process and relationship. Patient internalizes aspects of therapy that are positive, sustaining.
2.

Associated Tasks

1. Review and recapitulation of therapy course, accomplishments, unmet goals.
2. Address relational meaning of ending, including
   - issues of loss, separation,
   - transference, and
   - countertransference.
3. Evaluate patient's internalization of therapy process, therapist's function.

Outcomes

1. Reinforcement and consolidation of process and gains.
2. Resolution of issues in therapy relationship.
3. Preparedness for maintaining healthy functioning outside therapy.

Time

Working Phase

Termination Phase

Figure 3.1. The termination phase model.

TABLE 3.1
Comparison of Characteristics of the Working and
Termination Phases of Psychotherapy

Characteristic	Working phase	Termination phase
Trajectory of process	Linear, progressing toward treatment goals.	Oscillating, involving review alternating with anticipation of the future.
Focus of participants	Patient's view of issues and circumstances.	Emotional meaning of loss of therapy and therapist.
Relationship concern	Negotiating and maintaining a strong therapeutic alliance.	Separation, addressing positive and negative feelings, resolving issues.
Content	Patient issues may or may not discuss themes of separation and loss.	Themes of separation and loss predominate.
Overall aim	Achieve shared goals of treatment.	Reaffirm that patient has acquired the tools of therapy to be able to continue on own.

of the treatment objectives or approach, the termination phase has the potential to stimulate universal issues associated with the separation from or loss of nurturing relationships.

Features of different therapy approaches that may influence the importance of these issues in the termination process were discussed in chapter 2. Even if dealt with appropriately, or if less relevant in the therapist's approach, these issues can nonetheless color the ending of any therapy. A therapy that involves many of the factors discussed in chapter 2, or is reflected by greater preponderance of a few of these factors, will demand that the therapist pay particular attention to the therapy process during the termination phase. Even when these factors are absent in therapy, issues associated with the termination may nonetheless be latent in the patient–therapist interaction. The therapist should be aware of this possibility and use his or her clinical judgment with regard to the appropriateness of making these issues explicitly manifest for examination in the closing sessions with a particular patient.

The characteristics of the working and termination phases are qualitatively different; Table 3.1 briefly summarizes a number of these. The examination of specific issues during the working phase of therapy may have a cyclical or circular character. In general, however, the working phase of therapy has a linear trajectory—there is a consistent movement forward toward attainment of the goals of therapy. The focus during the working phase is on the patient's point of view in regard to his or her issues and situation. In contrast, the termination phase has an oscillating trajectory, between recapitulating work done earlier in therapy and applying the insights and associated changes to an imminent future without the therapy relationship. The focus of the participants also shifts during the termination phase, with primary attention to the patient's material regarding termination, that is, the meaning of separation from and loss of the therapy relationship and therapist. The therapist's experience of the ending of the therapy relationship should also be attended to as the process unfolds, in terms of how it may interfere with this process. As a general rule, this material is not brought into the discussion during sessions but does remain critical to the therapist's consideration of countertransference, be this on his or her own or in supervision.

The passage from the working phase to the termination phase can also elicit a number of changes in the therapy process and relationship. Intensity may return to the working alliance, the transference, and the process of working through persistent issues. Insights may be reformulated, and understandings and the associated changes in behavior and interaction may be reviewed and reworked. The working phase of therapy has the aim of achieving the agreed-on goals of treatment. The therapeutic process during the termination phase aims to reaffirm that the patient has acquired the tools to continue the course of change and increasing self-awareness on his or her own (Fieldsteel, 1990).

The task of termination is to allow the patient to weather the regressive pull of the separation and loss of the therapist as an "elected surrogate parent" (Pipes & Davenport, 1999, p. 329) and consolidate the gains made earlier in therapy (Shapiro & Ginzberg, 2002). In contrast to the forward-looking orientation of the working phase of therapy, the perspective taken during the termination phase is characterized by a review of the work accomplished and attention to the here and now of the therapeutic relationship. An important task at the time the working phase of therapy appears to be ending is to be explicit that this transition will have to occur, that is, getting the possibility of ending the therapy "on the table."

From a psychoanalytic perspective, Liegner (1986) described the ideal situation at the point of moving into a termination phase. Generalizing from this perspective, the description highlights the paradox of termination for both parties in most therapeutic relationships.

> [It is] that period of an analysis when the transference neurosis is well established, when conflicts appear to have been successfully resolved, when the patient's intrapsychic and external life meet most of the criteria of a healthy and well-functioning person. The patient and analyst are in a state of positive feeling for one another and working cooperatively toward the dissolution of the transference neurosis. But the patient may find himself trapped. He wants the satisfaction of functioning autonomously yet does not want to part with this emotionally significant person who has played such a vital role in his life. Despite his awareness of the analyst as a separate person whom he can view objectively, this emotional attachment remains, even though free of the neurotic expectation of gratification of infantile impulses. The analyst too may feel no wish to sever the relationship. He may feel good about having accomplished what

he was employed to do, but his patient has also assumed emotional significance to him. They have been on a long journey together. There is a feeling of mutual respect and affection uncolored by neurotic gratification, self-aggrandizement, or financial needs. The treatment seems to be working its way toward a healthy separation with both parties in a state of positive feeling. (p. 8)

The move into the termination phase of the treatment process may be hampered by (a) normal tendencies to avoid issues of loss and separation, (b) the therapist's greater comfort with relationship-building rather than relationship-uncoupling activities, and (c) less therapist emphasis on case management issues like termination (Ward, 1984). Negotiating the transition into the termination phase and completing the termination process will be smoother if patient and therapist were able to establish an explicit understanding of the goals of therapy at the beginning of treatment (Lanning & Carey, 1987). In effect, the therapist should consider the ending of therapy as a salient issue from the outset, not only when it emerges as a possibility late in therapy.

Hoyt (1979) suggested that "all the work of the therapy may be seen as prologue to (and part of) the termination" (p. 208). A number of authors (Ekstein, 1965; Gaskill, 1980; Grinberg, 1980; Rangell, 1966) have stressed that the end phase of analysis or analytic therapy is an intensive, summing-up process, reviewing and repeating in depth the various themes and conflicts of the treatment. This process is seen as a required one, to consolidate and integrate the gains of the therapy. The end phase is not only a period that involves attention to the consolidation of gains but also a test of the therapy, an examination of the stability of these previous achievements (Levy, 1986, p. 123).

As the termination begins to emerge as a possibility, the therapist should be prepared for the specialized work to follow. Golland (1997) proposed that four general principles should govern the therapist's conduct of the termination in open-ended, analytically oriented therapy. The first guiding principle is that the therapist follows the lead of the patient. For the termination experience to be truly reparative, patients must be allowed "to develop in their own fashion, move at their own pace, and end when they are ready" (Ruderman, 1999, p. 187). The second guiding principle is that the termination follows, in spirit, the technical style of the treatment itself, as it has developed in the individual case (see also Dewald, 1982). Termination is a phase of the therapy with characteristic issues, but except for the common practice of agreeing on a date, there is a general consensus that special techniques are neither required nor appropriate. Lipton (1961) explicitly indicated that this principle applies even in the closing session. The third principle is that therapeutic considerations continue to remain a priority during the closing phase of treatment. In other words, the therapist should consider each step forward toward termination in terms of its therapeutic value for the patient at that particular juncture. For example, would it be therapeutic for the patient at this point to address closing the working phase and initiating the termination phase? Are there any impediments to the patient moving into the termination phase of therapy and negotiating this phase successfully? The fourth guiding principle is the most important: Endings of treatment need time and thoughtful consideration. An open-ended, analytic therapy is designed to foster powerful transferential affects and fantasies. Ending such a treatment must, therefore, be a careful process in which patient and therapist pay close attention to the special issues that parting always involves (Golland, 1997). Kramer (1990) argued that it can only enhance the treatment if the therapist serves as a healthy role model, enabling the patient to deal with feelings about the ending and the loss, as well as the new beginning represented by the termination of therapy.

These guiding principles outline how the therapist should approach the work associated with the ending of therapy. In addition, two general objectives outlining what should be accomplished during the final phase of therapy can be considered. First, the therapist aims to have the patient achieve an emotionally balanced and realistic view of the treatment process and accomplishments and of the therapeutic relationship. This objective of balanced appraisal requires consideration not only of the gains realized in therapy but also of the limitations of the endeavor, in terms of what goals were not achieved or still require therapeutic examination. It also requires that the positive and negative qualities and experiences in the therapeutic relationship be addressed in equal measure. Therefore, the first and second termination outcomes are encompassed by this first general objective. As the second general objective, the therapist seeks to ensure that the patient takes away, or internalizes, something positive and sustaining from the therapy. Depending on the nature of the patient and his or her problems and the therapy approach implemented, this internalization could encompass (a) the experience of being supported and valued, (b) useful problem-solving skills, (c) the therapist's interpretive function, (d) the experience of a collaborative alliance, or (e) the actual process of therapeutic work. Whatever the aspect of therapy successfully internalized, the assumption is that the patient is able to make use of this aspect, following termination, to maintain healthy functioning and prevent the recurrence of problems. The third termination outcome is thus encompassed by this second general objective.

EMERGENCE OF THE TERMINATION CRITERIA

Three criteria for termination were introduced in chapter 2. In contrast to the list of idealistic and abstract criteria described by Firestein (1978), the three criteria presented in the previous chapter can be characterized as readily observable and concrete. They include (a) reasonable fulfillment of the shared goals of therapy, (b) a change in the quality of the patient–therapist relationship, and (c) a shift in the patient's concerns toward the future and extratherapeutic circumstances and relationships. In this section we examine these termination criteria in more detail, highlighting the material the therapist can identify as evidence for their emergence.

Attainment of Goals

The evaluation of the termination criteria begins with an assessment of the degree to which the goals of treatment have been attained by the patient. These goals are shared by the patient and therapist, based on a mutual agreement established at the outset of therapy. The assessment of goal attainment is by definition much broader in therapies that are open ended and long term, relative to briefer approaches that focus on a circumscribed problem. Ward (1984) presented a list of areas useful for evaluating patient goal attainment. This list was originally articulated by Maholick and Turner (1979, pp. 588–589) and is applicable across many treatment formats and orientations. The assessment can include the following:

- examining whether initial problems or symptoms have been reduced or eliminated,
- determining whether the stress that motivated the patient to seek therapy has dissipated,
- assessing increased coping ability,
- assessing increased understanding and valuing of self and others,
- determining increased levels of relating to others and of loving and being loved,
- examining increased abilities to plan and work productively, and
- evaluating increases in the capacity to play and enjoy life.

Shift in the Therapy Relationship

In an open-ended treatment, the patient's first communications regarding termination are often implied and not expressed as conscious thoughts and feelings. In the majority of instances, the patient does not speak explicitly of termination. The reporting of significant dreams is often taken as an indirect indication that the issue of termination has assumed intrapsychic importance for the patient, albeit outside of his or her awareness (Liegner, 1986; Usher, 1999). For instance, the patient may repeatedly dream of departures, extended trips to unfamiliar locales; in other dreams, the patient may find him- or herself in isolated areas, at funerals, or in a new or refurbished home. Alternately, the patient may dream of meeting the therapist outside the office, on social occasions.

Allusions to the ending of therapy may also be implied in the content of the patient's verbal material. The patient's discourse may more frequently and intensely refer to experiences of separation and loss by death. These experiences may be from the past or the present, and the patient may have experienced the loss personally or reflect on the losses experienced by others. The shift in the relationship may also occur more directly in the form of a patient question about how long therapy usually lasts or how termination of the relationship will take place. In a minority of cases, the patient may be explicit about feeling better and thinking about leaving treatment.

The patient's preconscious awareness of termination as a possibility can also give rise to changes in the therapy relationship that reflect resistance, anxiety, and strain. Ward (1984) listed a number of behaviors that may signal the onset of the termination stage in this way. This list was drawn largely from the group treatment literature and generally refers to patient actions that reflect a resistance to the idea of termination and separation. These behaviors may include a decrease in the intensity of the work of therapy; lateness, joking, and intellectualizing; missed appointments, apathy, acting out, regression to earlier and less mature behavior patterns, withdrawal, denial, expression of anger, and mourning. In addition, the patient may express feelings of separation and loss, dissolution, futility, impotence, dependency, inadequacy, and abandonment (p. 22). If the patient increasingly engages in some of these listed behaviors or feelings but does not verbalize a desire for termination, then it may become necessary for the therapist to explicitly initiate the process.

Shift in the Patient's Current Concerns

A change in the patient's conscious concerns often heralds that the time for termination has arrived. The patient's discourse may more frequently and intensely refer to current and past relationships that involve changes in him- or herself, or experiences of separation and loss by death. Contrasting references to reunions and encounters with former significant others may be given importance in the session. The patient may spend several sessions reporting how well they have been feeling and how well they are handling areas of former difficulty. A future orientation may emerge as the patient begins seriously to consider new jobs or moving to another city, all changes that might prevent him or her from continuing treatment without this possibility being directly mentioned.

Over time and through the experience of a number of therapy cases, practitioners become sensitive to the cues associated with termination. The therapist, if the overall context of the treatment process suggests it, will identify allusions to or expressions of thoughts of nearing actual termination in the material.

When the therapist interprets it in those terms, patients often are taken aback and alarmed as they may be by interpretations of other unacknowledged motivations and connections, interpretations that bring repressed or vaguely felt, unformulated ideas and intentions to the surface. (Loewald, 1988, p. 162)

When these become evident, the patient can be asked directly whether he or she is having thoughts or feelings about ending. If the possibility of termination is a conscious issue, the therapist's verbal expression will initiate discussions and plans for the ending process. If the patient's intentions to terminate are unconscious, discussion may stimulate thoughts and feelings about the therapist's observations of goal attainment, changes in session content, or shifts in the therapeutic relationship (Kramer, 1990, p. 157).

Raising the Issue of Ending

The transition into the termination phase (i.e., the pretermination phase) may be divided into two stages (Loewald, 1988). During the initial stage and with the therapist's help, the patient arrives at a decision about whether or not to terminate. This first stage is initiated by the various indications that the patient "unconsciously or consciously approaches the question of terminating treatment with more than casual glances" (p. 155) and is also characterized by the review of the termination criteria. The patient's responsibility for deciding to terminate is central to this discussion. An important message the therapist can communicate to the patient is that "ending by choice . . . implies faith in the future" (Murdin, 2000, p. 1). The therapist also underscores that this responsibility encompasses a willingness to openly explore the question of "readiness" for termination. The second pretermination stage involves a crystallization of the patient's decision to end therapy. It is ushered in when patient and therapist are able to come to agreement on a number of important points: (a) that the patient, implicitly or more directly, has been seriously and rather consistently thinking about actually ending treatment; (b) that termination in the near future makes sense; and (c) that the therapy can conclude with the participants having a clear perspective on the quality of the treatment outcome.

After discussion of the subject of termination has been initiated, it is necessary that the therapy process be restructured to focus on issues associated with the evaluation of therapy progress and the patient's readiness for termination (Ward, 1984, p. 22). The therapist takes the patient's contributions to an assessment of therapy goal attainment into account. The therapist also considers the reliability of the patient's statement that he or she is ready to leave therapy. However, according to Loewald (1988), "it is the therapist's responsibility, and an aspect of his competency, to make an objective assessment" of the termination criteria, "so as to agree or disagree with the patient about termination" (p. 159). In an open-ended therapy, disagreement about the appropriateness of termination, in general, can suggest one of two possibilities: first, that the therapist's perspective is correct and a furthering of the working phase should be considered, or, second, that the patient's perspective is correct and therapist countertransference is clouding the issue (see the discussion of countertransference in "The Termination Phase" section). To repeat, for therapeutic purposes, the final decision about proceeding toward termination remains with the patient.

If, after the topic of termination has been explicitly brought into the therapy process and the other termination criteria are positive, the patient remains uncertain about his or her ability to maintain gains without therapist support, then ending the therapy process may be inappropriate (Ward, 1984). Reassessment should be conducted to determine whether the lack of readiness stems from unfinished therapy work related to the goals of treatment, a hidden dependent transference on the therapist, or the stimulation of intense affective issues related to previous loss experiences. A "recycling" back into the working phase of therapy may have to be undertaken (Ward, 1984, p. 24).

The therapist's own feeling about the potential ending is one of the most reliable indicators of the patient's readiness to terminate. Two patients may bring the possibility of ending into the process and demonstrate fulfillment of the termination criteria in the same way, but only one patient may actually be ready to leave treatment. The only detectable difference will be in the therapist's internal response to the emergence of the topic and evidence for achievement of the termination criteria (Murdin, 2000, p. 64). A key element of the therapist's response is his or her sense of the patient's level of anxiety in conjunction with the focus on the possibility of termination.

Firestein (1978) stated that the actual "setting of the date makes termination more real" (p. 238) to the patient. The concrete action of setting the date can stimulate intense regressive reactions in many patients. These reactions do not in every instance indicate that a recycling back into the working phase is necessary. The critical question is the degree to which the patient has the resiliency and capacity to successfully resolve these reactions, using the therapy relationship and the skills acquired through the course of treatment. The quality of the process and manner of resolving these reactions can also provide further evidence for the patient's fulfillment of the termination criteria (Levy, 1986). Conversely, if "new" material emerges after a date has been set, the possibility of prolonging the termination period has to be considered. Even if the new material is understood as a reaction to the idea of terminating, this is an indication that the patient is not feeling quite ready to end and may, legitimately, need more time. If the new material is something that the patient had not been conscious of until the time for ending was negotiated, the therapist should flexibly extend the termination phase for a period to help the patient understand and deal with this information (Usher, 1999, p. 104).

Thus, the actual setting of the date for termination is an event that involves reality testing for the patient. Rather than being viewed as a process between the patient and therapist, the "negotiation" of the ending date is more appropriately regarded as a representation of the patient's ambivalence about the termination. In most instances of open-ended therapy, the patient will experience competing feelings about the ending. The negotiation reflects the patient's effort to find an affective balance and be able to acknowledge his or her readiness to say goodbye to the therapist and therapy. A central task associated with the setting of the end date is to help the patient acknowledge that ending is a real event that is inevitable. The establishment of this fact in the therapy relationship most likely has a similarly profound effect on the clinician (Kramer, 1990, p. 29) and reinforces the importance of reflection on possible countertransference feelings.

A Comment on the Group Therapy Situation

The presence of multiple therapy participants in the group context (i.e., fellow group members, cotherapists) increases the complexity of the issues associated with the emergence of termination criteria, as previously discussed. For example, another group member may identify a patient's apparent readiness for termination, or the possibility of ending therapy may be explored mutually by several patients simultaneously. A focus on the issue of ending therapy by one patient can frequently trigger similar concerns for or about other patients. The therapist in the group situation therefore has to contend with examining not only the ramifications of a possible termination with the patient in question but also how the termination impacts the other patients in the group.

The determination of the patient's readiness to terminate, and the negotiated setting of the final date, may also involve greater complexity in the group situation. A range of options is available to the group leaders. Decisions regarding the timing of termination can remain the province of the individual patient, but the other members may be used as consultants in the patient's evaluation of the associated issues. Given the different relationships the patient may have with each group member certain opinions may carry a great deal of weight, whereas others may be discarded. Alternatively, the decisions associated with the transition to a termination phase may be based on the consensus of all members. The evaluation of the appropriateness of termination by the therapist may or may not incorporate the perspectives of those members who are remaining in the group. These considerations increase in complexity still further when the group is led by cotherapists.

The group therapists may thus need to define a strategy with regard to patient termination prior to beginning or early in the life of the group. Frequently, prospective patients are informed about the expectations in regard to termination prior to entering the group. Once the group is under way, the focus of the leaders is on the development of group norms that govern how the members address the possibility of ending and moving into a termination phase.

THE TERMINATION PHASE

At the point where the possibility of ending has been entertained and a date has been set to make it a reality, the therapeutic relationship should be characterized by a consistency of mutual respect and productive collaboration. In other words, the therapeutic alliance will be strong and resilient, all the more for having been through "rupture and repair" sequences during the working phase of therapy. Kramer (1990) argued that over and above attention to the health of the alliance, the therapist must also cultivate a respectful attitude toward the patient—seeing the patient as autonomous, proactive, and self-directive—to facilitate healthy, productive endings. Throughout the termination phase, the therapist's capacities to be empathic, tolerant, and nonmanipulative are critical.

Greenson (1992) described four elements of the therapy process that the therapist must be cognizant of when going through the termination phase. The description was written for the analytic situation but applies equally well to a long-term, dynamically oriented psychotherapy. The first consideration during the termination phase is that all of the patient's material, apart from what else it may refer to, must carry some reference that the therapy is ending. It is extremely important for the therapist to be continually wondering how the patient is reacting to the upcoming ending, what thoughts and fantasies the patient may have about it, and what plans the patient has for the period immediately after termination. "In fact, once the topic has been introduced, the eventuality of termination should be raised at *every* opportunity and should constitute a part of all the therapist's conceptualizing and formulating of the patient's material and behavior" (Usher, 1999, p. 109). The second element requiring scrutiny is the therapeutic relationship in its various guises. "One must pay attention to the patient's transference reactions, to the state of the working alliance, and to the real relationship" (Greenson, 1992, p. 341). The third element is the form of the patient's depressive reaction to the notion of termination. The patient should be able to recognize that he or she is going to miss the therapist and the therapy, while at the same time feeling the anger, disappointment, or other affects that emerge around the close of the relationship. In other words, the patient's recognition and expression of ambivalence, in relation both to the therapy and to outside life, is characteristic of a healthy termination process (Mander, 2000). The final element is the increased likelihood the patient will do more acting out during the termination phase. "In part, this is a means of testing out the old neurotic patterns to see if they still give gratification, partly to say goodbye to the old neurotic pleasures, and partly to make a transition from reenactment to memory" (Greenson, 1992, p. 342).

Each of the outcomes of termination must be addressed during the final phase of therapy. Whatever the treatment approach or modality, a review and consolidation of the treatment process and gains is central to the termination phase. Attention to the resolution of issues in the therapeutic relationship will vary as a function of the importance of the relationship in the process, but issues of separation and loss will likely need to be acknowledged in the close of any treatment. The therapist should also reflect on transference and countertransference reactions to the termination, whether or not these are brought into the therapeutic discussion. Fear, uncertainty, sadness, and grief, as well as anger, disappointment and resentment, but also a sense of mastery and hopeful anticipation, are all affects that may be aroused in the patient by the move toward the ending of the therapeutic collaboration (Tyson, 1996). The final termination outcome, reinforcing the patient's preparedness for maintaining healthy functioning, is essentially seeing the patient safely out of the therapy relationship and into a life without therapy. For those patients characterized by structural deficits or a strong dependency on the therapist, this particular outcome may be difficult to achieve. For other patients, the primary consideration is the degree to which a strong sense of autonomy and a self-analytic function has been established.

Murdin (2000) pointed out that "a good ending needs to be in the present" (p. 134). The patient and therapist can value what they achieved together and the quality of their relationship at this juncture in the therapy but can also look toward a future that includes separation without undue anxiety. "This attitude allows for the stage in which ending becomes part of the discourse that makes up the therapy but is neither dreaded nor desired to an extent that creates unbearable anxiety" (p. 136).

Addressing the Outcomes of Termination

On the basis of a review of the behaviors reported to occur most frequently during the terminations of 72 brief therapy clients, Marx and Gelso (1987) described the typical termination as consisting of three objectives:

- looking back (reviewing the therapy and goal attainment),
- saying goodbye (an examination of the patient's feelings about the ending), and
- looking ahead (moving toward an agreed-on date for the final session and discussing future plans, including additional therapy).

Quintana and Holahan (1992) found that unsuccessful therapy cases involved endings that were characterized by less review of the course of therapy, less activity bringing closure to the patient–therapist relationship and the patients' affective reactions to termination, and less frequent discussions of life following the end of therapy. Each of the results identified in these studies has a parallel with an outcome of termination, and each is important in effectively negotiating the termination phase and contributing to a successful treatment. Although a discussion of the practical accomplishments of the therapy is important, the critical focus of the participants is on the *meaning*, in affective terms, of the course of therapy, the nature of the patient–therapist relationship, and the prospect of life without therapy after termination (Levinson, 1977). Exhibit 3.1 highlights the objectives, session content, therapy process, and therapeutic strategies associated with each of the termination outcomes.

Reinforcement and Consolidation of the Treatment Process and Gains

The first outcome of termination requires a review and recapitulation of the work accomplished over the course of therapy and the gains realized through this process. By a review of treatment, we mean a planned or spontaneous discussion of where the patient started compared with where he or she is at the conclusion of treatment in terms of presenting problems, life difficulties, interpersonal relationships, and other aspects of change and growth. This review and summing-up process should include a discussion of how to maintain treatment gains as well as areas the patient can continue to work on by him- or herself after treatment ends (Kramer, 1990, p. 154). It is frequently noted in the literature that this process should actually start at the beginning of treatment. In the early stages of the therapy endeavor, the therapist and patient must resolve the discrepancy between idealistic, grandiose, perfectionistic goals and obtainable, realistic ones (Kramer, 1990, p. 17). If this distinction has not been made, the termination phase may not be established and the process of ending therapy not engaged, because both therapist and patient, consciously or unconsciously, may be continuing to strive for the impossible. It is also frequently recommended in the literature that the patient's progress be discussed throughout the course of psychotherapy. The review process during the termination phase can thus be a summary of previous reviews. The patient's perceptions and input are critical to this ongoing progress review as a check on the therapist's point of view; the critical nature of the patient's evaluation is highlighted further at the time of termination.

Frequently, the process of review is characterized by the reemergence of the patient's initial symptoms, chief complaints, and problem areas that may have been regarded as resolved or at least to have received a good deal of attention during therapy. In most instances, when prior difficulties do reappear during the termination phase, "it is as if the whole difficulty is repeated in compressed and attenuated form in a short period of time" (Levinson, 1977, p. 485). This reemergence may be associated with unfinished work on the salient issues, occur because the patient is prepared to work at a deeper level on the same problems, or serve as an active test of the achievements of

EXHIBIT 3.1
Termination Outcomes: Objective, Content, Process,
and Therapeutic Strategy

1. REINFORCEMENT AND CONSOLIDATION OF THE TREATMENT PROCESS AND GAINS

Objective

- Attainment of this termination outcome involves a review and recapitulation of the work accomplished over the course of therapy.
- The patient's understanding of issues, now resolved, can be tested by anticipating future problem situations.

Content of sessions

- The review compares where the patient started with where he or she is in terms of presenting problems, life difficulties, interpersonal relations, and other aspects of growth.
- The discussion focuses on how to maintain treatment gains, areas the patient can continue to work on, and the degree of transfer of therapy process and gains to life outside therapy.

Therapy process

- The process is often characterized by a reemergence of the initial symptoms: chief complaints and problems, even if resolved, frequently reflect the patient's attempt to deal with loose ends or test the strength of therapeutic gains.
- The process may also involve the patient's introduction of "new" issues, frequently reflecting some form of resistance to the idea of ending the treatment.

Therapeutic strategy

- The patient's perceptions and input regarding work accomplished, satisfactions and dissatisfactions, and confidence regarding the future are examined.

2. RESOLUTION OF ISSUES IN THE PATIENT–THERAPIST RELATIONSHIP

Objective

- There is open exploration and discussion of feelings associated with the dissolution of the relationship; ideally, the interaction around the topic is characterized by immediacy.

Content of sessions

- Feelings associated with previous losses in the patient's life may emerge and should be addressed in the same way as other issues during treatment.
- Feelings associated with the loss of the "old self" or previous and maladaptive ways of seeking gratification are also likely to be stimulated.
- The patient's transference at the time of termination can reflect a resurgence of themes addressed earlier in the therapy, the reenactment of earlier relationship losses (including oedipal disappointments), or manifestations of resistance to the idea of ending the treatment.

Therapy process

- For the patient, termination involves the loss of a valued change process, the person of the therapist, and the therapeutic relationship; addressing these losses involves mourning as a conscious process.

- For the patient, a difficult aspect of dealing with the termination is realistically acknowledging the limitations of the therapy and therapist.

Therapeutic strategy

- The patient is encouraged to articulate all feelings in regard to the loss of the therapy relationship; this can span a broad range of affects, both negative and positive.
- The therapist contrasts the patient's perceptions of rejection or abandonment with the reality of the termination; that is, the goals for treatment have been achieved and the patient is ready to go on without therapy.
- The therapist actively encourages the patient to engage in a goodbye to the therapy and the therapeutic relationship; in contrast, quietly witnessing the goodbye to the old self is often sufficient.
- It is critical for the therapist to deal thoroughly with negative aspects of the patient's transference at the time of termination.
- The termination can stimulate a range of countertransference feelings in the therapist, depending on the characteristics of the case, the therapist's own issues with loss, or the gratifications the therapist derives from involvement with the patient.
- The therapist should rigorously attend to countertransference feelings both within sessions and over the course of the termination phase; this is particularly true when he or she is unilaterally considering an end to the therapy (i.e., forced termination).
- The therapist's feelings and conflicts in regard to loss are also stimulated by the termination; these as well as countertransference issues should be dealt with (e.g., in supervision, peer consultation) to prevent any negative impact on the patient's goodbye.

3. PREPAREDNESS FOR MAINTAINING HEALTHY FUNCTIONING

Objective

- Maintenance of healthy functioning after therapy is contingent on the patient's internalization of the functional aspects of the therapy; an objective appraisal of the positive contributions of the patient to the therapy process can underscore his or her increased psychological resources.

Content of therapy sessions

- The content of discussion is commensurate with the objectives of treatment, for example, skills development, resolution of interpersonal conflicts, or modification of character structure.

Therapy process

- The therapist helps the patient anticipate future problematic situations.
- Consideration is given to transferring the lessons of therapy to dealing more adaptively with future difficulties.

Therapeutic strategy

- The therapist draws attention to, and validates, the steps the patient has taken toward health.
- The therapist can focus on transformations in the patient's contributions to the process over the course of therapy, highlighting the development of greater skill in the tasks of treatment (e.g., capacity for reflection, contributions to the alliance).
- The therapist expresses confidence in the patient's ability to independently continue the work of therapy.

the therapy. Either way, the establishment of an ending date often provides a stimulus for the patient to return, consciously or unconsciously, to the issues that originally brought him or her to therapy, as a "last chance" to accomplish the outstanding work that may still need to be done (Usher, 1999). Foreknowledge of this phenomenon allows the therapist to explore the underlying meaning for the reemergence of the central issues, rather than taking the patient's report at face value.

Another common occurrence is the introduction of new problems by the patient. Some patients may initiate a discussion of new stresses and problems to deal with during the termination phase and even during the final session (Lipton, 1961). In contrast to the reemergence of familiar symptoms or issues, the introduction of new problems is more likely to reflect some degree of resistance to the termination of therapy. This behavior may have a range of motivations associated with the termination (Levinson, 1977; Murdin, 2000):

- the patient's pursuit of self-perfection;
- a wish to ensure the continued maintenance of the therapy relationship rather than face the forthcoming separation;
- an attempt to appeal to or even seduce the therapist's concern to persuade the therapist to extend the therapy; or
- an attempt to master the fear that if the "real truth" is known the patient will be humiliated or abandoned by the therapist.

Clearly, then, the therapist should not simply dismiss these behaviors as attempts at seduction or minor phenomena of the termination phase. The behaviors can serve as an indication of the patient's unarticulated opposition to the prospect of termination and, thus, inform the participants' examination of issues associated with concluding the therapeutic relationship.

A major consideration in regard to the first outcome of termination is the degree to which the patient has generalized the insights or learning achieved within therapy to his or her life outside (Pipes & Davenport, 1999). This has been referred to as the issue of "transfer," both of the process of therapeutic work to dealing with life issues and crises and of the gains realized in treatment to outside relationships and circumstances (Lanning & Carey, 1987). Developing a summary of the learning that has occurred during the working phase of therapy is one means of ensuring that this generalization will occur. Another productive way of focusing on the specific gains is to ask the patient how he or she might recognize old, unproductive patterns of behavior if they began to reoccur or anticipate future situations in which they would be likely to revert to old patterns. A discussion of how newly learned behaviors might apply in these situations is also generally helpful. In the more supportive approaches or those emphasizing skills development, actual rehearsal of the new behaviors in a role play might be considered. Alternatively, Ward (1984) suggested a number of exercises to facilitate a review of goal attainment, including having the patient prepare a written progress report, reviewing an earlier recorded therapy session, or making use of standardized outcome measures early and again at the end of therapy. In short, it is beneficial to help patients acquire a set of procedures to correct themselves in potentially stressful situations, an effort that also serves to communicate trust in the patient's abilities (Lanning & Carey, 1987).

Review and consolidation of the therapy process and achievements can also include the patient's attempt to actually try out new or differently used behaviors. Invariably, new and possibly unintegrated ways of coping and the inevitable conflicts associated with the patient's effort at change in ongoing relationships will involve varying degrees of anxiety, failure, or disappointment. In response, the patient may be tempted to revert to less adaptive but familiar old patterns. Alternatively, new patterns of thinking, feeling, or behavior may serve to underscore the advantages of renouncing past satisfactions, wishes, or relationships, and highlight how much of the patient's previous life might have been lost or wasted. Consequently, the patient's awareness of his or her degree of health relative to pretherapy can activate feelings of pain, sadness, or shame (Dewald, 1982). This reinforces the point made earlier—even a practical review of the changes made in therapy can stimulate a strong affective response. The therapist can remind the patient that the usual therapeutic examination can be brought fruitfully to bear on these feelings, very much as during the working phase of treatment.

Resolution of Issues in the Patient–Therapist Relationship

In an open-ended psychotherapy, termination can give rise to profound feelings associated with the dissolution of the therapy relationship. In most instances, dealing with these feelings will demand more of the participants than a review of the therapy process and gains (the first termination outcome) or preparing for the maintenance of healthy functioning (the third termination outcome). These issues can be especially problematic in the case of "forced" terminations. This topic is addressed at length in chapter 7 but is given some consideration here, as well. Following this, three topics of some complexity are addressed: issues of separation and loss at the time of termination, transference, and countertransference.

Opening and inviting exploration of the issue of separation is a primary strategy for dealing with affective issues surrounding the cessation of therapy and working through the closure of the therapeutic relationship. Throughout the termination phase, the therapist encourages the patient to explore feelings that arise during the process, especially those of loss, grief, abandonment, and related affects. The therapist can emphasize that although it may be easy and somewhat natural to avoid and deny such feelings, they are very important for the successful conclusion of therapy. An important strategic orientation during this phase is that of immediacy or encouraging a direct discussion of the patient's feelings toward the therapist and toward their relationship.

> More than any other single indicator, the presence or absence of this increased attention to and working through of relationship factors discriminates between approaches that use the termination process most effectively as a facilitative or therapeutic mechanism in its own right and those that do not. (Ward, 1984, p. 23)

The goal of this emphasis is the expression of an appropriate and meaningful goodbye at the actual conclusion of therapy. An essential guideline in regard to the therapist's attention to affective and relationship factors during termination is that, if used, therapist disclosures are never detrimental to the patient (Ward, 1984).

In the group therapy context, Schermer and Klein (1996) noted that the multiple meanings and impacts of termination must be examined not only in terms of intrapsychic and interpersonal functioning but also in terms of the group as a whole. Patients engaged in terminating from group therapy can therefore experience the same range of feelings and conflicts with regard to the loss of the group as they experience vis-à-vis the loss of the other members or group leaders. This experience can encompass a process of mourning; the affects of guilt, shame, and aggression in response to the "dying" group; or the experience of a shortcoming or absence associated with the loss of the functions provided by the group (e.g., support and soothing, a sense of belonging).

Forced Terminations

Many therapist-initiated terminations (ruling out events such as death, moving, or retirement) can be related to countertransference issues (Kramer, 1990, p. 30), especially if the patient gives no cues or suggestions in regard to termination and no clearly observable criteria for termination emerge. Discussion of the therapy case with colleagues or formal supervision can help determine whether this is a possibility and perhaps offer a means toward resolution. There are, of course, cases where the therapist has the clear perception that further contact will not be beneficial to the patient or that problems in the therapeutic relationship are such that productive collaboration is unlikely. In these occurrences, the patient may experience the termination as a clear rejection or narcissistic injury to the self-esteem (Levinson, 1977, p. 482).

If the contract had not stated that there would be an ending at a particular time, then patients will at best have mixed feelings on being told that the therapist will not continue the work beyond a certain date. On the one hand, there may be feelings of anger and disappointment over being abandoned. Depression associated with feelings of powerlessness and displaced grief might well be expected. Given the time constraints, the therapist should encourage a full expression of these feelings. In addition, it can be helpful to express understanding for the patient's reaction, acknowledge responsibility for the decision to end, and provide for validation of the patient's experience of rejection if present. For some patients, the response to the therapist's announcement might translate directly into action, such as demonstrating independence by being late for sessions or threatening to leave therapy before being left. Once again, commenting on these behaviors and the underlying affects, in the context of a truncated therapy, can assist the patient in making the best of a perceived bad situation. On the other hand, some patients work as hard as possible in the time remaining to achieve as much as possible before concluding with the therapist. The patient may express a wish to end well with the therapist in order that the therapist can be retained as a good, conscious image to be called on as needed (Murdin, 2000, pp. 80–81). In these instances, the therapist can capitalize on the patient's stance by highlighting what has been achieved and the patient's maturity in dealing with the abrupt termination in this way.

In the context of a termination initiated unilaterally by the therapist, the general recommendation is to shift the focus to immediate relationship issues between the patient and therapist. This shift will help foster a quick transition to an abbreviated termination phase. Depending on the time allowed before the final session, the therapist might have to restrict the discussion to relationship issues (the second termination outcome) and forego much in the way of examination of gains or planning for the future (the first and third termination outcomes). The conclusion of treatment should be presented as a logical and inevitable step in the change process to minimize the patient's feelings of rejection by the therapist (Lanning & Carey, 1987, p. 172).

Issues of Separation and Loss

For the patient facing the termination of a significant psychotherapy experience, issues of loss can be pervasive. First and foremost is the separation from the therapist and the loss of the therapeutic relationship. Both parties are faced with the ending of a rewarding, stimulating, and productive collaboration. The patient's treatment may have involved exploration of conflicts and feelings experienced in the transference to the therapist and achievements based on the working through of these transference manifestations. These developments should be discussed in the review of the treatment process and gains, that is, during consideration of the first termination outcome. Of course, feelings in regard to the struggles and victories in the process of working through the transference will emerge, and the impending end of the therapy may color many of these affects. However, over and above elements of the transference-oriented work engaged in during treatment, the patient should be encouraged to consider the variety of helpful elements and experiences in the therapeutic relationship itself (Dewald, 1982; Garcia-

Lawson & Lane, 1997). The therapist's patience, tolerance, capacity to listen and understand, reliability, and empathy likely constitute a unique interpersonal experience for the patient. The transference elements of the termination itself, that is, how the separation from the therapist has meaning in the context and under the influence of the patient's life history, also certainly require examination (see the *Transference* section later in this chapter). "But there remains the irreducible fact that precisely this form of experiencing and understanding is itself about to end, is itself about to become part of the historical past" (Loewald, 1988, p. 156).

This fact indicates why the termination stands apart from other aspects of the therapy process: It involves doing the work of *mourning*, that is, experiencing and working through the various affective reactions that are stimulated by the anticipation of separation from and loss of the relationship with the therapist. During the termination phase of psychotherapy, the object being mourned is present, engaged with the patient, and listening. In other words, the therapist's presence during the termination process not only makes mourning a conscious experience for the patient but also highlights those features of the therapy process that the patient can make his or her own. This can be critical to achieving a successful ending, one characterized by closure on the issues present in the relationship and internalization of the therapist's function.

The patient's reactions can include a general sense of loss, sadness, or depression, or more acute separation rage or anxiety. The patient's affects may also be bound in new symptoms or concerns, physical complaints, fantasies about the therapist (Fortune, 1987), underestimations of the amount of progress made, or idealizations or devaluations of the therapy (Donoghue, 1994; Strupp & Binder, 1984). The patient might struggle with impulses to flee therapy or engage in behaviors (e.g., coming late, canceling sessions) indicative of attempts at flight. Conversely, the patient might manifest increased dependency on the therapist, reflected in attempts to postpone termination (e.g., presenting new symptoms or crises) and protect against anxious and angry feelings related to experiences of rejection, abandonment, and separation. Positive reactions are, of course, possible and include an expressed sense of maturity or feelings of achievement, confidence, and relief. However, these reactions often tend to be communicated in the context of patient ambivalence. Often, simply asking how the patient perceived the therapist and their collaboration over the course of treatment will help bring the patient's experience of the therapeutic relationship under direct review.

The therapist may also identify critical incidents in the course of the therapeutic relationship and highlight how the relationship may have changed over time (Lamb, 1985). Statements by the therapist that link symptoms, fantasies, or behaviors to possible feelings about the impending separation can encourage their articulation by the patient. The patient may defend against the work of mourning at termination by denying the existence of painful or intense affects, trying to avoid expressing such feelings, or maintaining that a minimal expression will suffice (Dewald, 1982). The therapist counters this defensive stance by underscoring the importance of dealing with all aspects of the loss experience, and encouraging a continuation of the usual therapeutic attitude. As was the case throughout the working phase of treatment, the patient's experience is clarified, examined, and understood in terms of the dynamics of his or her internal and interpersonal functioning.

The therapist contrasts the patient's perceptions of the imminent separation as a rejection or abandonment with the reality of the termination, that is, that the patient has achieved what were set out as therapeutic goals and is ready to move on in life without therapy. The patient's separation anxiety can be somewhat normalized by noting the importance of the work done together and the difficulty of giving up any relationship of similar value. The task is to facilitate the patient's adaptive experience of the separation anxiety by encouraging a full discussion of the various affects stimulated by the imminent ending (Garcia-Lawson & Lane, 1997). "Mourning work and healthy growth are accomplished only when a relationship is given up which is realistically over and when giving it up can be differentiated from a sense of being deprived or rejected" (Fleming & Benedek, 1966, p. 175). Throughout, the therapist can model openness to a frank discussion of the relationship, including appropriate disclosure in regard to his or her experiences within the frame of the treatment (Lanning & Carey, 1987). Reciprocal disclosures can help to reestablish equity in the patient–therapist transaction, an important element in achieving relationship closure at the time of ending.

The immediacy of the therapeutic relationship at the time of termination may stimulate memories of earlier losses in other relationships. This is particularly likely for those patients with a history of significant object loss and for those cases where loss, separation–individuation, and dependence–independence represented important themes in the therapy (Donoghue, 1994; Marx & Gelso, 1987). The resurgence of feelings associated with previous losses is addressed in the same manner as other material brought into the therapeutic situation. First, the therapist and patient consider the affective impact of those early separation experiences and their impact on current relationships. Second, they examine parallels and contrasts between feelings in the transference and those in regard to the end of the therapeutic relationship. Frequently, the patient's view of these earlier experiences from the perspective of the therapy and its ending can bring about a revised representation of those experiences, an integration that promotes further change (Loewald, 1988). The therapist should seek to reinforce the patient's recognition that the ending is not as difficult as feared and that it can be experienced as empowering, a new beginning rather than amounting to a frightening abandonment (Murdin, 2000).

In a reasonably successful open-ended therapy, the patient will likely need to address the personal loss associated with giving up archaic wishes, now recognized as impossible to fulfill. There is potentially a conscious recognition of frustration and loss of previously desired psychic goals, and acceptance of the fact that the opportunity for certain forms of satisfaction and fulfillment and pleasure appropriate to an earlier period in life may now be irretrievably gone (Dewald, 1982). In related fashion, because of the transformations he or she may have realized during therapy, the need to mourn the "old self" and the gratifications linked to previous maladaptive behaviors can also confront the patient (Levinson, 1977). "There is no immediate comfort for these losses as they belong to the process of maturation and individuation" (Schubert, 2000, p. 113). The therapist will likely need to actively encourage the patient to say goodbye to the therapeutic relationship and therapy process. By contrast, quietly witnessing and acknowledging the patient's goodbye to "who I was" is often sufficient.

For the therapist, the termination brings with it the loss of a patient with whom he or she has had a prolonged and intimate experience. The termination also comes at a time when the patient has achieved a degree of healthy functioning and may be perceived as more attractive by the therapist. The therapist in addition faces the loss of work with the patient and the gratifications—not always monetary, but associated with shared achievement and a personal sense of mastery—this work has provided. Finally, the therapist must contemplate a future where information regarding the patient's situation is no longer forthcoming; in effect, the therapist must contend with not knowing how "the story comes out." In contrast to these difficult feelings, and addressed less frequently in the literature, the therapist may also experience positive feelings of pride and joy for the patient's accomplishments, gratitude, and a sense of freedom or relief.

The termination also has the potential to reawaken the practitioner's own conflicts about previous losses, stimulate anxiety about the patient's ability to function without treatment, or prompt feelings of guilt for not providing all that the patient desired from therapy (Fortune, 1987; Viorst, 1982). Boyer and Hoffman (1993) reported that both therapist loss history and perceived patient sensitivity to loss were predictive of therapist affective reactions—specifically, anxiety and depression—to the termination. The therapist's equanimity during the termination phase depends a great deal on being able to see the patient as a separate and whole person, and not using the patient as a repository of his or her own projected insecurities and impairments associated with previous losses (Murdin, 2000). The therapist's self-analysis or supervision is the appropriate vehicle for working through these termination impacts; bringing these experiences into the therapeutic relationship can be intrusive and interfere with the patient's own process of mourning. Lamb (1985) suggested that it may be appropriate for the therapist to discuss the value and meaning of the relationship with the patient, as well as the general dilemma of parting when life events are going more smoothly for the patient.

Transference

In this section, transference themes that are commonly manifest during the termination phase are considered. The discussion emphasizes identification of these themes and suggestions for addressing them therapeutically during the termination phase. Examination of the patient's transference feelings toward the therapist characterizes many approaches to psychotherapy. This may be a central consideration in analytic forms of treatment, and an important aspect of the work in dynamically oriented approaches, be the format individual or group. In the more supportive therapy approaches, the therapist may be aware of but choose not to address transference issues.

The nature of the transference during the working phase of therapy will be, in part, a reflection of the agreed-on goals of treatment and the therapeutic strategy adopted to meet those goals. The termination may exaggerate transference themes addressed earlier in the therapy, particularly in those cases where the transference involvement has been high and there have been strong wishes to be gratified by the therapist (Levinson, 1977). The termination may also stimulate the emergence of new transference themes associated with endings, separations, and losses. These latter manifestations can serve to complicate the examination of separation and loss issues as described previously or serve as impediments to this important termination work. Because the patient and therapist are in the real situation of stopping a relationship, the transferential responses will at times be related to this, and at times be displacements from figures in the past. When a symptom worsens or new material emerges during the termination phase, possible manifestations of transference reactions have to be considered. "All of the resistances to dealing with feelings about ending and possible transferences will have to be commented on and interpreted in the context of this ending and of past endings in the patient's life" (Usher, 1999, p. 115).

With some patients, the therapist's attention and consistency lead to the emergence of a strong maternal transference, in which the patient's wish for an all-giving and perfectly understanding mother–therapist becomes evident. If such a regressive dependence has been a theme at times during the therapy, then the loss of the therapist implied by the termination can arouse considerable anxiety (Kauff, 1977; Tyson, 1996). Intense negative transference reactions may develop as the patient recognizes the final frustration implied by the termination (Dewald, 1982). The patient may withhold the full intensity of anger or rage associated with feelings of helplessness to preserve the therapeutic relationship, while maintaining unconscious hopes that the infantile wishes will still be fulfilled. With the futility of these hopes finally recognized in the context of the termination phase, the patient can feel that there is nothing in the relationship with the therapist worth preserving. Intense rage may follow, and the associated anxiety and helplessness can reveal certain limitations to the accomplishments of the therapy. If a severe regression ensues and the patient appears to lose the gains of treatment, such as the capacity to maintain object constancy, then the therapist and patient might need to revisit the topic of termination even if an ending date has been set (Tyson, 1996).

The process of termination may also stimulate unresolved oedipal wishes, conflicts, and associated guilt. Although these themes might have been a part of the treatment throughout, they can often arise in a new, different, and more intense way during termination. That is, recognizing the impending loss of the therapist and the therapeutic relationship forces the patient to acknowledge that the oedipal libidinal wishes that were revived in the transference will never be satisfied. Intense anger, envy and jealousy, longing and sadness—that is, the painful affects associated with early childhood oedipal wishes and disappointments—may arise. These may be directed toward other patients, toward the therapist's spouse and family, or directly toward the therapist. The therapist's technique is now challenged with balancing the patient's need to express and work through these affects and the frequent result—that the guilt and anxiety associated with these affects tend to undermine the patient's self-esteem. Titrating the associated anxiety becomes an imperative task requiring tact and sensitivity. The patient must give up the possibility of gratifying, through the therapist, whatever preoedipal and oedipal fantasies were stimulated during the course of treatment and come to terms with the recognition that the therapist has a real life outside the treatment from which the patient is and will be excluded (Tyson, 1996, pp. 503–507).

The process during the termination phase demands that the patient actively leave the therapist, rather than simply passively experience the loss. One of the crucial tasks in this process is the deidealization of the patient's representations of the therapist (Shechter, 1993). Often, painful affects are aroused during the termination phase as the patient asks, "Is this all there is? Why am I not better?" Patients often anticipate that a sense of emptiness will accompany the loss of the therapist, and they experience fears, anxieties, and uncertainties about their future and about their capacity to deal effectively with future conflicts without the help of the therapy (Tyson, 1996). The struggle with disappointments and disillusionments concerning the therapist and the therapy process cannot be shirked. Patients must come to recognize that the therapist cannot protect them from the pain of current intrapsychic conflict or ensure against the pain of conflicts that may appear at any time in the future. In short, the patient must acknowledge that the outcome of therapy has its limitations. If these disappointments can be addressed during the termination phase, then the patient may have less difficulty with disappointment following the conclusion of therapy.

Although each patient's experience of the ending is unique to some degree, Kupers (1988, p. 58) highlighted certain identifiable patterns of transference that arise in response to the termination phase:

- the client who so deeply resents what he experiences as rejection or abandonment by the therapist at the time of termination that he attacks the work of the therapy and undoes or fails to make use of the gains of treatment;
- the client who becomes so anxious and feels so helpless whenever the therapist takes a vacation or mentions termination that a regression occurs and the dependency seems interminable; and
- the client who refuses to become dependent on the therapist in the first place, or denies the dependency that has developed, and is being truthful when, at the time of termination, she or he says, "It's OK, I won't miss you."

Kupers highlighted these patterns to underscore the importance of addressing aspects of negative transference at the time of termination (see also Werbart, 1997). He contended that if the negative feelings are not brought to the surface during therapy, and especially during the termination phase, it is likely they will increase in intensity after termination and undermine the benefits of the treatment. During the termination phase, then, it is critical that the therapist helps the patient articulate the negative feelings, particularly disappointment regarding the therapist or therapy. In this way, the patient can develop a balanced emotional perspective on the treatment and "decide that though there are the negative feelings, the therapy has accomplished a great deal" (Kupers, 1988, p. 59).

A common theme in many treatments is the patient's desire to hang on to therapy in part to avoid life's risks (Kramer, 1990). The therapist must try to be sensitive to the sometimes subtle presence of this phenomenon. For example, during the termination phase, the patient reports developing an interest in the mental health professions. Besides possibly expressing a need to hold on to the therapy by identifying with the therapist (possibly indicating that there are problems with internalization), this may also be an indication of the patient's envy of the therapist, of feelings of sibling rivalry, or possibly of all three. Whatever the motive, the feelings, wishes, and fantasies associated with this interest have to be explored, and the question of their relationship to the therapist's work with the patient must be posed.

Another transference reaction that sometimes emerges during the termination phase is the patient's suggestion that the relationship be carried on in a different form after termination (Usher, 1999). If the purpose for prolonging the relationship is curiosity, something that may emerge more strongly as the termination of the therapy is discussed, the transference fantasies can be explored. During the termination phase, many patients express a yearning for others to serve as a substitute for the therapist. They may displace transference wishes and affects onto new or other key figures in an attempt to avoid working through the disengagement from and loss of the therapist.

Because such activities frequently serve as defenses against the affective experience of loss, the problem for the therapist is to separate genuine behavioral change, on the basis of independence from previous conflicts, from continuing transference displacements. According to Dewald (1982), it is usually possible to recognize the latter situation by the context in which the new behavior occurs, the abruptness of its emergence, its similarities to the therapeutic relationship, and the decrease in intensity of the termination work that results from the new involvement (pp. 445–446).

The patient's negative transference or intense feelings of pain, disappointment, or grief are occasionally accompanied by a wish to frustrate or punish the therapist. Wishes for revenge may motivate the patient to sacrifice the therapeutic gains of a termination process and move toward a premature termination. This can represent a manipulative effort to disappoint and arouse guilt in the therapist for the perceived failure of the therapy process. Other patients may remain in therapy but use a wide range of defensive maneuvers, such as denial, displacement, and devaluation. Some who have formed an intensive transference involvement may devalue the therapist, the therapeutic relationship, and the progress achieved in the attempt to feel reassured that nothing of significance will be lost (Garcia-Lawson & Lane, 1997).

The termination situation can thus promote an intensification of transference reactions or bring new manifestations to the fore. The separation anxiety and depressive affects that can be stimulated originate from all developmental levels. Schafer (1973) considered the transference potential of the termination phase in this way:

> The potential for virtually every significant human emotion resides in the termination situation. . . . The ideal termination would explore all these emotions—for example, feelings of deprivation and longing, guilt and unworthiness, gratitude and envy, triumph and defeat, love and betrayal, disappointment and elation, rage and grief, from all levels of psychosexual and ego development—insofar as they were accessible and significant. (p. 146)

The crucial task for the therapist is to help the patient experience the full emotional meaning of the termination without the interference of countertransference feelings or enactments (Schubert, 2000). The therapist's difficulties with countertransference at the time of termination are considered in the following section.

Countertransference

The issue of ending therapy necessarily involves the therapist in a personal sense (Usher, 1999). Weddington and Cavenar (1979) suggested that the dearth of clinical literature on termination reflects that therapists have difficulty coping with their countertransference feelings. The therapist can encounter difficulties at the time the patient brings up terminating for the first time, particularly if the therapist is not in agreement with the patient's expressed intent. Kramer (1990) emphasized that therapists should not verbally disagree with patients' decisions to terminate, even if they do not believe it is appropriate to end treatment. "There is much to lose and little to gain from the practitioner interjecting personal feelings and needs into the termination decision" (p. 40). During the termination phase itself, the therapist can be vulnerable to a whole range of such needs and feelings (Martin & Schurtman, 1985). Problems arising as a result of countertransference are more likely when there is a break in the empathic bond between patient and therapist. Given the characteristics of the treatment and patient, therapists may become overwhelmed by the intensity and special quality of the patient's resistance, regression, and transference associated with the termination, and may find themselves in a situation where countertransference creates difficulty in recognizing the strength and resources of the patient.

The prospect of separating from a patient with whom the therapist has had an intimate and frequently gratifying experience can induce a deep sense of loss (Maar, 1989). For the therapist, termination can invoke many different kinds of loss: the loss of a whole, real object; the loss of some identified-with part of the object (e.g., the "safe" or "protected" patient); the loss of a healing symbiotic relatedness; the loss of some especially pleasing role; the loss of a host of professional and therapeutic ambitions; and the loss of the therapist's dream of his or her own perfection (Viorst, 1982, p. 416). The more common countertransference reactions are

- conscious or unconscious rage against the patient arising from hurt and loss;
- a tendency to infringe the boundaries of the therapeutic relationship; and
- in an open-ended therapy, postponement of the date of the final session.

Because of these countertransference difficulties, the therapist may even seek to gratify the patient's transference wishes, attempting to provide fulfillment of possibly inappropriate wishes as a way of decreasing the turmoil of the ending.

Liegner (1986, p. 10) suggested that the therapist may face a number of obstacles to resolving his or her own resistances to the termination. For example, the therapist

- may need the patient for financial reasons,
- may need the patient for reasons of self-esteem,
- needs to be needed,
- wants the patient to feel obligated,
- does not want to feel like a failure,

- wants gratitude and appreciation,
- wants to remain in the controlling position,
- does not want to feel inadequate or impotent, and
- may have some transference needs served by the patient.

Levinson (1977, p. 484) also described a number of attitudes, often held unconsciously by the therapist, that have the potential to be inimical to the patient's growth and an obstacle to successful completion of the termination phase—even unnecessarily prolonging the treatment. These attitudes encompass the following:

- The therapist is motivated by his therapeutic ambition to produce a "perfect" case;
- the therapist may expect and demand more from his patient than the patient's motivation, capacity, or situation warrants;
- the therapist may derive gratification from the patient and be unwilling to let go . . . , view[ing] the intimacy involved in the treatment process as a compensatory means of making up to the patient and himself for their childhood traumas, deprivations, and losses;
- the therapist may prolong the treatment, because it reflects his own helplessness and sense of limitation as feelings of defeat and inadequacy are aroused within him as the therapy continues;
- the therapist may prolong the patient's treatment in order to shield and protect himself against hurtful feelings of loss of a person with whom he has experienced a great deal and for whom he has come to feel deeply; and
- the therapist may react compensatorily with the patient for losses that the therapist is currently experiencing in his own life.

For the therapist, as well as for the patient, the completion of therapy may also signify the cessation of a learning experience. When the patient as "teacher" discontinues treatment while the therapist is still actively learning from him or her, the therapist can feel disappointment. A different kind of experience results when the therapist has been receiving vicarious enjoyment from tales of the patient's exploits. The patient may not have been confronted in regard to self-destructive behavior in exchange for the therapist's pleasure in following the patient's misadventures. The therapist may find it difficult to give up this form of voyeurism (Mathews, 1989, p. 32).

The therapist's intent at the time of termination should be to allow the process to unfold without interference and to facilitate the patient's attending to the many issues that may arise. To realize this goal, the therapist needs to examine the possibility that any of these feelings or attitudes exist and to address them sufficiently, by way of self-analysis or supervision. In addition, therapists may need to carefully monitor their countertransference during sessions, being particularly attuned to angry feelings toward the patient. The failure to resolve unfinished business in regard to less-than-satisfactory terminations may impact the therapist's willingness and ability to connect with future patients.

Problems with countertransference at the time of termination are, thus, not unusual. The main problem is not the existence of unresolved conflict or character problems in the therapists, but that they may be unaware of their existence and of their harmful effects on the work of therapy (Noy-Sharav, 1998). Developing an awareness of countertransference needs or feelings can be useful in developing greater empathy for patients, thus helping them to clarify their feelings about termination and the linkages to important early experiences of loss and separation (Ruderman, 1999). How tolerant, empathic, and accepting the therapist is of the patient's reactions to ending therapy will depend on several factors (see Usher, 1999), including

- the therapist's past personal experiences with endings and losses;
- the therapist's history of separation experiences with parents, and the parent's ability or inability to allow for an appropriate separation;
- the therapist's current needs to go on seeing this patient (gratification of providing treatment, other gratifications);
- the therapist's possible guilt over being relieved to "get rid of" this patient; and
- the ending of the therapy relationship coinciding with other endings in the therapist's life.

The quality of the therapist's reflections on the case and its termination, and of the therapist's supervision, can also be added. Empathetically sharing the patient's termination process while mastering countertransference responses offers the therapist the opportunity to be available for new meaningful therapeutic endeavors (Tyson, 1996, p. 520).

Preparedness for Maintaining Healthy Functioning

Internalization is seen as one of the most powerful therapeutic agents (Blatt & Behrends, 1987) and effective management of the termination is considered vital to the reinforcement of internalizations in psychotherapy (Mann, 1973; Quintana, 1993; Strupp & Binder, 1984). The work done in regard to the first two outcomes of termination—reviewing and consolidating the treatment process and gains and resolving issues in the patient–therapist relationship—can go a long way to ensuring that the patient is prepared to maintain healthier functioning following the end of therapy. The review allows the therapist to reinforce both the minor and major accomplishments achieved by the patient over the course of treatment. Attention to the quality and upcoming loss of the therapeutic relationship allows the patient to develop an emotionally balanced and realistic view of the therapist and therapy. In effect, the patient becomes able to acknowledge what was helpful and positive in the relationship while also developing a realistic view of the limitations of the therapist and the therapy.

The therapeutic work around these termination outcomes provides opportunities for patient internalization, for example, patients can acquire a representation of themselves as working capably to resolve problems, or they can retain a representation of a supportive relationship in which they experienced being valued. Thus, during the termination phase, representations of the therapist's function within the therapy relationship, as well as the patient's "self-in-therapy," can be internalized. In turn, these internalizations increase the probability that the patient can continue to make use of aspects of the therapy (a supportive relationship, a particular way of addressing problems) in the absence of the therapist.

To maximize the likelihood that useful internalizations will occur, that is, to ensure attainment of the third termination outcome, there are a number of strategies therapists can implement during the termination phase. First, the therapist needs to draw attention to each step that the patient takes toward health—these steps should be acknowledged, accepted, and supported. An important transformation in the therapist–patient relationship is that it becomes progressively updated to incorporate patients' growth (Geller, 1987; Quintana, 1993), not that it is simply lost or ended as the therapy concludes. For this transformation to occur, patients need to acknowledge the steps they have taken toward more mature functioning. This should be accomplished during the work associated with the first termination outcome. Perhaps most important for the patient is for the therapist to acknowledge and validate the patient's sense of accomplishment.

Second, in attempting to promote internalization processes, the therapist should focus on subtle and continuous transformations in psychotherapy. The changes in the quality of the therapeutic relationship, particularly as the patient's transference reactions to the therapist are examined and resolved, usually provide a number of excellent examples. The therapist can also encourage patients to internalize images of themselves that reflect their participation in the therapeutic process. Patients should be given and encouraged to assume credit for much of the progress they have achieved. During the termination phase, the therapist can point out specific examples of how the patient made significant contributions to the therapy process. Furthermore, one of the most beneficial outcomes of therapy may be patients' development of observing ego or self-observational functions involving self-support, self-understanding, and self-affirmation skills. The internalization of these skills allows patients to recapitulate functional aspects of the therapeutic relationship (Quintana & Meara, 1990).

Internalization of these aspects may be promoted by having the patient identify the functions of therapy that were particularly therapeutic. Therapists may assist by offering their perspective on what elements of therapy were productive and by reflecting on their general experience of what aspects of therapy tend to be effective. Noticing and pointing out when the patient's activity indicates that he or she has already assimilated some of the functional aspects of therapy can reinforce the patient's internalizations. Patients should be encouraged to do more of the work around how the termination experience is represented "so that self-analytic capacities are enhanced during this period" (Dewald, 1982, p. 450). The therapist does this by communicating that the patient should take greater responsibility for the work during sessions, and expressing confidence that the patient will continue to experience further growth on his or her own (Levy, 1986).

Novick (1988) argued that a useful indicator that the patient can establish a self-analytic function and can continue the work of therapy on his or her own is the quality of the therapeutic alliance. Patients who internalize constructive images of their participation in the working alliance may best be able to recapitulate their role in the therapeutic process after the termination of treatment.

Third, a realistic approach needs to be taken toward the last phase of therapy that neither over- nor underemphasizes the meaning of the ending. This is in contrast to the attention given to the patient's idiosyncratic experience of feelings of loss as the end draws near, and the earlier roots of those feelings. It may be important for therapists to make a distinction between losing and outgrowing a valued process or relationship. If therapy has been constructive and if patients have internalized important aspects of therapy, then they are likely to have outgrown much of the need for the formal structure of therapy at this time in their ongoing development. It is important that patients end therapy with a realistic view of themselves, their therapists, and therapy. Patients who idealize therapy or their therapists may underestimate their own internalized resources and may fail to recognize nonprofessional sources of support in their social network. Thus, perhaps one of the more critical transformations for patients during termination is their deidealization of the therapeutic process. Patients for whom therapy has been demystified may be able to take the necessary steps to be their own therapist after termination.

Termination as Interruption

In a number of instances, the patient may intend to be in therapy only until symptoms are resolved, with the further intent to return when these or other symptoms become a problem in the future (Kupers, 1988). Alternatively, structural deficits or dependency may characterize the patient's functioning, and the therapy approach is characterized by supportive interventions aimed at assisting the patient through a period of crisis. With either case, a deeper therapeutic relationship might not develop and many of the issues associated with termination might not emerge or, if so, not play an important role at the time of ending. A more pragmatic perspective on termination is required of the therapist in these cases. Certainly, it is important to achieve agreement with the patient that the symptoms or crisis situation have, in fact, been resolved. In terms of internalization, however, the therapist must be content with ensuring that the patient has assimilated the message that another course of therapy can and will be made available when the need arises. Therapists, thus, assure patients that they may return for treatment at any time and do not emphasize the ending as a distinct closure on the relationship (Kramer, 1990). Budman and Gurman (1988) argued that it is valuable in these circumstances to explicitly invite the patient to return, especially when the therapy has not been an expressive, psychodynamic approach. Whether the therapist emphasizes an absolute end of treatment or focuses more on termination as partial and a raincheck on future contact, each approach implies that treatment is an ongoing, evolutionary process; that it offers a relative rather than an absolute cure; and that the therapist will remain sensitive to changing needs or situations in the patient's life (Kramer, 1986, p. 531).

Reaching the Ending

If patient and therapist are able to work well together and achieve a mutually satisfactory attainment of the three termination outcomes, the actual close of the therapy can proceed quite smoothly. Less than satisfactory attainment of any of the three outcomes will likely leave a sense of loose ends with the patient, the therapist, or both. It remains important that the participants continue to openly address any concerns as the last session approaches, as well as during the final session itself. This section briefly considers the issue of technical modification as therapy approaches the ending, as well as considerations in regard to the last session.

Issues of Technique and Technical Modification

The nature of the patient's response to the termination will be affected by the knowledge, skill, experience, and willingness of the therapist to remain sensitively observant, empathic, and skillfully responsive to the patient and his or her efforts to feel secure with the ending of therapy (Levinson, 1977, p. 482). The therapist's ability to appreciate the significant impact of the termination process is a necessary prerequisite to helping the patient integrate the achievements of the treatment and master the feelings evoked by the ending, and thus achieve an optimal therapeutic outcome (Dewald, 1982). If the underlying dynamics of termination are not understood or the therapist is not prepared for the manifestations of the termination process and the work required in regard to the termination outcomes, then the result may be discouragement, a sense of failure, a feeling of guilt, a willingness to postpone the patient's termination, or a temptation to abandon the therapeutic position in favor of more active, manipulative, symptom-oriented or supportive activity (Dewald, 1982, p. 449).

The crucial variables associated with a positive therapeutic ending are largely within the control of the practitioner (Kramer, 1990). These include (a) formulating realistic and obtainable goals and educating the patient about each participant's role and the process of therapy at the beginning of treatment, (b) watching for emergence of the termination criteria, (c) engaging in a discussion of termination as early as possible after the termination criteria make their appearance, (d) conducting a thorough review of treatment and addressing issues of loss, (e) maintaining empathy and being aware of countertransference issues, and (f) sustaining respect for the patient's autonomy. Although the majority of terminations in therapies oriented to the facilitation of insight frame the ending as closure on the relationship, Kramer (1990) also argued that "keeping the door open," that is, indicating to the patient that the therapist would be available should a further course of therapy be considered necessary, is also related to positive endings. Another important termination-related task for the therapist is to come to a comfortable recognition of the limitations of what the therapy interventions and process can accomplish (Tyson, 1996). No course of psychotherapy and no termination are ever perfect. The therapist's realistic appraisal of what did and what did not get accomplished in treatment should be communicated to the patient. This communication can help the patient achieve the emotionally balanced view of the relationship and the therapy process that ensures the patient's internalizations will be of maximum usefulness following the conclusion of the treatment.

The Final Session

The last session, dedicated to the actual saying of goodbyes, can be a difficult one for both patient and therapist. Attention to the termination outcomes and associated issues in the sessions leading up to the final contact can greatly lessen the emotional load in the last meeting. It remains possible that feelings about the ending may not have been completely worked through, and either the patient or the therapist may be left feeling bereft or unsatisfied during or after the final session (Usher, 1999).

Some patients attempt a flight into complete health in an effort to reassure themselves and the therapist that they feel confident to move on in life without therapy. This may be motivated by a defense against the sadness or fear they may be feeling in regard to the impending loss or a wish to remain a "good" patient to the end. Patients may panic and wish to change their mind and not part after all. Even when the idea of termination has been explored at length, the blunt reality of the ending during the final session can upset a smooth passage toward closure. The therapist should attend empathetically to these anxieties, and once again express confidence in the patient and the expectation that he or she can function in a healthy manner.

The therapist needs to attend to the dissolution of the therapeutic relationship in the final session. An appropriate stance for the therapist is to assume a natural attitude, to "be seen and reacted to as a normal figure and no longer the object for continued transference displacement" (Garcia-Lawson & Lane, 1997, p. 252). This attitude will fall somewhere between the therapeutic attitude maintained from the outset of treatment through both the working and termination phases and the intimacy of a social relationship. The therapist can communicate this attitude by acknowledging the shared therapeutic journey and expressing the wish—usually with some genuine fondness—for the patient's future well-being.

Given the quality of the work done in regard to the outcomes of termination during the final phase of treatment, it is possible that the therapy will not end with sadness being the primary affect. The ending may have a celebratory note and the patient may express optimism and energy about the future. In the same way that the patient's anxieties are countered by the therapist's expressions of confidence, an excessively positive view of the therapy and the future without therapy can be leavened by again summarizing what has and has not been done. "To recapitulate what both agree has not been possible or only marginally achieved is to face as far as possible the reality of the relationship and its shortcomings" (Murdin, 2000, p. 146). As is the case throughout the termination phase, the therapist aims at facilitating a balanced view of the treatment and therapeutic relationship during the final session.

CLINICAL PRINCIPLES

The termination phase of open-ended therapy can be a demanding one for both patient and therapist but at the same time has the potential to substantially add to the quality and accomplishments of the treatment. It is evident from the discussion that there are myriad issues the therapist needs to be cognizant of and explore with the patient. This complexity underscores the importance of allocating sufficient time and attention to the ending of the therapy and the therapy relationship. On the basis of the preceding discussion in this chapter, the following clinical principles appear to assume key importance during the termination phase:

1. The patient's responsibility for deciding to terminate and determining the pace of the ending should be encouraged. The therapist's functions are to ensure that a focus on termination is maintained and that a thorough review of the treatment, examination of the therapy relationship, and preparation for the future without therapy are instigated.
2. The therapist seeks to meet two primary objectives during the termination phase: First, the patient is able to develop an

emotionally balanced and realistic view of the treatment process and accomplishments, and of the therapeutic relationship. Second, the patient is able to take away, or internalize, something positive and sustaining from the therapy.

3. Observations of therapy goal attainment, a positive change in the quality of the therapeutic relationship, or a shift in the patient's current concerns signal that a focus on terminating therapy is appropriate. The necessity of the therapist articulating the move into the pretermination phase will vary as a function of the patient's conscious awareness of this shift. The therapist's sense of the appropriateness of a move toward termination will be reflective of the patient's "readiness" to conclude treatment. The pretermination phase involves examination of the termination criteria and marks a transitional period between the working and termination phases. The transition from the pretermination phase to the termination phase proper should be explicitly marked, usually accomplished by the negotiated setting of a date for the final session.

4. During the termination phase proper, the therapist maintains a respectful attitude toward the patient and endeavors to be as empathic, tolerant, and nonmanipulative as possible.

5. Attention is given to each of the termination outcomes during the ending phase of treatment. The critical focus of the participants is on the affective meanings associated with the course and accomplishments of treatment, the quality of the patient–therapist relationship, and the prospect of life without therapy, following termination.

6. The patient's perceptions and input are critical to the review and consolidation of treatment gains, that is, the first termination outcome. The therapist's task in regard to this outcome is to ensure that sufficient transfer of the gains to the patient's life outside therapy has occurred.

7. The second termination outcome, that is, resolution of issues in the patient–therapist relationship, is frequently associated with the most demanding and difficult work of the termination phase. To facilitate this work, the therapist capitalizes on the immediacy of the patient–therapist relationship and emphasizes the importance of addressing affective issues. Feelings associated with separation and loss should be thoroughly examined, with attention to links to the patient's earlier loss experiences. Feelings of loss may also emerge in conjunction with the patient's renunciation of earlier, maladaptive ways of functioning (i.e., the old self). A range of transference themes can emerge in response to the termination. A com-

prehensive examination of these reactions, particularly those involving negative transference, is critical.

8. The therapist's countertransference reaction to the patient's termination can take many forms. If left unaddressed, it is likely that these reactions will interfere with or even preclude effective work toward the ending. Attention to these reactions through self-analysis, peer consultation, or supervision is therefore critical. Awareness and containment of countertransference feelings can facilitate the therapist's empathy for the patient's experience as the final session draws near.

9. Preparedness for maintaining healthy functioning, that is, the third termination outcome, is largely a function of the patient's internalization of aspects of the therapy process and relationship. The therapist should highlight the patient's contribution to the work of therapy and the changes, subtle or otherwise, that occurred in the quality of the therapeutic relationship over the course of treatment. At the same time, attention should be given to the limitations of the treatment outcome and the tasks that remain unfinished.

10. No treatment and no termination are perfect. A "good enough" termination involves the development of a realistic evaluation of the treatment and balanced appraisal of the therapeutic relationship. Conveying the message to the patient that "the door remains open" is an element of positive therapy endings.

TERMINATION PHASE MODEL

The termination outcomes described in chapter 2 and process of termination described in this chapter are reflected in the termination phase model presented in Figure 3.1. The model was developed to increase the likelihood that the outcomes and processes described would generalize across different forms and modalities of psychotherapy. However, the model does not fit all therapeutic situations equally well. Variations exist. These variations may be associated with the form of therapy being provided (e.g., supportive therapy), the structure of the therapy (e.g., short-term, time-limited therapy), or particular patient characteristics (e.g., borderline personality traits). The next three chapters will consider such variations.

CONCLUSION

The termination phase model depicted in Figure 3.1 is a condensed representation of the extended discussion of the process of termination provided in this chapter. From the discussion, it is evident that negotiating the termination phase can be a complex process that poses significant demands for both patient and therapist. A full and comprehensive examination of the myriad issues and themes that arise during the termination phase is perhaps only possible in an intensive, open-ended form of therapy, with an extended series of sessions being devoted to the process of ending. In other therapies, a consistent focus on the three termination outcomes, attention to the tasks associated with each outcome, and the provision of sufficient time for an effective termination process can increase the likelihood of a positive ending.

4

ORIENTATION OF THERAPY
AND TERMINATION

We believe that termination is a critical phase of the psychotherapeutic process. However, the central role of termination has not always received the attention it deserves. Proponents of different orientations to psychotherapy have differed in their views of termination. It appears that the more treatment is structured and focused on skills acquisition, and the less the therapeutic alliance is addressed and used in treatment, the less emphasis termination has received. Accordingly, the termination outcomes that we have described (i.e., consolidation of the therapy process and gains, resolution of issues in the therapy relationship, preparedness for maintaining healthy functioning) may take on different meanings and may be approached in a different manner, depending on the therapist's orientation.

In this chapter, we consider variations in the termination process associated with four different orientations of therapy: interpersonal therapy, cognitive–behavioral therapy, supportive therapy, and experiential therapy. The chapter is organized around the three termination outcomes of the general model, described in chapters 2 and 3. This chapter discusses how therapists working from these four therapy orientations approach the termination outcomes. Because the general model of termination that is described in this book is based on long-term psychodynamic psychotherapy, a psychodynamic perspective on termination has been thoroughly described in the two preceding chapters and, thus, is not further developed here.

Termination has different meanings for each of these four orientations of therapy. In interpersonal therapy, the termination phase is an essential component of treatment. It is a specific stage of therapy during which the patient faces the task of giving up an important relationship and establishing a sense of competence to deal with future problems without the therapist (Klerman, Weissman, Rounsaville, & Chevron, 1984). The patient is given a chance to consolidate progress, discuss feelings about the therapy relationship ending, discuss concerns about relapse and the possible need for future therapy, and formally say goodbye (Wilfley, MacKenzie, Welch, Ayres, & Weissman, 2000). In interpersonal therapy, termination is viewed as a time when many complicated and conflicting feelings are brought up. If managed successfully, termination can promote expectations for successful living and application of newly learned living skills that continue long after treatment is finished.

Cognitive–behavioral therapy is a skills acquisition model of psychotherapy. The therapist's goal is to assist the patient in acquiring the skills to deal with internal and external stressors that are a part of life. Clearly defined goals are formulated at the beginning of therapy. When objective rating scales, patient reports, therapist observations, or feedback from significant others confirm that these goals have been reasonably achieved, the therapist moves toward termination of therapy (Freeman & Reinecke, 1995). Termination in cognitive–behavioral therapy is not viewed as a distinct phase of treatment. Rather, it is viewed as a point in treatment where the distinctive characteristics of therapy are faded out and the aspects of the patient's natural environment that may help maintain treatment gains are accentuated (Hayes, Follette, & Follette, 1995). This fading out means that sessions are gradually tapered (i.e., reduced in number) to facilitate the transfer and maintenance of treatment gains in the patient's daily environment. This also helps to reduce the abruptness of the ending once it actually occurs. Relatively little emphasis is placed on the ending of the patient–therapist relationship in cognitive–behavioral therapy (Goldfried, 2002).

In supportive therapy, termination is regarded as an important phase of treatment. However, the termination is often managed differently in supportive therapy. In many instances, it may not be a complete termination but instead a gradual attenuation of the relationship that may extend over a period of several years (Werman, 1984). This is particularly common with patients with long-term disorders such as schizophrenia or recurrent affective disorders. Thus, the structure of the termination process in supportive therapy is arranged to minimize stress and loss (Dewald, 1994). Termination in supportive therapy is a specific stage of treatment during which the patient faces the task of functioning with greater independence from the therapist, but with the reminder of the therapist's continued availability. The patient's progress is reviewed at this time, feelings about therapy ending are discussed, and arrangements for future contact may be made.

Experiential therapy does not espouse a particular theory of termination, nor does it view termination as an especially important phase of treatment (Greenberg, 2002). Nevertheless, termination demands a great deal of the therapist's attention in experiential therapy. For example, separation and loss are discussed openly and thoroughly. The therapist makes an effort to empower the patient so that the patient feels a sense of ownership in the accomplishments of the therapeutic work they did together. New meanings that were constructed during therapy are consolidated and reviewed (Elliott, Watson, Goldman, & Greenberg, 2004). Relapse is discussed and the possibility of any future contact between the patient and therapist is clarified. Foremost in experiential therapy, the termination is addressed as the phase of a human relationship in which two people have developed a close bond and now are separating (Greenberg, 2002). This involves, for both the patient and therapist, acknowledging and discussing feelings of sadness at the ending of the relationship and joy at starting on a new path (Bugental & Sterling, 1995).

REINFORCEMENT AND CONSOLIDATION OF THE THERAPY PROCESS AND GAINS MADE IN TREATMENT

The general model of termination that we have described posits that the first termination outcome entails a review and recapitulation of what has transpired between the patient and therapist over the course of treatment. This includes reviewing the patient's accomplishments as well as objectives that may not have been met. The review process may stimulate the reemergence of old symptoms or problems or the introduction of new ones. Thus, new challenges may arise during this part of the termination process.

A review of the patient's achievements in therapy is universally endorsed among the four orientations of therapy discussed in this chapter. Similarly, the absence of a focus on the objectives that were not achieved is also common across the four orientations. Nevertheless, there are differences in how each orientation addresses this aspect of the termination process. Table 4.1 provides a comparison of the strategies used in each of the four therapy orientations, relative to the general psychotherapy, to address the first termination outcome.

Interpersonal Therapy

Interpersonal therapy, for example, encourages a thorough discussion of the progress that the patient has made, thus, helping to consolidate the

TABLE 4.1

Reinforcement and Consolidation of the Therapy Process and Gains Made in Treatment: Variations to the General Model

General model	Interpersonal therapy	Cognitive–behavioral therapy	Supportive therapy	Experiential therapy
Review important events that transpired over the course of therapy.	Consolidate the work that was done during therapy.	Review the extent to which the treatment effects have transferred to the patient's natural environment.	Review the extent to which the patient has returned to adaptive, independent functioning.	Summarize patient's new narrative about self and the world, and review problems and their experientially derived solutions.
Review the patient's accomplishments.	Engage in thorough discussion of the patient's progress.	Identify how changes patient has made in cognitive processes have led to improvements in functioning.	Review accomplishments, underscoring ways in which improvements are consequences of patient's actions.	Attribute change to the patient's efforts.
Review objectives that were not met.	**Minimize attention to unmet objectives.**	**Minimize consideration of objectives that were not met.**	**Minimize attention to unmet objectives.**	**Minimize attention to objectives that were not achieved.**
Attend to the introduction of new symptoms or re-emergence of old symptoms.	**Minimize attention to old or new problems that are introduced.**	Address the emergence of new or old symptoms as opportunities to apply new skills.	**Delay termination if old or new symptoms emerge and put patient at risk for poor independent functioning.**	**Minimize attention to old or new symptoms that may emerge.**

Note. Boldface-type entries indicate divergence from the general model.

work that has been done and to enhance a sense of independent competence in the patient (Wilfley et al., 2000). It is common for patients (particularly depressed patients for whom interpersonal therapy was initially developed) to view themselves in a critical fashion. They may have difficulty recognizing improvement in themselves or be quick to attribute change to the efforts of the therapist. Identifying and crediting change to the patient is important for enhancing the patient's sense of self-efficacy (Weissman, Markowitz, & Klerman, 2000). Failure to point out important changes or to allow patients to own responsibility for these changes could erode their confidence in their ability to maintain these successes without treatment.

From the beginning of interpersonal therapy, the patient should receive the message that the therapy relationship is not a substitute for outside relationships but, rather, was established to assist the patient in learning how to better manage those outside relationships (Klerman et al., 1984). The basic strategy in interpersonal therapy is for patients to assume responsibility for monitoring their own life, relationships, and involvement in social activities. Thus, during therapy, the therapist should emphasize how the patient is beginning or has begun to successfully manage relationships outside of therapy. Patients can be helped to recognize that these outside relationships are now more available because of the effort they have invested in making better use of the social environment (Wilfley et al., 2000).

There is little focus in interpersonal therapy on the objectives of treatment that have not been met. Presumably, such a discussion does not occur because it may work against the strategy of bolstering the patient's self-confidence as the ending nears. Similarly, the interpersonal therapy model makes few references to the possibility of old problems reemerging or new ones being introduced by the patient. However, it is acknowledged that a patient may experience slightly distressing symptoms as termination approaches, which may be interpreted by the patient as a relapse (Klerman et al., 1984). Thus, patients should be told that toward the end of therapy, it is common to have feelings of apprehension, anger, or sadness about ending, but these feelings do not portend a return of old problems (Weissman et al., 2000).

Cognitive–Behavioral Therapy

A review of the patient's accomplishments is also considered important in cognitive–behavioral therapy. The review has the primary aim of gauging the extent to which the treatment effects have transferred to the patient's natural environment (Nelson & Politano, 1993). The therapist helps the patient see how changes in cognitive processes in therapy have led to changes in the patient's functioning. Similar to interpersonal therapy, the therapist tries to foster a sense of self-efficacy. According to cognitive theory, the extent to which patients acquire the expectancy that they can now master or deal effectively with difficulties is a primary factor that mediates the outcome and maintenance of gains of cognitive–behavioral therapy (Bandura, 1989). This part of the termination process is particularly important in cognitive–behavioral therapy because it marks the transition from the need for regular visits (associated with the working phase of treatment) to the need for only intermittent visits (associated with the maintenance phase of treatment, also called *fading out*; Goldfried, 2002). Fading out will be described in more detail in the section addressing the third termination outcome later in this chapter. Rehearsal of new behaviors or cognitive processes is also a strategy that is used to help consolidate treatment gains.

In cognitive–behavioral therapy, the therapist allocates little time to consideration of objectives that were not met in treatment. There is an assumption that some of the patient's problems will remain unsolved at the end of treatment, but the therapist communicates to the patient that the patient now has the tools to approach and independently solve these problems (Nelson & Politano, 1993). The therapist maintains a pragmatic approach toward the issue of old or new symptoms being introduced by the patient as the end nears. Such reactions provide opportunities for the cognitive–behavioral therapist to help the patient test out his or her new approach to cognitive processing and ascertain whether the reactions are irrational or dysfunctional (Nelson & Politano, 1993). The therapist can help diminish problems by emphasizing the educational nature of cognitive–behavioral therapy. That is, the therapist can communicate to the patient that therapy has been a training period, where the patient has learned new ways of dealing with his or her problems and now has a capacity to use these new tools to deal with any new problems that may arise (Nelson & Politano, 1993).

Supportive Therapy

Supportive therapy generally considers a review of treatment gains as necessary for deciding when to wean the patient from therapy. The goal of supportive therapy is to have the patient return to adaptive, independent functioning as much as possible. Thus, accomplishments should be reviewed, underscoring the ways in which freedom from symptoms or better functioning and positive experiences are consequences of the patient's actions (Pinsker, 1997). This strategy will help improve the patient's sense of self-efficacy and move the patient toward independence. Similar to cognitive–behavioral therapy, supportive therapy uses rehearsal of newly acquired skills to help solidify the accomplishments of therapy and to help ensure that gains are well integrated into the patient's everyday functioning (Misch, 2000). If some symptoms or problems remain, then they should be identified and discussed. The patient may feel that he or she can handle them independently, with only minor support, or not at all, which would suggest that termination be postponed.

Consistent with the objective of supportive therapy to minimize all sources of distress, the therapist should provide the patient with information about typical reactions to termination and how they can be handled (Pinsker, 1997). This will help minimize some of the fear, anger, or sadness that can occur. Similarly, acknowledging that old problems may surface will help reduce the likelihood of disappointment if it occurs and can help initiate a problem-solving strategy in anticipation of the possibility (Pinsker, 1997). It is also recommended that the therapist not initiate or continue with the termination process if the patient is exposed to some acute stressor (e.g., loss of a job or a relationship) even though the goals of therapy may have been achieved (Rockland, 1989).

Experiential Therapy

In experiential therapy, termination entails consolidation of new meanings formed during treatment. This is consistent with the goal of experiential therapy of helping the patient achieve new awareness and create new meanings from emotional experiences. Thus, themes that were identified are clearly symbolized and reiterated (Greenberg, 2002). The patient's emerging new narrative about the self and the world that was constructed during therapy is summarized (Greenberg, 2002). As well, the problems that were focused on and their experientially derived solutions are reviewed (Elliott et al., 2004). In experiential therapy, as in other forms of therapy, it is important to attribute change to the patient's efforts. This helps to empower the patient and create a sense that continued success is possible without the therapist.

Experiential therapy appears to minimize attention to goals that were not achieved in therapy. This is likely because the termination in experiential therapy is viewed as a choice point (of the patient) and not as the attainment of a certain end (Greenberg, 2002). The change process that began in therapy is part of an ongoing growth process that will continue after therapy (Elliott et al., 2004). Thus, the patient will likely resolve problems that were not addressed in therapy as this change process continues. Similarly, there is little discussion in the experiential therapy literature of the reemergence of old problems and presentation of new ones as termination approaches.

RESOLUTION OF ISSUES IN THE THERAPY RELATIONSHIP

The second termination outcome described in the general model of termination concerns the resolution of issues linked to the ending of the patient–therapist relationship. Separation and loss are often predominant themes in the discussion. These themes may be associated with aspects of the transference as well as with the real loss of the therapy relationship. Countertransference issues also require the therapist's attention. In the frame of general, open-ended psychotherapy, this second termination outcome demands the most attention and energy of any of the three termination outcomes.

There is considerable variability among the four orientations of therapy addressed in this chapter, regarding attention to issues associated with the ending of the therapy relationship. However, there is consistency among the four orientations in that none focus on resolving issues related to the transference and none address the topic of containing countertransference feelings. Table 4.2 presents a comparison of the four therapy orientations, relative to the general psychotherapy, with respect to the second termination outcome.

Interpersonal Therapy

In interpersonal therapy, recognizing termination as a potential time of grief and discussing negative feelings about terminating the therapy relationship are important tasks of the termination process (Weissman et al., 2000). As the ending of treatment nears, patients often develop anxiety about losing the therapy relationship and being alone. Sad feelings may lead to fears of relapse and a return of symptoms. The therapist in interpersonal therapy addresses the theme of loss as an analogue of grief (Wilfley et al., 2000). Grief is one of the four key problem areas (with interpersonal conflict, role conflict, and role transitions) that are targeted in interpersonal therapy. Some of the same strategies that were used to address grief issues during the working phase of therapy are used to address issues related to the impending loss of the therapy relationship. These include guiding the patient toward involvement with others outside of the therapy setting (i.e., using one's existing social network) and exploring the feelings (positive and negative) associated with the loss.

Patients have a variety of responses to termination. In interpersonal therapy, it is important to encourage the patient to verbalize any negative feelings (e.g., sadness, anger, and abandonment) about the ending of the therapy relationship. Expressing and discussing such feelings allows for cognitive mastery of them so that they are not left as a "resentful residue of the therapeutic experience" (Wilfley et al., 2000, p. 151). Working through these feelings is regarded as a lesson in how to deal with many of life's disappointments. Positive aspects of termination (e.g., having greater confidence in oneself, excitement at the prospect of moving on with life) are also important to identify. This identification helps to create a more balanced, realistic perception of therapy and the patient–therapist relationship.

Cognitive–Behavioral Therapy

Relatively little emphasis is placed on the ending of the patient–therapist relationship in cognitive–behavioral therapy. However, some

TABLE 4.2

Resolution of Issues in the Therapy Relationship: Variations to the General Model

General model	Interpersonal therapy	Cognitive–behavioral therapy	Supportive therapy	Experiential therapy
Address the patient's reactions to separation from the therapist and loss of the therapy relationship.	Explore the patient's negative and positive feelings associated with the loss of the therapy relationship (treat the loss as an analogue of grief).	Explore the patient's thoughts and feelings about termination and schemas and assumptions regarding separation and loss.[a]	**Minimize the loss of the therapy relationship and ending of treatment (emphasize termination simply as an interruption in treatment).**	Openly address issues of separation and loss, as well as positive aspects of the separation.
Address the patient's transference reactions associated with endings, separation, and loss.	**Minimize attention to the patient's transference reactions to loss and separation.**	Examine how termination can activate memories, schemas, and behavioral responses from separations to other important people in the patient's life.[a]	**Do not interpret the patient's transference reactions to separation and loss, but correct such reactions by focusing on the real aspects of the therapy relationship.**	**Minimize attention to the patient's transference reactions to loss and separation.**
Attend to one's own countertransference reactions to endings, separation, and loss	**Minimize attention to one's own counter-transference reactions to separation and loss.**	**Minimize attention to one's own counter-transference reactions to separation and loss.**	**Minimize attention to one's own counter-transference reactions to separation and loss.**	**Acknowledge one's own feelings associated with the ending of the therapy relationship.**

Note. Boldface-type entries indicate divergence from the general model. [a]This is not standard practice in cognitive–behavioral therapy.

cognitive–behavioral authors have sought to incorporate psychodynamic concepts to address certain phenomena in this form of therapy, in particular, the handling of the ending of the therapeutic relationship (e.g., Nelson & Politano, 1993). Freeman and Reinecke (1995) have suggested that, as the conclusion of treatment nears, the therapist should carefully explore the patient's thoughts and feelings about termination and the patient's schemas and assumptions in regard to separation and loss. Cognitive–behavioral therapists are beginning to recognize that termination of the patient–therapist relationship can have important meanings for the patient and can activate memories and schemas about separations from other important people in the patient's life (Freeman & Reinecke, 1995). Although cognitive–behavioral therapists rarely talk about transference, they do refer to transference-like phenomena as *shared behavioral responses* to current and historical contexts due to either their formal similarity (referred to as *stimulus generalization* in behavioral terms) or the patient's verbalizations that tie current events to past events (Hayes et al., 1995). If the patient's thoughts, feelings, and characteristic ways of coping with separation appear maladaptive, the therapist will, with the consent of the patient, turn attention to helping the patient establish new, more effective thought patterns and behavioral responses to separation (Hayes et al., 1995).

In cognitive–behavioral therapy, the therapist emphasizes the importance of the patient's independent functioning and use of resources in the outside social environment (Goldfried, 2002). However, cognitive–behavioral therapy views the role of the therapist as a consultant–collaborator and, thus, regards continued contact as appropriate and important (Freeman & Reinecke, 1995). Patients are invited to call and arrange future appointments in the event of an emergency. Patients may also call simply to get information or reinforcement of a particular behavior or to report a success. Thus, the continued availability of the therapist and continuation of the professional relationship between patient and therapist makes loss and separation less salient during termination in cognitive–behavioral therapy.

Supportive Therapy

In supportive therapy, the aim is to consider the termination as an interruption in the therapeutic contact (Werman, 1984). The therapist's effort is directed at minimizing the loss and stress of ending the treatment (Dewald, 1994). The therapist attempts to maintain a sense of continuity of the helpful therapeutic relationship and of the therapist's ongoing interest in and availability to the patient in the future (Dewald, 1994). The primary emphasis of the therapist in regard to the patient–therapist relationship is to reassure the patient that the relationship has not ended and that should the patient require further contact, it could be readily established (Rockland, 1989).

Reactions of the patient, such as sadness, uncertainty, and anxiety about the future without therapy, are addressed openly. However, their discussion is limited to only those responses that are already conscious to the patient (Dewald, 1994). Negative transference reactions are not interpreted, but they are corrected by focusing on the real aspects of the patient–therapist relationship. Resistance to experiencing feelings about the loss and mourning are not examined as in more exploratory therapies (Rockland, 1992). For example, the patient's attempts to minimize or deny affective responses to ending therapy may be gently questioned or treated with some scepticism, but they are not vigorously undermined (Rockland, 1992).

Experiential Therapy

Experiential therapy focuses on termination as a separation process. Termination is viewed as the end of a journey that deeply touched the psyches of both participants (Bugental & Sterling, 1995). Separation and loss are openly addressed. Feelings of sadness, regret, or anxiety, from the perspectives of both the patient and therapist, are acknowledged and discussed (Greenberg, 2002). New meanings of these emotional experiences for the patient are constructed. Positive aspects of the separation are also addressed. For the patient, there can be a bolstered sense of self-efficacy at being able to accomplish so much in therapy and excitement about starting a new path in life. For the therapist, there can be a sense of accomplishment and satisfaction.

Although separation and loss are emphasized as important topics during termination in experiential therapy, the patient is made aware of the continued availability of the therapist in the future should the need arise (Greenberg, 2002). The therapist indicates that they have formed a relationship that can continue indefinitely. The patient is informed that he or she may want to consult again in the future, and the therapist indicates his or her availability for future contacts. A parallel is drawn between the model of psychological service in experiential therapy and that of a family practitioner: The relationship does not require or encourage continuous contact but is available whenever there is a need (Greenberg, 2002).

In experiential therapy, therapists attempt to equalize the relationship as much as possible during termination. This equalization can include greater self-disclosure by the therapist to ensure that the patient sees the therapist as a fallible human being like anyone else (Elliott et al., 2004). In addition, the therapist emphasizes the therapy partnership and the efforts of the patient that led to the successes in therapy, thus, helping to empower the patient and encourage a sense of independent competence.

PREPAREDNESS FOR MAINTAINING HEALTHY FUNCTIONING

The third and final termination outcome is concerned with having patients demonstrate that they have developed the tools that allow for independent continuation of the therapeutic process. In essence, this means that patients should demonstrate that they have developed the capacity to function as their own therapist. With regard to the general, open-ended psychotherapy, this outcome refers to patients internalizing aspects of the therapy process (e.g., the self-analytic function) and the therapy relationship (e.g., the empathic, benign therapist) to serve as resources for patients to draw on when challenged by similar problems in the future.

The work associated with the first two termination outcomes described earlier in this chapter contributes greatly to ensuring that patients are prepared to maintain healthy functioning in the future. The general model of termination also describes other strategies that can be used by therapists who are implementing different approaches, as they work toward the attainment of the third termination outcome. This includes pointing out specific examples of how the patient made significant contributions to the therapy process. The therapist may invite the patient to identify the functions of therapy that were particularly helpful and then review how the patient successfully engaged in these functions during the course of therapy. The therapist may also offer his or her own perspective of which aspects of therapy tend to be the most effective and then discuss how the patient has used these and can continue to do so once therapy ends. Also, therapists should make an effort to demystify therapy to provide patients with the understanding that they are capable of continuing the therapeutic process on their own. Other strategies for preparing patients to maintain healthy functioning in the future are more specific to or receive more emphasis in different orientations of therapy. Table 4.3 presents the strategies associated with the four therapy orientations, relative to the general psychotherapy, involved in addressing the third termination outcome.

Interpersonal Therapy

In interpersonal therapy, for example, emphasis is placed on discussing possible future difficulties and strategies for handling them. According to the interpersonal therapy model, thinking about warning signs and symptoms and contingencies for handling future problems is of utmost importance for ensuring continued healthy functioning (Klerman et al., 1984). Specific action strategies are frequently rehearsed and perhaps even written down by the patient (Wilfley et al., 2000). By discussing these issues, patients receive the message that continued progress requires efforts similar to the work that was done in therapy. It encourages personal responsibility and bolsters feelings of competence.

Cognitive–Behavioral Therapy

In cognitive–behavioral therapy, fading out sessions during termination is regarded as a particularly useful strategy for ensuring maintenance of

TABLE 4.3
Preparedness for Maintaining Healthy Functioning: Variations to the General Model

General model	Interpersonal therapy	Cognitive–behavioral therapy	Supportive therapy	Experiential therapy
Acknowledge and validate the patient's accomplishments and steps taken toward healthy functioning.	**Discuss possible future difficulties and warning signs.**	**Gradually withdraw sessions so that naturally occurring consequences in the patient's environment reinforce new behaviors.**	**Discuss potentially difficult situations in the future.**	**Reduce the number of sessions to allow the patient to deal with issues more independently.**
Discuss which elements of therapy were most helpful (from the patient's and therapist's perspectives) and point out how the patient's activity indicates that these aspects have been assimilated.	**Review contingencies for handling future problems and rehearse specific strategies.**	**Assign homework so patient can self-monitor progress and also have the patient practice new coping strategies.**	**Rehearse newly acquired skills.**	**Discuss recognition of negative affective states, the meaning of such states, and what to do if they persist.**
Point out how the patient is capable of continuing the therapeutic process on his or her own.	Emphasize that continued progress requires efforts similar to the work that was done in therapy.	**Schedule booster sessions to monitor coping and provide reinforcement.**	**Schedule follow-up sessions and communicate the availability of the therapist if needed.**	**Indicate that the therapist is available for consultation in the future if required.**

Note. Boldface-type entries indicate divergence from the general model.

treatment gains (Goldfried, 2002). *Fading out* refers to the gradual withdrawal of the therapist and therapy. When targeted behaviors occur with enough frequency so that they can be adequately reinforced by naturally occurring consequences, the therapy and the therapist are systematically withdrawn (Nelson & Politano, 1993). Generalization and maintenance of changes made during therapy are enhanced as the patient assumes more control and responsibility for his or her progress and develops a growing sense of confidence.

Scheduling follow-up or booster sessions several months after the formal termination of therapy is also an important part of maintaining healthy functioning (Hayes et al., 1995). Booster sessions allow patients to report to someone who is invested in their improvement and can help them reassess their coping efforts as needed (Nelson & Politano, 1993). They also provide an opportunity for patients to receive reinforcement for their efforts at coping. Another strategy used by cognitive–behavioral therapists to help maintain treatment gains is assigning homework. Homework requires that patients self-monitor their progress and helps to ensure that patients review and reflect on their successes and experience a growing sense of mastery (Nelson & Politano, 1993). A final strategy used to help ensure maintenance is to practice dealing with anticipated problems. Patients are told to expect fluctuations in their adaptive behavior and feelings. Patients and therapists then discuss how to cope with such exacerbations. Patients may be encouraged to put themselves in a situation that previously would have been difficult for them to manage so that they can practice newly learned adaptive behaviors (Nelson & Politano, 1993). This practice prepares patients for challenges and struggles that will inevitably occur once therapy has ended.

Supportive Therapy

In supportive therapy, the therapist addresses the issue of maintaining healthy functioning in the future through two primary strategies. One strategy is to rehearse newly acquired skills. Just as in cognitive–behavioral therapy, the supportive therapist may review with the patient different situations in which the patient was able to successfully implement new problem-solving strategies (Pinsker, 1997). Therapists and patients may also discuss potentially difficult situations that may arise in the future and how these could be handled. The second strategy that is used is to schedule follow-up sessions or communicate the continued availability of the therapist should the patient need to resume contact (Werman, 1984).

Experiential Therapy

In experiential therapy, tapering of sessions is an important part of ensuring the maintenance of treatment gains (Greenberg, 2002). Much like the fading-out process in cognitive–behavioral therapy, tapering sessions allows for the patient to begin to deal with issues more independently but at the same time have the opportunity to consult with the therapist to report progress and to get further guidance. Discussion of relapse is also a useful strategy for maintaining gains achieved in experiential therapy. Patients are told that relapses into negative states or patterns are expected and a typical part of the change process (Greenberg, 2002). It is emphasized that falling back into old patterns or reactions is not a problem. Rather, becoming stuck in these old patterns or maladaptive states without awareness or being able to leave them is the difficulty. As Greenberg (2002) described, "getting depressed, being unsure, or arguing again are all part of a process of living and never go away completely" (p. 359). As long as relapses into these states do not endure for too long, their occurrence should not be taken as a sign of failure. Thus, discussion of relapse involves awareness of negative states, the meaning of such states, and what to do if these states persist. Finally, having the therapist communicate to the patient that their relationship will continue even though the sessions have formally ended facilitates maintenance of healthy functioning (Bugental & Sterling, 1995). Should the patient have the need for further consultation, the therapist will be available.

CONCLUSION

There are differences in how much emphasis termination receives in different orientations of therapy. Generally, the more the therapy focuses on the patient's relationships outside or inside of the therapy setting, the more attention is given to the termination process. Accordingly, the termination outcomes associated with the general model of termination that have been described in the previous chapters receive different emphases, depending on the orientation of therapy being offered.

Consolidation of treatment gains is universally regarded as an important termination outcome among the four orientations of therapy that were reviewed in this chapter. Each orientation also supports the examination of how learning has generalized to life outside of therapy. In all therapies, however, there may be little or no attention directed toward the discussion of problem areas not resolved during therapy. In a similar fashion, there is little discussion of how to handle new symptoms—or a reemergence of old symptoms—at termination. Some therapies may involve the rehearsal of new behaviors or skills to further solidify the gains made in treatment.

There are considerable differences among the therapies in how issues surrounding the ending of the therapeutic relationship are addressed. Some stress the grief and mourning associated with the separation and others stress that the relationship is not ending but will always be available. All of the therapies recognize the importance of addressing the feelings associated with the ending of the patient–therapist relationship. None, however, attend to the resolution of transference issues or containing countertransference reactions.

All of the therapies discussed in this chapter agree that a key to maintaining gains is having patients demonstrate the ability to continue the work of therapy on their own. Some therapies discuss potential future problems and approaches to resolving them. Making contingency plans for returning to therapy if needed is also a strategy used in some therapies for ensuring that gains are maintained.

A notable commonality among the four therapies is the task of helping patients develop a sense of empowerment during termination. Empowerment has been conceptualized as knowing oneself well enough to determine appropriate desires and goals, making decisions to achieve these goals, feeling secure enough to actively deal with life's challenges, and seeking appropriate resources and support when needed (Fisher, 1994; Harp, 1994). Although only experiential therapy directly refers to empowerment, the other orientations refer to aspects of empowerment such as self-efficacy, control, and mastery. All of the therapies emphasize how a review and consolidation of the therapy process and gains made in treatment contributes to patients' empowerment. A heightened sense of empowerment is considered essential for helping patients maintain their treatment gains. A belief in personal control will help patients move toward increased and continuing psychological well-being.

Variations in how the termination outcomes are approached depend not only on the orientation of therapy that is offered but also on the structure of the therapy. For example, each termination outcome is addressed in a different manner, depending on whether therapy is short term versus long term, time limited versus time unlimited, individual versus group. In chapter 5, we consider how differences in the therapy structure affect the termination outcomes associated with the general model of termination.

5

STRUCTURE OF THERAPY AND TERMINATION

As described in chapters 2 and 3, the criteria for the onset of termination resemble the criteria for the successful outcome of therapy. If the objectives of therapy have been achieved, it is usually time to initiate termination tasks. Thus, once the criteria are recognized, it is time that the therapist should attempt to engage the patient in the three tasks of termination (reviewing the work and gains of therapy, examining the patient–therapist relationship, and reinforcing the internalization of therapeutic functions). When these tasks have been accomplished successfully, the outcomes of termination include the consolidation of gains, the resolution of relationship problems, and the maintenance of healthy functioning. The question that is central to this chapter is how do variations in the structure of therapy affect the tasks and processes of termination, which then affect the achievement of the outcomes of termination, which then affect the outcomes of therapy? Stated more succinctly, how does structure affect the therapist's efforts to bring about a successful termination of therapy?

Unfortunately, there is little research that has addressed the central question of this chapter. In addition, the clinical and theoretical literatures have addressed the question only indirectly, usually as a tangential part of some other topic. The answers that are provided in this chapter largely reflect our experiences and our inferences from the clinical and theoretical literatures.

TIME AS STRUCTURE

For both individual therapy and group therapy, structure is most commonly defined in terms of time dimensions. For example, therapies differ in terms of their frequency of sessions, their duration of sessions, and the duration of therapy itself. Session frequency ranges from minimal levels, such as monthly maintenance sessions for certain behavior therapies, to maximal levels, such as four to five sessions per week, for psychoanalysis. In regard to session duration, the "50-minute hour" for individual sessions and the "90-minute hour" for group therapy sessions have been common standards. However, there are many exceptions to these session durations (e.g., 15-minute sessions for supportive therapy and medication review). In regard to the duration of therapy, the most common distinction is between short term and long term. Short-term therapies are usually 6 months or less in duration, although some therapists regard durations up to a year as short term. Long-term therapies are generally defined as those exceeding a year. Psychoanalysis, which commonly lasts several years, is usually regarded as representing the upper limit. However, a substantial number of patients who receive short-term treatments return for booster sessions, with therapy contacts that consequently span a long period of time. Others receive treatments at different times throughout their lives. In these cases, the duration of therapy is difficult to define. For example, it may refer to an episode of therapy that involves 8 weekly sessions or to a 3-year period of time that includes 3 such episodes of brief therapy. There is also the possibility of different combinations of frequencies and durations within the same treatment. For example, weekly hourly sessions of therapy for 6 months may be followed by monthly 30-minute sessions of follow-up for 12 months.

Another familiar time dimension distinguishes time-limited and time-unlimited therapies. In the case of time-limited therapies, both the patient and the therapist know the duration of therapy prior to its onset. Once determined, therapists almost always stick to the time limit. Time-limited therapies are usually also short-term therapies. In the case of time-unlimited therapies, the decision to terminate therapy is left to the judgment of the patient in collaboration with the therapist at an unspecified time. However, the patient and therapist often have in mind an initial estimate of the eventual length of therapy or at least the minimum length of therapy (e.g., 2 years). They usually allow ample room for modification of the estimate on the basis of the extent of the patient's progress in achieving the objectives of therapy.

PATIENT FEATURES AND CHARACTERISTICS AS STRUCTURE

In addition to the time dimensions cited in the previous section, group therapies have several structural characteristics that are defined in terms of their patients. For example, there are differences in regard to the patient's opportunity to join a group. In closed groups, all members must begin together, and no new members are added once the group has begun. Closed groups are usually short term and time limited. In contrast, a patient may join an open group whenever the therapist designates that there is a vacancy to be filled. Many therapists who conduct long-term, time-unlimited groups wait until there are several vacancies before recruiting new patients for the group. In this way, a patient who is joining an ongoing group has other patients who share the role of newcomer.

Additional patient characteristics that define the structural nature of therapy groups are the number of patients in the group (group size) and the composition of the group. *Composition* refers to the degree of diversity of the patients in the group in terms of specific variables. The greater the diversity, the greater the heterogeneity of the group. The lesser the diversity, the greater the homogeneity of the group. There are many patient variables on which to determine degree of diversity. They include demographic, diagnostic, personality, and presenting problem variables. Short-term, time-limited therapy groups often tend to be homogeneous in terms of diagnosis and presenting problems. Homogeneity is believed to facilitate cohesiveness among members, universality (recognition that many people have problems similar to the patient), and initial acceleration of affect expression and work. These processes can compensate for the overall brevity of short-term groups.

IMPACT OF STRUCTURE

Authors who consider the impact of structure on termination usually draw attention to the less-versus-more differences of the time dimensions. That is, they contrast the impact of fewer sessions, briefer sessions, briefer therapy, and time limits with more sessions, longer sessions, longer therapy, and the absence of time limits. As an example, consider short-term therapy and long-term therapy. In short-term therapy, patients have less opportunity to work on their problems than in long-term therapy. If the therapist's assessment of outcome in long-term therapy suggests that the patient's progress has been disappointing, in particular in comparison to what the therapist thinks the patient might have achieved, initiation of the three tasks of termination may be postponed. Or, if initial engagement in the tasks of termination reveals few gains, unsettled relationship problems, or minimal internalization of therapeutic functions, then the tasks of termination similarly may be postponed. Consequently, the therapist may not engage the patient in the tasks of termination until the very end of therapy. Or worse still, in an effort to provide as much treatment as possible, the therapist may forgo the tasks of termination entirely. Either way, termination issues are not adequately addressed. As a result, even modest gains resulting from therapy, such as relief of some symptoms, may be only short-lived.

Even if an assessment of outcome or the initial engagement in the tasks of termination suggests reasonably successful outcomes, there is less time to complete the tasks of termination (review of work and gains, examination of the patient–therapist relationship, and internalization of therapeutic functions) in short-term therapy. Thus, there is less time to achieve the outcomes of termination (consolidation of gains, resolution of patient–therapist relationship problems, and maintenance of healthy functioning).

PATIENT AND THERAPIST REACTIONS

The structure of time-limited therapy can have a direct bearing on how the patient and therapist approach termination. From the patient's perspective, a reminder from the therapist that termination is imminent can be experienced as intrusive and upsetting. Therapists may become the target of anger and emotional pressure by patients as the preset termination is approached. Patients may feel that they are a number to which a treatment has been assigned and then curtailed in an arbitrary manner, despite being aware since the outset that the therapy involved time limits. In turn, therapists may endure guilt feelings about abandoning patients who are still in need and a degree of helplessness at being forced to perform an impossible task (Noy-Sharav, 1998). Therapists must balance bringing closure to the work of achieving the goals of therapy with allowing sufficient time to address the ending of therapy and the therapy relationship.

BENEFITS OF SHORT-TERM THERAPY

Although there is clearly less time to complete the tasks of termination in short-term therapy, some clinicians have argued that it is an especially powerful medium for exploring the meaning, relevance, and impact of termination on the patient. This is because termination is always in the forefront of short-term therapy. It is also particularly the case if the therapy is time limited, which means that the exact time and date of termination are already determined and known by patient and therapist. Perhaps the most well-known advocate of this position in the individual therapy literature is James Mann (1973). His model of therapy emphasizes the meaning of time in individual life development, particularly in the experience of separation and loss. The objective of therapy is the mastery of separation anxiety as a basis for the mastery of other neurotic conflict. Therapy consists of 12 sessions, which he believes can be conceptualized as 3 distinct thirds of 4 sessions each. A smooth first third that is characterized by a positive transference and symptom reduction is followed by a difficult second third for the patient that is characterized by focus on the central conflict of separation without resolution from an ambivalently held object (person). The final third is devoted to the patient's reaction to the impending termination. It is an opportunity for the patient to explore and, with hope, resolve ambivalence toward persons who have been lost through separations, whether in the past or with the current therapy relationship.

As Bauer and Kobos (1987) emphasized, a key issue in this type of therapy is the definite and irreversible decision about the time of termination. This issue, in conjunction with the therapist's persistent focus, creates intense pressure to examine issues concerning attachment, loss, separation, the finiteness of relationships, and death and mortality themselves. From this perspective, there is often a crisis in the last few sessions of the time-limited arrangement. The crisis raises the question of whether the patient can maintain autonomy and self-confidence without the therapist and therapy. A successful resolution of this question can provide the patient with hope and greater self-confidence.

An important secondary benefit of short-term therapy, according to Mann, is the avoidance of overdependency on the therapist, which is always a risk in long-term therapies. Nelson and Politano (1993) also emphasized this point and argued that, by viewing the therapy as short term, the therapist counters dependency and forestalls beliefs that there will be a miraculous cure.

A final benefit is the pressure to work hard because time in treatment is known to be brief and limited. In most instances, the restricted and shrinking time frame prompts the patient to do concentrated work on his or her issues, if not over the entire course of treatment then usually in one or two "good process" sessions as the termination date approaches (Bauer & Kobos, 1987; Davanloo, 1978; Mann, 1973).

QUESTIONS REGARDING THE IMPORTANCE OF TERMINATION IN SHORT-TERM THERAPY

Some investigators have challenged the importance attributed to termination in short-term individual therapy. Quintana (1993) argued that the metaphor of crisis or loss as a consequence of impending termination in short-term therapy is an exaggeration. He believed that most patients view termination in short-term therapy as a temporary interruption of receiving services during their lifetime. He argued that a more accurate metaphor is that of development or transformation.

Quintana is not alone in believing that the importance of termination in brief therapy has been overestimated. Budman (1990) has highlighted several beliefs that he alleged have contributed to the "myth" of termination as a critical period in brief therapy. Historically, the beliefs mainly have been associated with long-term therapy, including psychoanalysis. The first belief is that an effective therapy cures the patient of his core psychopathologies. The second belief is that the cure is long lasting, often as long as the patient's life. Thus, the patient is not expected to return to the therapist. The third belief is that the termination of therapy is final. Because of the attachment that has developed between the patient and the therapist and the prospect of achieving a lifelong cure, the fourth belief is that the termination is a frightening, painful, and emotionally charged process that requires much careful and skillful attention on the part of both patient and therapist.

Budman (1990) challenged each of these beliefs along the following lines. In the case of short-term therapy, limited and circumscribed (focal) problems are addressed. At the initiation of therapy, the patient and therapist mutually agree on goals for the treatment that are realistic and attainable. Thus, basic personality change and long-lasting cure are beyond the scope of therapy. The patient is expected to encounter problems at future points in his life for which he is welcome to return for further treatments. Thus, the termination is not expected to be final. Because of the brevity of therapy, which limits the strength of the attachment between patient and therapist, and because of the expectation of future contact, separation is not particularly painful or emotionally charged. To strengthen his arguments, Budman cited previous research (Taube, Goldman, Burns, & Kessler, 1988) that suggests that termination is a subject that for many patients is not broached at all. This is, in part, due to the small number of sessions received by many patients. Charman and Graham (2004) noted that many trainees and their patients avoid the termination phase and that a planned negotiated termination is the exception rather than the rule.

Cummings (1990) expressed a similar belief that for many patients therapy can be conceived of as brief intermittent episodes to meet recurring crises throughout the life cycle. He believed that over the life span patients make repeated return visits to their therapists when various emotional crises occur, just as patients return again and again to their general practitioners when medical crises occur. Thus, the last visit never needs to be construed as a final visit. According to Cummings (1990, p. 173),

> In brief, intermittent psychotherapy throughout the life cycle, you can free yourself from the concept of the ideal therapist, where each of us has to be all things to all people. You can free yourself from the concept of cure, and you can free yourself from the bother of termination.

Barnett, MacGlashan, and Clarke (2000) argued that because of the shortness of therapy, many issues do not need to be worked on. They also suggested that if the length is predetermined, separation is less traumatic.

CONTRASTING VIEWPOINTS IN REGARD TO SHORT-TERM GROUP THERAPY

Similar to short-term individual therapy, there are contrasting viewpoints concerning the importance of termination and the processes of termination to the patient in short-term group therapy. It can be argued that although termination is very important, it can also be quite challenging for the patient because there is not only the bond between patient and therapist that will be broken but also the many bonds among the patients. MacKenzie (1997) argued that the closed, short-term group format provides the membership with an opportunity to address termination issues collectively and serves to intensify this termination focus. MacKenzie (1996) cited the paradoxical situation of patients becoming closer as the patients discuss separation. In addition, for certain types of patients (e.g., patients experiencing complicated grief), the termination of therapy is regarded as especially stressful and challenging because it represents the very type of situation with which the patients are having trouble dealing, namely separation and loss. For the same reason, termination is regarded as very important, given that the patients have a real opportunity to better understand why they are having difficulty adjusting to losses in their lives and an opportunity to handle the here-and-now situation in the group differently.

SHORT-TERM GROUP THERAPY FOR COMPLICATED GRIEF

We have shared these assumptions about the importance of termination in our clinical and research work with time-limited, short-term therapy groups for psychiatric outpatients with complicated grief. Since 1986, we have conducted over 80 such groups. Our program began with interpretive (insight-oriented) groups that attempted to identify and remove obstacles to normal bereavement. Obstacles were defined as conflicts between the patient and the lost persons. The unique symptoms associated with complicated grief (e.g., preoccupation with and yearning for the lost person) were conceptualized as derivatives of the unresolved conflicts. The groups met once weekly for 90 minutes for 12 weeks. About two thirds of the groups have been part of formal psychotherapy clinical trials. In 1992, we published the results of a controlled clinical investigation that investigated the efficacy of 16 of the therapy groups (McCallum & Piper, 1990a; Piper, McCallum, & Azim, 1992). Treated patients improved significantly more than control patients on 10 out of 16 outcome variables (mean effect size = 0.67). The improvements were clinically significant and maintained at the 6-month follow-up. The results clearly supported the efficacy of short-term interpretive therapy groups in treating complicated grief.

More recently, our program has also provided time-limited, short-term supportive therapy groups for patients with complicated grief. These groups emphasize support and problem solving to improve the patients' immediate adaptation to their life situations; they do not focus on underlying internal conflicts. We completed a clinical trial that compared the outcomes of eight interpretive groups and eight supportive groups (Piper, McCallum, Joyce, Rosie, & Ogrodniczuk, 2001). There were no significant differences in the outcomes associated with the two approaches. Patients in both conditions demonstrated considerable improvement according to the criteria of statistical significance, clinical significance, and effect sizes. The therapists in both treatment conditions highlighted the limited time and issues related to termination. Consequently, they were important topics that influenced the processes of the sessions in both treatment conditions.

Similar to short-term individual therapy, it can be argued that the importance of termination in short-term group therapy is questionable. The loss groups consist of only 12 weekly sessions and usually include eight to nine patients. Given these structural features, one may question whether there is time to become very attached to the other patients in the group and to the therapist and whether there is much time to engage in the tasks of termination. In regard to the attachment issue, it has been our experience that the topic of losing others through death is an emotionally charged one that bonds members rather quickly and facilitates an affectively charged beginning to the groups. For a given patient, there are almost always one or two other patients with whom the patient can easily identify. Although individual therapy patients may find it easy to envision return visits to their therapist to resume therapy, this is not the case for group therapy. Groups that finish are never resumed, at least with the same membership. Thus, the termination of a group is final. Even a patient's voiced aspiration to meet with other patients after the end of the group is rarely realized. Thus, although we understand the skepticism of some authors in regard to the importance of termination in short-term group therapy, our experience has been quite different. This may be because limited time is an especially sensitive topic for patients who are experiencing complicated grief. In regard to the limited time to engage in the tasks of termination in short-term group therapy, our experience has been promising. Although admittedly limited, time to engage in the tasks of termination tended to be used effectively given the affective intensity of the group climate.

According to Rutan and Stone (2001), the individual patient's termination in group therapy is more public and more complicated because the patient is leaving many members, not just one. They agreed that there is less time, because of the presence of the other members, for detailed discussions about the associations and memories that are stirred up in the departing patient. They believed that patients experience less regression than patients in individual therapy. Although there is less opportunity and time in group therapy to engage in the processes of termination at the level of the individual patient, the topic of termination need not be neglected. Feelings and concerns shared by all of the patients can be addressed through accurate group interpretations. The therapists who lead groups in our program are trained to be particularly sensitive to termination issues and to keep the patients continually attuned to the inevitability of separation and loss as they experience it in the group itself.

PATIENT CHARACTERISTICS AND GROUP COMPOSITION IN GROUPS FOR COMPLICATED GRIEF

As mentioned previously, the composition of therapy groups in terms of patient characteristics is another structural dimension that distinguishes groups. Our work with patients who have experienced complicated grief provides an example. In our clinical trial that compared interpretive groups with supportive groups, the patient characteristic known as *quality of object relations* (QOR) emerged as a potentially important composition characteristic (see also chap. 6). Although we found no significant outcome differences between the two types of groups, we found a significant interaction between the type of group and QOR. QOR was directly related to benefit in interpretive therapy and inversely, although minimally, related to benefit in supportive therapy. QOR is defined as a person's internal enduring tendency to establish certain types of relationships that range along an overall dimension from primitive to mature (Azim, Piper, Segal, Nixon, & Duncan, 1991; Piper & Duncan, 1999). As the word *quality* suggests, the kinds of relationships at high levels represent a more favorable and desirable set of circumstances for the person. QOR was assessed with a 1-hour semistructured interview. Lifelong relationships with recent and past significant persons and the immediate relationship with the interviewer were examined. Although the focus was on external relationships, it was assumed that they reflect the internal object representations and conflictual components of the patient's internal world. The administration and scoring of the interview were guided by a manual (Piper, McCallum, & Joyce, 1996).

In this comparative study, the composition of the groups was heterogeneous on QOR. Each group included patients who were high and low on QOR. Because of the significant interaction effect, we designed a subsequent composition study that is currently in progress. In this study, groups that are composed only of high-QOR patients are receiving interpretive group therapy and groups that are composed only of low-QOR patients are receiving supportive group therapy. Heterogeneous groups (i.e., groups mixed on QOR) are also being conducted with both approaches as in the comparative study. We are hypothesizing that the outcome of the homogeneous groups will be superior to the outcome of the heterogeneous groups. In addition to investigating outcome, we plan to investigate a set of process variables that will provide us with some insights into the differing processes of the therapy groups.

We predict that the processes of therapy will proceed more smoothly in the homogeneous groups in which patients have a greater propensity to work in a similar way. We hope to learn something about the extent to which the groups engaged in different termination processes. For example, will the high-QOR interpretive groups examine issues related to the patient–therapist relationship and other termination factors to a greater extent than the mixed-QOR interpretive groups?

Group composition studies are extremely difficult to conduct, which explains their near absence in the general group-therapy literature. A similar statement can be made about the scarcity of studies that have investigated the processes of termination. An exception is a study by Geller and Farber (1993). Geller and Farber (1993) found that the greater the number of sessions attended by patients in individual therapy, the greater the likelihood that patients will use representations of the therapist to continue the work of therapy following termination. Representations of the therapist appear to be good evidence of internalizing the therapeutic functions, which is one of the main tasks of termination. This raises the general possibility that the more that the structural characteristics decrease the amount of time that the therapist spends with the patients, the less the termination processes occur and the less the outcomes of termination are achieved. This is a hypothesis that deserves future research investigation.

CONCLUSION

We indicated at the start of this chapter that the literature concerning the impact of structural characteristics on the termination of psychotherapy is relatively small. Management of the time dimension of therapy was considered as a central structural consideration. The more the therapy extends toward the longer term, or has an open-ended structure, the more the termination phase model will apply. That is, with fewer constraints on the time afforded for the therapy, a more comprehensive termination phase becomes possible. With short-term therapy approaches, an in-depth examination of the impact of terminating treatment is less feasible. At the same time, many short-term therapies are also conducted in a time-limited format, meaning that patient and therapist are consciously aware of the end date from the start. This has the effect of making the eventual termination a salient issue throughout the course of therapy.

Patient characteristics were also considered in this chapter. They were addressed in terms of the structural aspect of composition in group therapy modalities. Composition can be seen to interact with the time dimension; that is, short-term groups tend more often to be homogeneous in composition while more open-ended groups are composed to reflect greater heterogeneity among the patients. Termination in the short-term group format is more often a shared experience for the patients, whereas in a long-term group, the diversity of termination experiences can heighten the learning potential of endings. The direct effect of patient characteristics on the termination process is considered in more detail in the next chapter.

6

PATIENT CHARACTERISTICS AND VARIATIONS IN TERMINATION PROCESSES AND OUTCOMES

There is clear evidence that personal characteristics and qualities of the patient have a major influence on the outcome of psychotherapy (Lambert, 1992). The field of psychotherapy research is currently emphasizing the importance of patient variables in interaction with both therapist and treatment variables (Clarkin & Levy, 2004). By contrast, almost no attention has been given in the literature to the influence of varying patient characteristics on the process and outcomes of termination. It seems a truism that patient characteristics would have as much influence on the process and outcomes of termination as they do on the process and outcomes of therapy, yet the clinical and empirical study of this specific topic is minimal. The purpose of this chapter is to examine those patient characteristics that have an impact on the process and outcomes of the termination of psychotherapy, on the basis of existing evidence or clinical commentary in the literature.

By necessity, then, the discussion in this chapter tends toward the speculative. Two working assumptions were made in conducting a review of the literature. First, as noted, a number of patient variables have been shown to predict therapy outcome. In addition, a number of patient attitudinal and personality characteristics have been shown to predict dropping out versus completing therapy. The literature concerning dropping out versus completing therapy is reviewed in detail in chapter 7. For heuristic purposes, then, these patient variables were considered as factors potentially influencing the likelihood of a successful therapeutic termination. Second, it was assumed that the supposed impact of these patient variables on the termination process and outcomes could be stated in terms of the termination phase model presented in chapters 2 and 3.

An important theme is evident in both current psychotherapy research and the literature on termination of psychotherapy. It suggests that more global interpersonal dimensions, for example, the patient's attachment style, quality of object relations, or personality organization (Kernberg, 1984), likely have a critical influence on the quality of the therapy process and various outcomes. "The client's past interpersonal relationships and current ability to form a positive and fruitful relationship with the therapist are, on the face of it, quite relevant to the continuation and success of the therapy" (Clarkin & Levy, 2004, p. 210). This statement could likely be extended to encompass the engagement in the termination process and successful attainment of the termination outcomes.

A final qualification should be offered. The effect of the patient's characteristics on the termination process and outcomes does not occur in isolation—the characteristics and skill of the therapist, and the nature of the patient–therapist relationship, will of course also have a bearing on the quality of the termination phase. Every patient is unique in terms of range and severity of problems, history, interpersonal style, and commitment to change. Many characteristics of the patient have the potential to influence the particular therapy case. The characteristics discussed in this chapter are considered in the literature, and many have moderate to strong empirical support as predictors of therapy process or outcome, even if not explicitly associated with the termination of psychotherapy. Psychotherapy is by definition an interpersonal process. Thus, the patient's behavior in therapy is influenced, in turn, by the characteristics and behavior of his or her therapist. The therapist's primary influence is on the patient's continued motivation for change and the nature of his or her participation in the process. In general, the patient variables considered as potential influences on the termination process and outcomes are seen to function as determinants of the patient's motivation and participation. They are also often the same characteristics that led the patient to seek treatment (Hilsenroth, Holdwick, Castlebury, & Blais, 1998) and frequently those "that may disrupt the therapeutic venture" (Clarkin & Levy, 2004, p. 211).

In a successful psychotherapy, then, the therapist will capitalize on the positive characteristics of the patient and accommodate to the negative characteristics. The literature may suggest speculations about which patient variables potentially have an impact on the termination and require attention on the part of the therapist. However, the timing of the ending, how to bring it about, and the degree of success attained, all have to be coordinated with the needs of the particular case (Liegner, 1986) and in terms of the patient's individual characteristics.

The following discussion is organized into three sections. In the first, we consider the attitudinal and personality variables suggested to influence the termination in the dropout-continuation and outcome research literatures. The second section discusses the impact of two global interpersonal dimensions, quality of object relations and attachment style, on the termination process and outcomes. The final section considers patient variation in general diagnostic terms. In this section, variations in the termination process and outcomes are considered for severe and chronic disorders, trauma disorders, and personality disorders (PDs). A substantial amount of the clinical and research literature addresses the therapy process, including the termination of therapy, with patients characterized by borderline personality disorder (BPD). An extended discussion of termination with borderline patients closes the final section.

PATIENT ATTITUDINAL AND PERSONALITY CHARACTERISTICS

Our discussion opens with a consideration of specific personality traits that are likely to impact the quality of the ending of therapy. These traits can range from simple attitudes toward the therapy endeavor to more complex groupings of personality elements representative of individual dispositions or tendencies (e.g., pessimism, self-criticism).

Attitudinal Variables

Attitudinal variables refer to cognitive-affective appraisals of issues, situations, or other people. Attitudes generally carry a certain valence (positive, negative) that will influence how the individual approaches the issue, situation, or other person. In this section we consider the likely impact of the patient's attitudes toward therapy and the importance of behavior change on the process of termination.

Positive Orientation for Therapy

Patients regarded as good candidates for psychotherapy are often those who express a desire for more interpersonal contact and affiliation. Past studies (e.g., Moras & Strupp, 1982) support this clinical observation—patients who express this objective tend to make better use of treatment. This motivational attribute has been associated with benefit for patients of varying levels of problem severity; that is, it is independent of the level of the patient's actual affiliative capacity.

Motivation that translates into behavior has also been associated with therapy outcome. Gomes-Schwartz (1978) analyzed process ratings from taped segments of therapy sessions and found that the feature most consistently predicting outcome was patient willingness and ability to become actively involved in the therapy. O'Malley, Suh, and Strupp (1983) found that patient involvement correlated significantly with all measures of outcome in the Vanderbilt Psychotherapy Outcome Study.

A primary constituent of patients' motivation and quality of participation in therapy is their continuing confidence in the therapist and treatment (J. D. Frank, 1971). The therapist's skill in facilitating and maintaining a productive collaborative alliance with the patient will be a major determinant of the patient's confidence, continuing motivation, and ongoing involvement. A well-conducted therapy will be characterized by all these elements; the therapy will also provide the patient with a favorable experience of interpersonal affiliation and change. During the termination phase, then, maintenance of the patient's confidence and productive involvement will ensure that the termination process will be largely progressive and the termination outcomes will be successfully attained.

The Patient's Stage of Change

The transtheoretical model of change (Prochaska & DiClemente, 1982, 1984, 1992) argues that individuals progress through a series of four general stages as they modify problem behaviors: (a) precontemplation, (b) contemplation, (c) action, and (d) maintenance. In certain presentations of the model, the action stage is divided into preparation and action stages. At the precontemplation stage, individuals are not adequately aware of their problems and have not formulated any intention to change behavior in the foreseeable future. It would be a clinical error to offer a patient in the precontemplation stage a course of psychotherapy: Individuals in precontemplation are resistant to change and would most likely drop out of treatment (Prochaska & DiClemente, 1984). Considerations of the termination process with these patients are therefore moot. In the contemplation stage, individuals are aware of their problem and addressing its ramifications but have not committed themselves to taking action, that is, actual behavior change. The action stage of change is characterized by their efforts to alter their behavior, experiences, and environment to actually overcome the problem. Finally, in the maintenance stage, individuals work toward preventing relapse and maintaining the gains they have achieved.

In terms of the termination process, patients in the contemplation stage would be unlikely to evidence termination criteria of any sufficiency. They would also be likely to express dissatisfaction with the outcome of therapy. This situation would probably occur most often in the briefer forms of treatment. Patients in the action stage would be most likely to make effective use of the therapy. In terms of the termination, the action stage patient would evidence some degree of success with the first termination outcome (i.e., a consolidating review of the therapy process and gains made in treatment) but might encounter difficulty achieving success with the third termination outcome (i.e., evidencing a solid preparedness for maintaining healthy functioning). All things being equal, patients in the maintenance stage would likely achieve satisfactory attainment of all three termination outcomes (Brogan, Prochaska, & Prochaska, 1999).

Affect-Related Variables

Affect-related variables refer to trait-like dispositions of the patient. That is, such variables reflect relatively stable tendencies of the individual to be, for example, hostile or anxious. These patient characteristics can influence the establishment of the therapeutic collaboration for good or ill, which in turn can impact on the quality of the termination process.

Mistrust and Hostility

The patient's characteristic level of suspiciousness or animosity toward others can emerge as a function of his or her relational history (e.g., experiences of physical or sexual abuse) or be a corollary of the presenting illness (e.g., paranoid PD or schizophrenia). The intensity of relational strains due to mistrust or hostility arising from a functional condition (e.g., schizophrenia) can frequently be alleviated by medication treatment. For other patients, the affective issue is predominantly based on characterological traits and, in turn, often a primary focus of any psychotherapeutic intervention that is offered. In- and outside of the therapy situation, these traits represent major interpersonal deficits that decrease the likelihood of stable, meaningful intimate relationships. These affective qualities (hostility, mistrust) represent negative dynamic factors in the treatment situation when they persist across hours of psychotherapy rather than characterizing transient misunderstandings or alliance "ruptures" (Frayn, 1992). If the patient is able to explore these feelings in the therapy relationship, then significant improvement may be possible. Often, however, the feelings may be entrenched defenses against a more profoundly feared vulnerability and thus more impervious to modification. In these circumstances, the therapy can often result in a stalemate and a discouraging outcome for both patient and therapist. Such a situation would render attainment of the second termination outcome—the resolution of issues in the patient–therapist relationship—extremely unlikely.

Conversely, the patient's intransigent mistrust or hostility can be expressed more covertly, by way of acting out in the therapy context or in the outside world during treatment, to stay sick and defeat the therapist, cause harm to others, or achieve a self-destructive objective (Groves & Newman, 1992). This goes beyond a question of patient resistance to the actual development of a "therapy impossible" situation (Groves & Newman, 1992, p. 340) and can frequently only be addressed by a forced termination enacted by the therapist. Research has demonstrated the particular importance of mistrust and hostility in the development of transference problems, negative therapeutic reactions, and treatment dropout in the psychotherapy of patients with BPD (Skodol, Buckley, & Charles, 1983; T. E. Smith, Koenigsberg, Yeomans, Clarkin, & Selzer, 1995; Waldinger & Gunderson, 1984). These issues are revisited in the final section of this chapter.

Denial and Anxiety Proneness

In contrast to those patients characterized by the chronic expression of the corrosive affects of mistrust and hostility, other patients may be marked by a tendency toward denial or increasing anxiety in the face of emotional demands in the therapy situation (Frayn, 1992). Again, the issue is whether the patient's denial or experience of anxiety is transient and episodic as the therapy process unfolds and can, thus, be worked with more or less effectively, or whether these responses are more persistent across the course of treatment. In the latter situation, the process is likely to be extremely difficult and strained unless the therapist's approach is primarily one of support and facilitating adaptation to current circumstances.

As the therapy moves toward completion, the patient's proclivity to engage in denial or experience anxiety is likely to be triggered in different ways as attention is given to each of the termination outcomes. For the first outcome, with the goal of reinforcing and consolidating the therapy process and gains, the patient's tendency to be self-critical or perfectionistic (Blatt, Quinlan, Pilkonis, & Shea, 1995) can trigger the use of denial or increased anxiety and derail the tasks of review and recapitulation. Vulnerability to extreme reactions in the face of loss can lead to the emergence of denial or anxiety in response to the therapist's efforts to resolve issues in the therapeutic relationship, the second termination outcome. Difficulties with autonomy or independent function, or problems maintaining a future orientation, can give rise to increased anxiety and denial in response to the effort to determine the patient's preparedness for maintaining healthy functioning.

Frayn (1992) noted that patients manifesting extreme levels of these affect-related characteristics should be identified during the preparation for, or early in the course of, psychotherapy. Identifying that these qualities may indeed pose obstacles to an effective process, let alone an effective termination, should lead the clinician to consider alternatives to expressive forms of psychotherapy, for example, skills-training interventions or support groups.

Ego Strength

Ego strength is reflected by the presence of a number of personality factors that, taken together, enable an individual to tolerate the anxiety associated with conflicting environmental demands or internal concerns, and to continually refine a flexible and differentiated coping style. A composite variable, ego strength reflects the traits of frustration tolerance, impulse control, introspectiveness, good reality testing, creativity in problem solving, optimism, and self-confidence. In the Menninger Psychotherapy Project (Kernberg et al., 1972), a significant relationship between ego strength and outcome in psychoanalytic psychotherapy was demonstrated; however, other researchers (Luborsky et al., 1980; Weber, Bachrach, & Solomon, 1985) were unable to replicate this relationship. In current parlance, ego strength would be represented by the concept of resilience (Kumpfer, 1999; Stein, Fonagy, Ferguson, & Wisman, 2000). Patients vary considerably in terms of ego strength or resilience; the more primitive or severely disordered patients show less development of this capacity. It is also certainly true that psychotherapy, particularly more intensive or longer term forms of treatment, would be expected to result in increased ego strength or improved resilience.

A patient of high ego strength would be expected to stay with the tasks of the termination phase, particularly the possibly more stressful exploration of issues in the therapeutic relationship associated with the second termination outcome. Conversely, a patient of low ego strength may experience the ending of the relationship to be quite painful and associated with feelings of hopelessness and fear for the future. The low ego strength patient would also potentially struggle with developing plans to deal with crisis or distress in the posttermination period.

Psychological Mindedness

Psychological mindedness (PM) refers generally to an individual's ability to understand people and their problems in psychological terms. More specifically, PM is regarded as a dynamic personality trait reflecting both an interest in inner life and the capacity to be introspective, qualities which in turn are held to be related to an ability to acquire insight (see Conte & Ratto, 1997; McCallum & Piper, 1997b). As a dynamic personality trait, "psychological mindedness tends to be identified with a *process* reflecting a *structure* leading to an outcome" (McCallum & Piper, 1997a, p. 247). PM has also been addressed as self-awareness (Marini & Case, 1994), private self-consciousness (Fenigstein, Scheier, & Buss, 1975), or personal intelligence (Park, Imboden, Park, Hulse, & Unger, 1992). The construct of alexithymia (Taylor, 1984) appears to represent the obverse of PM, as it is held to reflect difficulties identifying and accessing inner contents (i.e., feelings, thoughts, motives) or distinguishing these from physical, bodily sensations. PM has been operationalized by various investigators and measured by using self-report questionnaires, clinical assessments (e.g., response to trial interpretations), or composite scores from measures of associated variables.

Our research group has administered the Psychological Mindedness Assessment Procedure (PMAP; McCallum & Piper, 1990b, 1997b) to evaluate the construct among patients participating in clinical trials of various forms of time-limited, dynamically oriented psychotherapy. We operationally define *PM* as the ability to identify dynamic (intrapsychic) components and to relate them to a person's difficulties. The PMAP uses a scripted and simulated videotaped patient–therapist interaction as a standardized test stimulus. The person being assessed views the actress–patient describing a recent life event to her therapist. The vignette includes verbalizations that reflect dynamic components (e.g., conflicting wishes, defensive maneuvers) and links between internal and external events (e.g., links between internal experiences and behavior). After viewing the videotape, the person being assessed responds to the question, "What seems to be troubling this person?" The narrative response is scored according to a 9-point scale; higher scores reflect a greater appreciation of unconscious motivations and conflict, the motivating power of anxiety, and the purpose of defense mechanisms.

The PMAP has been shown to be reliably used by assessors. The PM score has also been shown to be independent of patient age or gender, level of education, intelligence, or other demographic variables, and indexes of psychiatric symptomatology or distress. The PM variable's association with attrition, process, and therapy outcome was investigated in a series of clinical trial studies. PM was predictive of remaining versus dropping out of short-term interpretive group therapy for complicated bereavement (McCallum & Piper, 1990a; see also Conte & Ratto, 1997). PM was consistently related to the patient's quality of "work" in group forms of dynamically oriented psychotherapy, for example, short-term group approaches (McCallum & Piper, 1990a) or intensive partial hospital treatment programs (McCallum, Piper, & O'Kelly, 1997; Piper, Joyce, Azim, & Rosie, 1994). The variable was predictive of benefit in day treatment (Piper et al., 1994) and in both interpretive and supportive forms of short-term, time-limited group (Piper, McCallum, Joyce, Rosie, & Ogrodniczuk, 2001) and individual therapy (Piper, Joyce, McCallum, & Azim, 1998).

The implications of these findings are relatively clear. PM appears to be a trait associated with the patient's ability to engage productively in psychodynamic forms of psychotherapy. We believe that PM reflects a general capacity of the patient to make effective use of therapeutic interventions and the therapy process to achieve problem resolution. Whether this pattern of relationships involving PM generalizes to other forms of psychotherapy has not yet been studied.

With regard to the termination of psychotherapy, high PM would be expected to facilitate the attainment of termination outcomes. In particular, a high-PM patient would be more likely to have awareness of transference issues and the range of feelings associated with ending the patient–therapist relationship. The patient would also be more likely to incorporate aspects of this relationship (e.g., the formulation of interpretations and responding to interpretation) and the functions of the therapist in looking ahead to maintaining healthy functioning following the termination of treatment. Conversely, the low-PM patient may not "speak the same language" as the interpretive therapist, which would impede the patient's ability to benefit from this kind of approach or to address the termination outcomes from an interpretive perspective. Low-PM patients may rely on greater input from the therapist to develop an understanding of their problems; that is, the constructed understanding would be largely communicated by the therapist rather than jointly developed. A more structured approach to the termination phase would also likely be required with the low-PM patient, the therapist systematically raising for discussion those issues associated with a review of the therapy, the ending of the therapeutic relationship, and the patient's preparation for healthy functioning after the end of the treatment.

Introjective Versus Anaclitic Configuration

Blatt and colleagues (Blatt et al., 1994; Blatt & Shichman, 1983; Blatt, Wein, Chevron, & Quinlan, 1979; Blatt, Wild, & Ritzler, 1975; Blatt, Wiseman, Prince-Gibson, & Gatt, 1991) have identified two primary configurations that encompass the psychopathologies seen in clinical settings. The two configurations are most evident among patients with major affective illness. The *introjective* configuration reflects a primary concern about self-regard and tends to be characterized by perfectionism, self-criticism, and shame. By contrast, the *anaclitic* configuration is focused primarily on the approval and caring of others and tends to be characterized by separation–individuation concerns and anxieties. Blatt et al. (1994) found that in a long-term psychotherapy, patients who were predominantly introjective (perfectionistic and self-critical) generally had better outcomes than clients who were predominantly anaclitic (concerned with abandonment and loss).

With regard to the termination, introjective patients might struggle with a negatively biased perspective on the process and gains of the therapy and, thus, may require a greater investment in addressing the first termination outcome. The priority would be to reinforce the connection between the positive contributions of the patient and the accomplishments of treatment. Anaclitic patients would approach the discussions around the second termination outcome with apprehension—addressing the end of the therapeutic relationship would in all likelihood recapitulate the entire treatment undertaking. Anaclitic patients could be expected to have a not entirely successful attainment of this termination outcome, even if demonstrably positive; that is, the patient may remain sensitive to experiences of rejection and abandonment despite satisfactory resolution of the issues in the patient–therapist relationship. This degree of attainment would consequently also have implications for the third termination outcome, the anaclitic patient's capacity to continue healthy function in the absence of the therapist's support. Primarily, the therapist would need to ensure that he or she felt confident in the patient's ability to be resilient. If this was in doubt, the termination might not be considered as an absolute (i.e., a definitive goodbye) but approached as an interruption relative to future contacts.

INTERPERSONAL DIMENSIONS

Relative to the preceding discussion, the focus in this section is on more global dimensions of personality. These broader characteristics are reflective of the individual's interpersonal style and tend to be evident across most, if not all, important relationships.

Quality of Object Relations

Establishing a sense of the patient's capacity for interpersonal relatedness (Clemental-Jones, Malan, & Trauer, 1990; Moras & Strupp, 1982) is commonly regarded as a critical therapist task during the preparation for psychotherapy or during the early stage of treatment. To this end, the therapist can address the patient's interpersonal history (e.g., significant losses, involvements and separations), the patient's interpersonal functioning in current close relationships, or the patient's characteristic way of viewing relationships. The latter perspective addresses the patient's perceptions of relationships, beliefs regarding relationship issues such as trust and reciprocity, and wishes and anxieties about the costs and provisions of relationships, all subsumed under the "quality of object relations." Generally speaking, object relations refer to the conscious and unconscious mental representations of past interpersonal interactions, developed through the processes of internalization over the course of the individual's interpersonal history. The representations of self and others include cognitive, affective, and experiential components and function to regulate and direct interpersonal behavior (Blatt et al., 1991).

A formulation of the patient's internal object relations can reflect his or her capacity to form a collaborative working relationship with the therapist. A predisposition to establish a relatively trusting give-and-take relationship with an authority figure is an important indicator for a positive therapy process, an effective termination, and treatment benefit. The object relations formulation can provide an estimate of the patient's capacity to tolerate frustrations in the therapy relationship and predictions regarding the transference reactions that are likely to emerge (Joyce & McCallum, 2004). These are also important considerations when looking ahead to the eventual termination of therapy.

A variety of measures and methods of assessment have been developed to evaluate patients' quality of object relations in clinical studies (Object Relations Inventory of Blatt et al., 1991; Reflective Functioning Scale of Fonagy & Target, 1997; Core Conflictual Relationship Theme of Luborsky & Crits-Cristoph, 1997; Social Cognition and Object Relations Scale of Westen, 1991; for a review of these measures, see Huprich & Greenberg, 2003). The Quality of Object Relations (QOR) Assessment developed by our group was introduced in chapter 5. We define QOR as a person's internal enduring tendency to establish certain types of relationships (Azim et al., 1991). These relationship patterns range along an overall dimension from primitive (characterized by destructiveness and instability) to mature (characterized by reciprocity and mutuality). The QOR construct, thus, refers to the recurring pattern of relationships over the individual's life span, rather than to relationships during any one period (e.g., recent interpersonal functioning).

The patient's QOR is assessed by an experienced clinician during a 1-hour semistructured interview. The interviewer solicits information regarding four areas of functioning: behavioral manifestations, affect regulation, self-esteem regulation, and antecedent (etiological) factors. The interviewer assigns greater weight to behavioral manifestations because they are observable, experience near, and often manifest during the interview itself. The interview is roughly divided into three segments in which relationships in the patient's childhood, adolescence, and adulthood are successively the focus of attention. Following the interview, the assessor distributes 100 points across 5 levels of the QOR dimension (primitive, searching, controlling, triangular, and mature), determined by the strength and number of criteria at each level that are met by the patient's interview contribution. A simple arithmetic formula is then used to generate an overall score that ranges from 1 to 9—the higher the QOR score, the more mature the patient's object relations.

The reliability and construct validity of the QOR variable are reviewed in Piper and Duncan (1999). In general, QOR has been found to be independent of demographic and historic characteristics of the patient. The construct has also not been found to be related to Axis I diagnoses. As one would expect, patients with lower QOR scores (i.e., less than 4.5) tend to show more symptomatic disturbance and are more likely to have an Axis II diagnosis than patients with higher QOR scores (i.e., equal to or greater than 4.5), although the overlap is not considerable. The QOR variable has emerged as a strong predictor of therapy process and outcome in time-limited forms of dynamically oriented psychotherapy. In general across a number of studies (Piper, Azim, Joyce, McCallum, et al., 1991; Piper, Azim, McCallum, & Joyce, 1990; Piper, de Carufel, & Szkrumelak, 1985; Piper et al., 1998, 2001), high QOR has been shown to function as an important patient-treatment match for interpretive forms of psychotherapy. The high-QOR patient's history of meaningful give-and-take relationships appears to allow for the establishment of a strong collaboration with the therapist and greater readiness to make use of the interpretive approach. High-QOR patients also appear to have greater tolerance for the therapist's use of transference interpretations (Piper, Azim, Joyce, & McCallum, 1991). Though the evidence is less strong, there is reason to believe that low-QOR patients stand to gain more from a supportive therapy approach. The treatment itself can provide the patient with the experience of a clearly bounded and gratifying relationship, countering a lifelong experience of depriving or abusive relationships (see also Høglend, 1993a, 1993b; Horowitz, Marmar, Weiss, DeWitt, & Rosenbaum, 1984). Low-QOR patients apparently have less capacity to work with transference interpretations, indeed appearing to find this therapist technique injurious (Ogrodniczuk, Piper, Joyce, & McCallum, 1999).

The patient's QOR should thus be considered a primary determinant of the approach to therapy and the therapist's strategy within sessions. The more mature the patient's QOR, the more likely an expressive therapy approach can be undertaken, and the more likely each of the termination outcomes can be considered in full. In other words, the general model of the termination process and the tasks associated with each of the termination outcomes can be applied with minimal modification when working with the high-QOR patient. The more primitive the patient's QOR, the more problematic the patient's representations of interpersonal relatedness and capacity for self-regulation. With these patients, a supportive and open-ended therapy approach is more feasible. In terms of the termination outcomes, extended attention to issues in the patient–therapist relationship, or discussion of the patient's functioning in the absence of access to the therapist, may be destabilizing for the low-QOR patient. Instead, it may be more appropriate to focus on the termination as an interruption of an ongoing treatment process, with emphasis on the availability of the therapist in the event of future crises.

Attachment Style

The individual's patterning of attachment behaviors, or attachment style, is similar to the QOR construct in being based on early transactions with significant others. Specifically, attachment style reflects the individual's disposition to seek proximity to significant others for security and protection in times of stress, initially established through the interaction between the developing child and the early caregiver, usually the mother. Secure attachment develops from engaging with a caregiver who is attentive and responsive to the needs of the developing child. Insecure attachment is manifested in different behavioral patterns, for example, excessive dependence or defensive separation, that develop in response to absent or inconsistent responsiveness on the part of the attachment figure. Following the seminal theoretical work by Bowlby (1970, 1980, 1988) and empirical studies of mother–infant relations by Ainsworth (1964), the attachment model has been used as the underpinning for countless studies of adult behavior. In the area of psychotherapy research, a clear parallel has been drawn between the infant's attachment behaviors toward a caregiver during times of stress and the patient in distress seeking help in the therapeutic relationship.

According to Bowlby (1988), four attachment styles in infants or young children can be identified: secure, anxious–ambivalent, anxious–avoidant, and disorganized. Corresponding maternal behaviors have also been identified, ranging from optimally responsive through inconsistent to rejecting or dismissing. Researchers of adult behavior, particularly in clinical settings, have identified variants of attachment behavior, such as a *dismissing* form of anxious–avoidant attachment and a *preoccupied* form of anxious–ambivalent attachment (e.g., Bartholomew & Horowitz, 1991).

Patient attachment styles have been associated with positive therapy process and beneficial outcome, but there have been inconsistent results across studies. These inconsistencies suggest that there may actually be interactions between the patient's attachment behavior and the particular treatment approach, but these have yet to be identified. Certainly, securely attached patients tend to engage in the therapy process more easily and to achieve greater benefit. Among a group of outpatients presenting with heterogeneous Axis I disorders, those with a secure attachment style manifested less symptomatology at pretreatment and greater improvement after treatment (Meyer, Pilkonis, Proietti, Heape, & Egan, 2001). Securely attached patients have also been found to establish stronger alliances with the therapist (Satterfield & Lyddon, 1998) and are able to do so in the earlier stages of therapy (Eames & Roth, 2000).

Patients presenting with an anxious–avoidant attachment style tend to have the most problems establishing and maintaining an alliance. Dozier (1990) reported that patients characterized by dismissing attachments are often resistant to treatment and have greater problems making use of the help offered by the therapist. Dismissing individuals often become disorganized when confronted with the emotional demands of the therapy process (Dozier, Lomax, & Tyrell, 1996, cited in Clarkin & Levy, 2004). However, Eames and Roth (2000) reported that patients with dismissing or preoccupied attachment styles showed improvement in the quality of the therapeutic alliance as treatment progressed, suggesting that the therapy process was itself having a modifying impact on the patient's attachment behavior. Among nonpsychotic inpatients with severe PD engaged in an intensive hospital treatment program, Fonagy et al. (1996) found that those classified as insecure–dismissing in their attachment behavior showed the best response to the intervention, relative to other attachment subgroups.

Taken together, these findings generally suggest that patients who experience a high degree of anxiety about attachment relationships and who consequently have difficulty engaging in intimacy will also likely have problems establishing and making use of a healthy therapeutic alliance. Research has also indicated that variations in patient attachment style call for different responses from the therapist (Diamond et al., 1999). Hardy, Stiles, Barkham, and Startup (1998) reported that therapists focused more on affect and relationship issues with patients characterized by a preoccupied attachment style, but employed a more cognitive strategy with those patients marked by a dismissing attachment style. At the same time, the evidence to date suggests that even problematic insecure attachment styles can be engaged in the therapy process over time, to good results. As with the QOR construct, the more problematic the patient's attachment style, the more modifications will be required to the therapist's treatment approach to allow the patient to experience safety and trust in the relationship. In a long-term therapy, it may be possible as treatment goes on for the therapist to bring in certain types of interventions (e.g., comments regarding the transference) that earlier in the course of therapy would have proven too threatening to the patient. Knowledge of the patient's characteristic approach to attachment relationships can inform the therapist in regard to the "best fit" treatment approach, as well as sensitizing the clinician to changes in the patient's usual attachment behaviors.

With regard to the termination of therapy, a number of predictions involving patient attachment style can be advanced. Patients with a secure attachment style, like the patient of more mature QOR, should be able to engage comfortably in the various tasks associated with termination, as well as showing successful attainment of the termination outcomes. Patients characterized by anxious attachment will respond to the focus on the second and third termination outcomes (resolution of issues in the therapeutic relationship, preparing for maintenance of healthy function after the end of therapy) with increasing anxiety. In most instances, this will necessitate a greater use of supportive interventions or some limitation in the goals associated with these termination outcomes (e.g., overlooking unexpressed negative transference, emphasizing that the therapist can be available in the future). Addressing the review of therapy gains and the ending of the therapy relationship would likely be problematic for patients characterized by avoidance in their attachment relationships. The therapist can recall instances where the collaboration proved effective in dealing with particular issues to reinforce the usefulness of interpersonal engagement. Patients characterized by preoccupied or dismissing attachment behavior will both encounter difficulties dealing with the issues in the patient–therapist relationship, but perhaps for different reasons. The preoccupied patient may find it difficult to bear giving up the therapist, whereas the dismissing patient may find it problematic to acknowledge the importance of the therapist in the treatment. Ideally, the quality of the alliance and work accomplished in the therapy process (Eames & Roth, 2000) can allow these patients to acknowledge their particular difficulties at the time of terminating therapy.

PATIENT DIAGNOSIS

A broad perspective is also taken in this section. The focus of the discussion is the impact of general diagnostic distinctions on the ending of therapy. These include the severe functional conditions associated with Axis I of the *Diagnostic and Statistical Manual of Mental Disorders* (4th ed., rev.; American Psychiatric Association, 2000), those disorders associated with traumatic experience, and the extremes of personality functioning represented by the categories of Axis II. The section concludes with a specific focus on the demands of ending therapy with those patients diagnosed with BPD.

Severe and Chronic Disorders

By definition, patients with severe and chronic conditions such as bipolar illness or schizophrenia require long-term, even open-ended, treatment contracts. Psychotherapy interventions may be provided at intervals, usually as adjuncts to the primary modality of care (e.g., psychopharmacology, rehabilitation services, ongoing support groups). A formal termination of the therapy on each of these occasions, that is, with attention to each of the termination outcomes in the context of an absolute ending of the patient–therapist relationship, is inappropriate. The probability is high that the patient will return at some point for another course of therapy, when life stresses again become intolerable or the patient experiences fluctuations in his or her psychiatric condition.

Ideally, the patient and therapist should conclude a course of therapy in such a way that the dialogue can be picked up without discontinuity at the time of the patient's next presentation. With regard to the first termination outcome, the gains achieved as a result of the latest engagement in therapy can be reviewed and consolidated; the therapist may also link these achievements to the goals attained in previous contacts with the patient. In regard to the second termination outcome, successes and strains in the relationship during the latest course of therapy can be highlighted, with attention to how the patient and therapist negotiated an effective collaboration, for future reference. There is less emphasis placed on saying goodbye; instead, the patient and therapist approach the separation as a temporary one or "until we meet again." The therapist can address the third termination outcome in terms of the current successes and their application in the patient's life, as another link in the chain of therapeutic accomplishments attained over the series of intermittent contacts.

The situation is somewhat different if the therapist will not be available for future contacts with the patient. For example, the therapist may be completing training and moving into private practice, or the clinician may be contemplating retirement. In these situations, the ongoing care of the patient will frequently be turned over to a replacement therapist, but the particular relationship between the patient and therapist must be concluded. The patient should be reassured that therapy will remain available as required, albeit with a new provider. The history of involvement with the current therapist can be reviewed. Stone (2005) emphasized that patients with chronic and severe disorders do have the capacity to express and work with affects associated with termination in these circumstances. He emphasized that this is facilitated by the use of supportive interventions that address the "forward edge" of the patient's efforts at adaptation (Tolpin, 2002, p. 167), that is, clarifying the accommodation to the loss the patient is attempting to develop. This intervention strategy is seen to be of greater therapeutic value than the use of an interpretive focus on the here-and-now relationship or transference. The therapist is also more revealing about the reasons for the ending than might be the case with higher functioning patients.

Trauma Disorders

Psychologically, the task for the patient dealing with trauma is to fashion a personal meaning for the experience that can allow it to be assimilated and made a part of the individual's history and character. This is often phrased as the movement from being a victim of trauma to being a trauma survivor. In clinical practice, the trauma patient's capacity for trust, willingness to form an attachment relationship, and willingness to risk personal exposure will be critical concerns, in terms of demarcating the severity of the disorder, predicting possible difficulties in the therapy process, and specifically managing the termination.

More expressive forms of psychotherapy are generally offered for patients dealing with interpersonal trauma, as opposed to impersonal trauma (e.g., disaster). These latter types of traumatic response respond well to the cognitive and skills development therapies. Trauma can also be differentiated in terms of frequency or intensity, that is, a single episode of posttraumatic stress disorder (PTSD) relative to repeated or chronic trauma disorders. Regarding this distinction, more intensive or long-term therapies tend to be provided for the repeated or chronic forms. In addition, different types of treatment may be particularly useful as a function of the stage of recovery from trauma. For example, a homogeneous group of trauma patients may represent a useful treatment strategy early in the recovery process, whereas a heterogeneously composed group could offer more during the latter stages of recovery (see Buchele, 2000). In the following brief discussion, these distinctions are not considered in terms of specific implications for treatment strategy during the termination. The literature does not provide evidence to support any specific assertions. However, the implications within the frame of the termination phase model are considered.

The thesis has persisted since Freud (1937/1964a) that the prognosis for an effective conclusion of treatment is more favorable in cases where the etiology is traumatic (Blum, 1987; Ferraro, 1995). This would be the case, figuratively speaking, because trauma invariably involves some kind of loss or separation, whether of a real person (e.g., in a car accident) or of a certain state of functioning (e.g., sense of personal safety or sense of trust in others following an assault). From this perspective, the end of therapy is held to assume the form of a new trauma, stimulating separation anxieties and a reactivation of the earlier traumatic experience, independent of the quality of the treatment outcome. Liegner (1986) emphasized the importance of addressing the patient's positive and negative transferences at the time of termination to mitigate these separation anxieties: "If these are sufficiently diminished, the patient can then cope with the feelings of loss caused by the termination and with that part of mourning which he has to carry on by himself" (pp. 13–14). Consequently, for patients dealing primarily with experiences of trauma, addressing the issues in the patient–therapist relationship (the second termination outcome) can assume critical importance at the conclusion of treatment. The objective regarding this outcome would be to develop a realistic portrayal of the ending of the patient–therapist relationship, free of the distortions associated with the patient's anxieties and depressive feelings experienced in earlier traumatic situations. In effect, the work around this issue should demonstrate to the patient that the termination of therapy is not equivalent to trauma, given the resources the patient has developed through the process and in partnership with the therapist.

Lindy and Wilson (2001) argued that many cases of PTSD are lifelong conditions where the degree of integration achieved may be limited and treatment may be necessary on an intermittent basis. In these cases, the offer of a brief therapy would be inappropriate. Termination should be framed as an interruption of treatment rather than an ultimate ending. In longer term therapies, Lindy and Wilson argued that the therapist should be specific in determining when attention to the trauma has been sufficient and termination can be considered. They suggest that a useful endpoint may be when the patient has resumed engagement in certain phase-appropriate life tasks. This can be facilitated by attending to the patient's everyday life circumstances as part of the treatment effort from the outset.

Personality Disorders

There is clear evidence, across a number of symptom disorders (e.g., depression, anxiety, eating disorder), that treatment effects are attenuated for those patients with co-occurring PD in contrast with their counterparts without Axis II pathology (Clarkin & Levy, 2004; Diguer, Barber, & Luborsky, 1993; Shea, Widiger, & Klein, 1992). This is apparently associated with the problems that arise in the therapy relationship or process as a direct function of the patient's personality pathology: "It is important to consider that the same personality features that led the patient to seek treatment will inevitably intrude into the treatment itself" (Hilsenroth et al., 1998, p. 164). Therapists working with patients with PD "should plan treatment for more modest gains, anticipate and address potential early patient dropout, and plan for disruptions in the treatment adherence and alliance" (Clarkin & Levy, 2004, p. 202).

Two aspects of PD pathology have been highlighted in the literature as having a possible bearing on the quality of the termination process and the degree of successful attainment of the termination outcomes. The first is the nature of the patient's disorder-driven interpersonal style. Hilsenroth et al. (1998) investigated the relationship between therapy continuation and the individual diagnostic criteria for the Cluster B PDs (histrionic, borderline, narcissistic, and antisocial). Five individual criteria were found to be independent and nonredundant predictors of continuing in therapy, that is, moving toward therapy termination. Three variables were positively associated with continuation: "Frantic efforts to avoid real or imagined abandonment" (borderline PD Criterion 1); "Inappropriate, intense anger or difficulty controlling anger" (borderline PD Criterion 8); and "Considers relationships to be more intimate than they really are" (histrionic PD Criterion 8). These variables all reflect affective issues in interpersonal relationships, frequently the focus in a psychotherapy that emphasizes the expression of feelings, both generally and in relation to the patient–therapist relationship. Thus, patients meeting these diagnostic criteria may have found therapy useful to them and continued. Two Axis II criteria were negative predictors of continuation: "Requires excessive admiration" (narcissistic PD Criterion 4) and "Lack of remorse, indifference to or rationalising having hurt, mistreated, or stolen from another" (antisocial PD Criterion 7). These variables reflect a high degree of self-centeredness and little concern for others, a relational stance that would not be conducive to a productive patient–therapist collaboration. As a consequence, PD patients with these characteristics may protect themselves from becoming too deeply engaged and may be unable to use the time in therapy effectively. Their restricted engagement protects the patient from the feared intense or overwhelming responses to termination (Charman & Graham, 2004).

The second aspect of PD that has a bearing on the termination of psychotherapy is the difficulty these patients may have successfully internalizing aspects of the therapy relationship. Bender (1996, cited in Arnold, Farber, & Geller, 2004) found that the more patients manifested aspects of avoidant, dependent, passive–aggressive, self-defeating, or schizotypal character styles, the greater the likelihood they would not report making use of their therapy experience at the time of follow-up. This difficulty was attributed to the patient's fixed and rigid representations of relationships, leading to an undervaluing of the positive aspects of the therapy relationship.

Borderline Personality Disorder

BPD is by far the most intensively studied of the Axis II categories (Clarkin, Marziali, & Munroe-Blum, 1991). The sheer size of the literature in regard to clinical problems in the psychotherapy of patients with BPD is rarely found for any other disorder. Much of this literature concerns factors associated with the high rate of premature termination of psychotherapy by patients with BPD (Horner & Diamond, 1996), estimated to be approximately 67% across clinical settings (Skodol et al., 1983; Waldinger & Gunderson, 1984; see also Horner & Diamond, 1996; T. E. Smith et al., 1995). The literature is also replete with recommendations for enhancing the retention of patients with BPD in psychotherapy. Beyond retention, however, and similar to the wider psychotherapy literature, research data regarding termination experiences with BPD patients are sparse (Sansone, Fine, & Dennis, 1991).

There are many factors encouraging this intensive study of patients with BPD. Behaviors regarded as characteristic of the disorder can frequently put the borderline patient and others at severe risk of harm. As a group, patients with BPD tend to be quite heterogeneous in terms of presenting problems and coping style. This wide range of behavior demands that treatment strategies be comprehensive and that therapists have extensive experience (Aronson, 1989). Development of effective treatments for BPD can be advantageous for the treatment of other conditions that may present similar behaviors in attenuated form.

Assuming that the patient has been successfully retained in treatment, many features of BPD can contribute to problems with the process of termination and limited attainment of the termination outcomes. Patients with BPD may present with many of the characteristics, discussed earlier, which can negatively affect the termination phase:

- The patient's willingness and ability to become or stay involved in the therapy process may be absent or highly variable, as a function of conflicting anxieties about abandonment (loss of the other) or engulfment (loss of the self in overdependence).
- Confidence in the therapist and therapy may wax and wane considerably as tendencies to idealize and devalue are stimulated by the therapy process or as malevolent self–other representations come into play.
- Patients with BPD are frequently characterized as being unable to trust or as extremely hostile in the therapy context, each a stance taken to ward off fears of vulnerability. Mistrust and hostility are associated with the development of transference problems or negative therapeutic reactions among BPD patients (see Skodol et al., 1983; T. E. Smith et al., 1995; Waldinger & Gunderson, 1984).

- Patients with BPD are also prone to intense anxiety (the so-called fragile patient) and denial of responsibility for problems and may frequently present with impulsivity, poor frustration tolerance, and inadequate reality testing (i.e., poor ego strength).
- By definition, patients with BPD tend to function at a more primitive level of object relations and to engage in insecure (anxious, preoccupied) attachment behaviors. The therapist is often faced with crises associated with the patient's poor affective regulation and use of primitive defenses (e.g., denial, avoidance, acting out, projection and projective identification, splitting). The termination of therapy would likely be a period characterized by these crises.
- Patients with BPD frequently present with a history of severe relational trauma, and this can often be reenacted at the time of termination.

Sansone et al. (1991) offered a snapshot of clinicians' experience with BPD patients in psychotherapy. Respondents to the survey noted that premature termination was more the rule than the exception with these patients. The two most frequently endorsed reasons for premature termination were "the patient does not see the purpose of treatment" and "the patient terminates through acting-out behaviour." Respondents also indicated that the goal of therapy was characterological change or improvement but without the expectation of personality resolution to "normality." A "successful and complete" treatment was regarded as one in which the patient had shown "psychological movement to a higher level of organization." When asked about their primary concerns during the termination of BPD patients who had not successfully completed treatment or sufficiently stabilized, respondents emphasized problems because of (a) regression to previous levels of functioning, (b) acting-out behavior, and (c) self-destructiveness during the termination phase. These problems were attributed to the BPD patients' extreme sensitivity to separation and abandonment.

In psychological terms, contradictory and affectively extreme internal representations of self and other lie at the core of BPD. On the basis of these object relations, the BPD patient tends to oscillate dramatically in perceptions of others and interpersonal behavior. At one extreme the patient will perceive the other as a highly positive, even idealized, nurturing object and engage in behaviors aimed at maintaining proximity and avoiding abandonment. At the other extreme, a relationship partner will be perceived as highly negative and rejecting and consequently a target for intense feelings of rage. These oscillations can be prompted by the object's (other person's) actual behavior or by behavior perceived to meet one or the other of the patient's extreme object representations. These primitive, split-object relations are seen to arise from profoundly inconsistent caregiver relations during the patient's early years. The absence of integrated object representations that are essentially positive also leaves the patient with difficulty regulating intense affect and aggression. In effect, the patient has few resources for self-soothing if in distress or experiencing sadness, or for modulating feelings and expressions of rageful aggression into assertiveness. Frequently, the patient's rage at others who are perceived as depriving is experienced as destructive to the internal representation of that object, leaving the patient feeling empty. These characteristics of the BPD patient's internal world constitute a particular challenge for sustained psychotherapeutic treatment (Horner & Diamond, 1996).

At the core of the psychotherapeutic endeavor with BPD patients, then, is the effort to integrate a split internal world (Yeomans, Clarkin, & Kernberg, 2002). Much of this work will occur by way of attention to fluctuations in the immediate patient–therapist relationship, particularly at those times when the patient is faced with a separation, for example, the end of sessions, therapist vacations, or other breaks in the course of treatment. The patient's frustration, rage, and hatred toward the therapist require containment and examination. Needless to say, the therapist must bring a degree of resilience to this work. Frequently, the therapist must contend with impulses to discharge the patient rather than endure the intensely negative affects that can emerge in the process. "Yet these are the very feelings that enable (the therapist) to understand patients' life histories and parental attitudes" (Liegner, 1986, p. 6). Moreover, if the patient is able to explore these feelings in a therapy characterized by safety, clearly articulated boundaries and limit setting, and consistent attention to affect modulation, significant improvement may be possible (Hilsenroth et al., 1998; T. E. Smith et al., 1995).

The therapist's skill in structuring the therapy so as to contain the patient's affective storms and limit destructive behavior can substantially contribute to the continuation of psychotherapy. Indeed, an explicit focus on the BPD patient's reactions to the structure of the psychotherapy relationship has been linked to an improved therapeutic alliance and a decreased incidence of therapy dropout (Stevenson & Meares, 1992; Yeomans, Selzer, & Clarkin, 1993).

A successful psychotherapy with the BPD patient will be evidenced by progress toward greater integration of object representations and modulation of affect. Yeomans et al. (2002) highlighted a number of indications, including decreased acting-out behavior coupled with increased conscious awareness of affect, greater self-reflection and use of the therapist's interventions, increased tolerance of conflicting feelings (e.g., hatred and love for the therapist or others), and a move from a paranoid stance toward a capacity for true relatedness (p. 178). In addition to achievement of the patient's own goals for therapy, these indications are relevant to considering when the patient is ready for termination.

Raising the possibility of termination can be an extremely delicate proposition with a rejection-sensitive BPD patient and can prompt a resurgence of the more primitive object relations that have been the focus over the entire course of the treatment. That is, when the issue of termination is broached, the therapist may once again be perceived as someone who uses and then disposes of the patient. Alternatively, if the patient has manifested a move into the depressive position, the fantasy may be that his or her needs have depleted the therapist and that the patient deserves to be abandoned.

> Discussion and interpretation of these fantasies help the patient accept the realistic limitations of what the therapist, and others, can offer and help the patient understand that these limitations are due neither to the therapist's meanness nor to the patient's badness. (Yeomans et al., 2002, p. 180)

A realistic mourning of the therapy and therapy relationship then becomes possible. Thus, attention to the resolution of the issues in the patient–therapist relationship—the second termination outcome—will be of primary concern when concluding therapy with the borderline patient.

Yeomans et al. (2002) made two recommendations in regard to the termination with BPD patients. First, therapists should allow for 6 months of therapy contact before the final session to deal with the issues stimulated by initiation of the termination process. Second, patients should be scheduled for a return consultation 6 months after the final session for a review of whether the patients' split internal world continues to be integrated and has resulted in a more adaptive organization in their life. At this time, patients and therapists can address whether it would be helpful for patients to engage in further therapy aimed at addressing higher developmental (i.e., neurotic) issues. Generally, termination from therapy is not presented as precluding future contact between patients and therapists. Therapists communicate that opportunities for consultation remain available, and the 6-month hiatus is implemented so that the end of therapy "will be real and not a pseudotermination" (p. 181). The termination outcomes that concern a review and consolidation of treatment gains and establishing preparedness for maintenance of gains following treatment are framed in terms of the follow-up consultation and the likelihood of additional therapy involvement in the future.

CONCLUSION

It is clear from the foregoing that the patient characteristics identified as likely to influence the process of termination, for good or ill, tend to be highly interrelated. For example, it will often be the case that a particular patient will present with primitive object relations, an insecure attachment style, anxiety proneness, poor ego strength, and so on. Taken together, it is also evident that the variables discussed are associated in some way with the patient's capacity for interpersonal relatedness. Frequently, these variables are also very much associated with the issues that initially prompted the patient to seek out psychotherapy and often the focus of the work engaged in by the patient and therapist. In work with patients who present with a number of these characteristics, the transition to the termination phase can have a major impact and result in a reemergence of issues already addressed. Often, then, the work conducted by patient and therapist during the course of treatment is likely to be recapitulated in the termination phase.

Characteristics of particular patients may require that therapists modify their approach to therapy. It is likely the case that the more this is required, the more adjustments will also need to occur when attention to the termination outcomes becomes the central task of the relationship. For certain patients, for example, those with severe and chronic disorders, the termination outcomes are considered in limited form, from an orientation that the particular course of treatment is an instance of a longer term series of intermittent contacts. For other patients, for example, those with profound attachment issues, poor quality of object relations, or BPD, engagement in the tasks of the termination phase must be balanced against protection of the patient's newfound level of integration from trauma. This can involve an extension of the time involved in addressing the termination, a more extensive consideration of issues in the therapy relationship, or the provision of a time frame for systematic follow-up.

All things being equal, the general model of the termination process and outcomes can be applied to most therapy situations. In the real world of the therapy setting, the deficits and strengths presented by the particular patient will be a significant influence on the therapist's application of the general model of termination.

7
PATIENT-INITIATED TERMINATION

Ideally, patients and therapists are able to agree about the timing of the termination of psychotherapy. However, not all terminations of psychotherapy are successfully negotiated or mutually determined events. Sometimes terminations are the result of a unilateral decision to end therapy by the patient or therapist. Therapist-initiated termination is discussed in chapter 8. In this chapter, we consider patient-initiated termination.

The objectives of this chapter are threefold. First, we consider the incidence of patient-initiated premature termination, emphasizing the consistently high rates across various settings. Second, we provide a brief summary of the factors that research and theory have suggested may be associated with unnecessary and avoidable patient-initiated premature terminations. We highlight factors that appear to be particularly promising as predictors of patient-initiated premature terminations, such as the interpersonal functioning of the patient and perspective divergence between patient and therapist. Third, we review different strategies that may be useful for preventing or minimizing patient-initiated premature terminations. Nine strategies are discussed. This is an area that deserves much greater attention to inform efforts to retain patients in treatment and increase the possibility of a successfully negotiated termination.

Some patients terminate therapy earlier than planned as satisfied consumers because they have received sufficient help or their problems have diminished during their abbreviated stay. Other patient-initiated terminations are unavoidable or necessary. That is, some patients are forced to terminate therapy because life circumstances (e.g., a geographical move) make continuing in therapy impossible. Others may become physically incapacitated (e.g., illness, difficult pregnancy), thus making termination necessary. Although all of these terminations occur sooner than expected, they can be considered to be appropriate. Frequently, once the patient's circumstances have resolved, it is possible to resume the abbreviated treatment.

Other patient-initiated terminations are considered inappropriate. For example, a patient's sudden decision to end therapy against the therapist's recommendation is considered to be a premature termination. *Patient-initiated premature termination*, also referred to in the literature as unilateral termination, discontinuing, or dropping out, is generally recognized as a negative event in psychotherapy and a significant obstacle to the effective delivery of mental health services. Accordingly, this chapter regards patient-initiated premature termination as a negative event that occurs unnecessarily and is potentially avoidable.

DIFFICULTIES ASSOCIATED WITH PATIENT-INITIATED PREMATURE TERMINATION

Patient-initiated premature terminations pose several problems. From a clinical perspective, the patient may not receive the full potential benefit from treatment, including the benefit of a worked-through termination. The patient often experiences a sense of dissatisfaction or failure that can result in a worsening of problems. Indeed, patients who terminate prematurely report less therapeutic progress and more psychological distress (Pekarik, 1992). Premature terminators are more likely to be characterized as chronic patients, with a tendency to overuse services, in some cases contacting mental health services at twice the rate of patients classified as appropriate terminators (Carpenter, Del Gaudio, & Morrow, 1979).

In the context of group therapy, patient-initiated premature terminations can be even more disruptive. Discontinuation disrupts group solidarity and can precipitate other premature terminations (Fieldsteel, 1996; Rice, 1996). Patient-initiated premature terminations may destroy or delay meaningful work for the rest of the group, often leaving other group members feeling insecure, worried, or angry.

Most commonly, it is acknowledged that patient-initiated premature termination can be demoralizing to therapists, particularly for beginning therapists (Garfield, 1994). Therapists may believe that they have failed or were rejected by the patient. Such a belief may, in turn, impair clinical confidence and effectiveness. When they experience a premature termination, therapists may be left with a sense that they have wasted their time and effort. Narcissistic injury is also common among therapists. That is, for therapists whose own self-esteem is closely tied to their ability to help others, the loss of a patient through premature termination threatens their sense of self-worth. Painful reactions to losing a patient through premature termination, such as hurt, rejection, or anger, may interfere with other aspects of the therapist's professional or personal life, for example, interfering with the therapy of another patient who may be similar to the one who prematurely terminated.

From an administrative perspective, financial and human resources are not used efficiently when patients prematurely terminate. Appointment times that premature terminators fail to show for could be used to see other patients. This contributes to increasingly long wait lists. Therapists or clinics also lose income. Because patients who prematurely terminate are likely to be high users of mental health services, there are opportunity costs associated with other patients being deprived of access to needed services.

Finally, from a research perspective, patient-initiated premature termination results in a loss of data, which can significantly reduce the ability of the study to adequately test its hypotheses. Furthermore, premature termination can compromise the design of a study. For example, a randomized trial that experiences uneven premature termination among the conditions of the trial may not be able to compare the conditions as originally intended. These consequences of premature termination affect how a study's findings are interpreted.

INCIDENCE

Differences in how patient-initiated premature termination has been defined have confounded attempts to derive accurate estimates of its incidence. Many studies have defined patient-initiated premature termination as the failure to attend a specified number of sessions. Unfortunately, researchers use different cutoffs. Patients who are considered premature terminators in one study are viewed as appropriate terminators in others. In some studies, the criterion is the failure to complete the fixed time period for the therapy. Other studies have relied on therapist judgment to define patient-initiated premature termination. The discontinuities among studies enable one to make only gross estimates of incidence rates.

Reported rates of patient-initiated premature termination of psychotherapy are typically high. In a meta-analytic review of 125 studies of different forms of psychotherapy, Wierzbicki and Pekarik (1993) reported an average rate of 47%, which is consistent with rates reported in previous reviews (Baekeland & Lundwall, 1975; Garfield, 1986). Individual, group, family, and couples therapy had comparable rates (Klein & Carroll, 1986). However, rates for time-limited therapies may be lower. Sledge, Moras, Hartley, and Levine (1990) reported a rate of 32% for brief therapy that had a definite time limit compared with a rate of 67% for brief therapy that did not have a definite time limit and 61% for long-term therapy. The rates may be even lower for manualized time-limited therapies that are provided in clinical research units that make use of rigorous patient selection criteria. Hunt and Andrews (1992) reported a rate of 17% for time-limited cognitive–behavioral therapy that was provided in a clinical research unit, which stands in contrast to a reported rate of 50% for time-unlimited cognitive–behavioral therapy that was provided in a private practice setting (Persons, Burns, & Perloff, 1988). Relatively low rates were also reported by Elkin et al. (1989) for the manualized forms of time-limited interpersonal psychotherapy (23%) and cognitive–behavioral therapy (32%) that were provided in the National Institute of Mental Health collaborative treatment study of depression. Even though the rates of patient-initiated premature termination for manualized time-limited therapies in clinical trials appear to be lower than those for therapies provided under other conditions, the rates remain higher than desirable and are generalizable to only a small minority of practitioners. Rates for private practice or general clinics appear to be much higher and reflect the reality that patient-initiated premature termination represents an enormous problem for most providers of psychotherapy.

FACTORS RELATED TO PATIENT-INITIATED PREMATURE TERMINATION

The ability to accurately predict whether a person might leave treatment prematurely would prove invaluable to clinicians and administrators. Toward this end, a considerable amount of research has been conducted investigating the potential effect of several different factors on patient-initiated premature termination. The majority of studies have involved individual psychotherapy. Prediction of patient-initiated premature termination from group psychotherapy is a neglected topic in the literature. Studies investigating the prediction of premature termination have spanned several decades and have been summarized in many reviews (Garfield, 1994; Reis & Brown, 1999; Roback & Smith, 1987; Wierzbicki & Pekarik, 1993). It is not our intention to provide another comprehensive synthesis of the premature termination research literature but, instead, to offer a brief summary of the main findings of existing reviews and also to highlight promising themes that have emerged in the literature. Exhibit 7.1 provides a list of the factors that we describe in this chapter.

Patient Factors

The patient characteristics evaluated in studies to identify predictors of patient-initiated premature termination can be organized into four general

Patient factors

- Non-Caucasian racial status
- Poor education
- Low economic standing
- Unmet patient expectations
- Nonreadiness for change
- Interpersonal functioning

Therapist factors

- Insufficient knowledge of theory
- Lack of technical skill

Administrative factors

- Long wait-list length
- Inadequate patient preparation
- Lack of time-limited treatment structure
- Patient noncompliance

Interactive factors

- Unfavorable initial impressions of therapy participants
- Problem disagreement
- Weak therapeutic alliance
- Perspective divergence

Group factors

- Highly critical interpersonal feedback
- Excessive stimulation
- Low group cohesion
- Scapegoating
- Lack of positive affective experience early in treatment
- Low therapist cohesion to patient
- Difficulty expressing oneself in group
- Lack of participation in group

groupings. These include demographic characteristics, patient expectancies, patient readiness for change (Prochaska, Norcross, & DiClemente, 1994), and dimensions of interpersonal functioning.

Demographic Characteristics

Patient demographic characteristics have been the variables most often investigated by researchers, undoubtedly because of the ease of securing demographic information. In a comprehensive meta-analysis of 125 studies, Wierzbicki and Pekarik (1993) found that three patient demographic characteristics were consistently associated with patient-initiated premature termination: racial status, education, and economic standing. Patients are more likely to terminate prematurely if they are non-Caucasian, poorly educated, and have a low income. The relationship between these variables and patient-initiated premature termination has typically been attributed to the educational disadvantages related to a low socioeconomic standing. These educational disadvantages have been assumed to result in reduced psychological mindedness and verbal skills as well as limited ability to engage in abstract thought and fantasize. Considering the roles of race, education, and economics with regard to patient-initiated premature termination, clinics should promote the hiring of culturally sensitive therapists and the implementation of training regimens to educate therapists about culturally specific issues, rather than avoid offering services to high-risk populations.

Other variables that have received consistent support in regard to their effect on patient-initiated premature termination include patient expectancy, readiness for change, and interpersonal functioning.

Expectancy

Patient expectancy refers to the understanding or belief by a patient that a specific event will occur in therapy. Patients may have various expectations about psychotherapy, and if these are incongruent with what actually occurs, then the patient could become dissatisfied and withdraw from therapy. Patients who terminate prematurely were more likely to report expectations that they would have a relatively passive role in their treatment and receive specific advice (Reis & Brown, 1999). Furthermore, these patients typically expect very brief treatments, anticipating sessions to be 30 minutes or less, improvement to be actualized by at least the fifth session, and treatment to be completed in 10 sessions or less (Garfield, 1994). Such expectations are inconsistent with the reality of most psychotherapies. Thus, it appears that patients are more likely to prematurely terminate from psychotherapy if they have expectations of a relatively brief, fast-acting treatment that they passively receive from a mental health treatment provider. Such expectations are more consistent with treatments for medical illnesses than psychotherapeutic treatments for mental health problems.

Support for the association between patient expectancy and patient-initiated premature termination also comes from studies that have found that patients with little or no prior experience with psychotherapy are more likely to terminate prematurely (MacNair & Corazzini, 1994). Previous experience in psychotherapy contributes to the development of more realistic expectations regarding duration of treatment, patient and therapist roles, and what can be achieved.

Readiness for Change

Readiness for change refers to the degree of a patient's willingness to address a personal problem in therapy. Prochaska et al.'s (1994) transtheoretical model of psychotherapy change has been used to define different levels of readiness. Their model asserts that individuals progress through various motivational stages in an attempt to change their behavior. The model describes five stages of change: precontemplation, contemplation, preparation, action, and maintenance. In precontemplation, the individual either is unaware of or has no desire to change. In contemplation, the individual is aware of a problem but has not made a formal decision to change. In preparation, the individual has decided to take action shortly with regard to the problem or has unsuccessfully acted on it in the recent past. In action, the individual has begun effectively to change behavior but has not changed to the desired level. The final stage, maintenance, is characterized by significant behavior change and attempts to prevent relapse or to consolidate previous changes. A patient who enters therapy in the preparation, action, or maintenance stage already recognizes the problem or behavior that needs to be changed and is ready to begin to change or has initiated change. A patient in the precontemplation stage, however, may be unaware of or unwilling to recognize the existence of a problem. A patient in the contemplation stage may be undecided as to whether to act on the problem. Prochaska et al. (1994) have argued that patients who enter therapy in the precontemplation or contemplation stage are less ready to initiate change and may be more likely to terminate therapy prematurely. Several different research groups have found support for these hypotheses (Brogan et al., 1999; Derisley & Reynolds, 2000; K. J. Smith, Subich, & Kalodner, 1995).

Interpersonal Functioning

Recently, researchers have begun examining how various aspects of a patient's interpersonal functioning may affect one's decision to terminate psychotherapy prematurely. Patients vary in their capacity to develop positive relationships with others, and this may be a deciding factor for how successful a patient is in engaging in a therapeutic relationship. It has been argued that the highly personal, intense nature of a therapeutic relationship may be overwhelming for some patients, thus leading to premature termination (Rosenthal, 1998). However, a trend that appears to be emerging from research in this area suggests that *better* interpersonal functioning is associated with an increased likelihood of prematurely terminating psychotherapy. Specifically, researchers have found that patients who have a tendency to establish more cooperative relationships, experience more positive affect in relationships, and have more positive expectations for interpersonal relationships are more likely to terminate psychotherapy prematurely (Ackerman, Hilsenroth, Clemence, Weatherill, & Fowler, 2000; Hilsenroth, Handler, Toman, & Padawer, 1995). It is interesting to note that these same patients were found to have a lower need or desire to invest emotionally in relationships (Ackerman et al., 2000; Hilsenroth et al., 1995). Thus, the picture that emerges of the person who prematurely terminates psychotherapy is someone who may have more productive relationships outside of the therapeutic setting and may have less need for close contact with a therapist.

One possible explanation for why patients with better interpersonal functioning may be more inclined to terminate psychotherapy prematurely concerns the *flight into health* phenomenon. The term *flight into health* is often used to describe patients who respond very quickly to therapy. The quick response is interpreted as an escape tactic. That is, the quick responses are attempts to avoid the pain and anxiety of further exploration and self-disclosure (Frick, 1999). Patients who are relatively well when they enter therapy, such as those with better interpersonal functioning, may more easily act out a flight into health. A higher dropout rate among such patients may be the result.

Ackerman et al. (2000) speculated that interpersonal functioning and patient expectancy may interact to affect patient-initiated premature terminations. They hypothesized that patients for whom expectations are not met are more likely to terminate prematurely if they have more positive interpersonal relationships outside of therapy. The reasoning is that these patients can more easily fall back on their relationships outside of the therapy setting to seek the help that they expect and, thus, are more willing to end their relationship with their therapist if their expectations are not met.

It is important to point out that the association between higher levels of interpersonal functioning and increased likelihood of premature termination has been found only in studies of individual psychotherapy. Studies of premature termination from group psychotherapy have found an opposite relationship; that is, poorer interpersonal functioning is associated with a greater probability of premature termination (MacNair & Corazzini, 1994; Roback & Smith, 1987). Patients with maladaptive interpersonal functioning may feel more vulnerable in a group setting, being fearful of disclosure or attack, and, thus, may be more likely to flee (i.e., prematurely terminate) the group. It is also possible that the maladaptive behaviors of a patient with poor interpersonal functioning (which are more likely to be apparent in a group setting) elicit negative reactions from the other group members who respond by confronting the individual, ostracizing the patient from group activities, or scapegoating. This interaction may precipitate premature termination. As noted by Dies and Teleska (1985) in their discussion of negative outcomes in group psychotherapy, "maladaptive interpersonal styles which have led [a patient] to seek therapy in the first place, may unfortunately prove to be self-defeating in that context as well" (p. 123).

Therapist Factors

Research exploring therapist factors that may be associated with patient-initiated premature termination has focused primarily on demographic characteristics (primarily gender) and level of experience. Findings of this research have been inconsistent. For example, results variously indicate that patient-initiated premature termination is higher among male therapists (Betz

& Shullman, 1979), female therapists (Epperson, 1981), or does not differ between male and female therapists (Jenkins, Fuqua, & Blum, 1986). Similarly, although some studies indicate that patient-initiated premature termination is less prevalent among highly experienced therapists (Scogin, Belon, & Malone, 1986), others indicate no relationship between premature termination and experience (Jenkins et al., 1986).

Unfortunately, there has been little research conducted to explore other therapist variables as potential predictors of premature termination. Some authors have speculated that therapists' inability to understand the nature of the patient's problem and lack of technical skill may contribute to premature termination (Magnavita, 1994). Studies have not addressed these ideas directly. However, our research group has found indirect evidence to support the role that lack of technical skill may play in premature termination. We found that high use of transference interpretations may lead to a weak alliance and poor outcome for certain types of patients (Ogrodniczuk et al., 1999; Piper, Azim, Joyce, & McCallum, 1991; Piper et al., 1999). Our findings suggest that therapist difficulty with flexibly using the manualized treatment approach (reflecting low technical skill) may precipitate a patient's decision to terminate prematurely. Butler and Strupp (1993) have also found that manualized training of experienced therapists can result in sessions characterized by both rigid technical adherence and undesirable therapist interventions and behaviors. Intuitively, it would seem that a therapist might also contribute to patient-initiated premature termination by being insufficiently aware of factors that are associated with this event.

Administrative Factors

Administrative factors refers to variables that characterize the treatment or the clinic in which treatment is provided. It also refers to the processes of the clinic, for example, intake procedures. Administrative factors have been the least explored variables with regard to prediction of patient-initiated premature termination. Although significant effects for various administrative factors have been found in different studies, replication attempts either have not been performed or have failed. Thus, the literature is replete with inconsistent findings that prohibit making any firm conclusions about the association between administrative factors and patient-initiated premature termination.

Variables that appear to deserve further attention are wait-list length, patient preparation, time-limited treatment structure, and early signs of patient noncompliance.

Wait-List Length

Studies have found that the longer patients remain on a wait list, the more likely they will prematurely terminate once treatment begins (Baekeland

& Lundwall, 1975). This may reflect patients' decreased need for treatment with increased passage of time. It may also represent a retaliatory reaction. That is, patients may "fire" the therapist or the clinic in retribution for keeping them waiting so long.

Patient Preparation

Bernard and Drob (1989) found that inadequate patient preparation was one of the most consistently reported reasons provided by patients who terminated group psychotherapy prematurely. Patients who are inadequately prepared likely have expectations that are incongruent with the realities of psychotherapy. Confronted with a situation that contradicts one's expectations, patients may become dissatisfied or angry, choosing to prematurely terminate therapy as a way to act out their displeasure. In addition, psychotherapy presents many challenges to the patient who, if ill-prepared, may leave therapy to escape what they may perceive as too frightening or difficult.

Time-Limited Treatment Contracts

As previously mentioned in this chapter, short-term psychotherapy that has a definite time limit has been found to have approximately one half the rate of patient-initiated premature termination than short-term psychotherapy without a definite time limit and long-term psychotherapy (Sledge et al., 1990). Making the ending explicit and definite may help reduce patient tendencies to enact conflicts or fears about termination or the treatment by leaving therapy early.

Noncompliance

Finally, there have been serendipitous findings that patients who fail to comply with requests to complete questionnaires prior to therapy are more likely to prematurely terminate (Garfield, 1994). This may reflect an early warning sign of a general pattern of noncompliance or lack of motivation to cooperate in therapy. Similarly, Beckham (1992) has found that early missed therapy sessions are a strong predictor of patient-initiated premature termination. Missed sessions may be another indicator of noncompliance.

Interactive Factors

Thus far, we have considered various factors associated with the patient, therapist, or treatment setting that in some way create susceptibility to premature termination. In general, research on these isolated factors has produced few strong findings that can help clinicians reduce the incidence of patient-initiated premature termination in their practice. This state of affairs has led to the suggestion that it is time to turn our attention to more complex variables in the pursuit of identifying factors that are relevant to premature termination. It has been argued that the decisive component of patients' decisions in regard to premature termination is the quality of the human interaction in the therapeutic setting (Rainer & Campbell, 2001). This follows Luborsky et al.'s (1980) point that "the crucial predictive factors [for premature termination] may not be sufficiently apparent until the patient and the therapist have had a chance to interact" (p. 480). In this section of the chapter, we consider factors that reflect different aspects of the interaction between patient and therapist. Particularly relevant are findings from investigations of initial impressions of therapy participants, problem agreement, and the therapeutic alliance.

Initial Impressions

Initial perceptions and feelings about the other persons in the therapeutic setting may have considerable influence on patient-initiated premature termination. As in any social encounter, first impressions inform decision making in regard to likeability and trustworthiness of the other person and expected satisfaction of a relationship with that person. Ultimately, they form the basis for making the decision about whether to invest time and energy into developing a relationship with the other person. Studies have found that patients' initial impressions of the therapist have a significant effect on the likelihood of premature termination (Beckham, 1992; Hynan, 1990). Patients who terminate prematurely reported that they perceived the therapist as respecting them less, as less warm and empathic, and as less competent. It seems obvious that patients will be less willing to persevere in therapy if they perceive their therapists in such regard. Although less research has examined therapists' impressions of patients, findings of these studies are consistent with those studying patients' impressions of therapists. That is, therapists' negative impressions of their patients are associated with a greater probability of patient-initiated premature termination (Frayn, 1992; Lothstein, 1978; Ogrodniczuk, Piper, & Joyce, 2005). If the therapist regards the patient as unmotivated, overly defensive, hostile, or difficult in some other way, then it is conceivable that his or her attitudes may be communicated to the patient and influence the patient's participation and continuation in therapy.

Problem Agreement

Another promising area of research concerns problem agreement. Problem agreement, sometimes referred to as topic determination, is characterized as reaching agreement early in therapy in regard to the patient's presenting problem, as well as the goals and tasks of therapy. Investigators have found that patient-initiated premature termination is more likely to occur if the patient and therapist are unable to agree on what the patient's primary problem is or the cause of the problem (Epperson, Bushway, & Warman, 1983; Tracey, 1988). It is clear that such disagreement has the potential to create significant difficulties in the course of treatment and the therapeutic relationship, possibly leading to premature termination.

Some authors have also examined the degree to which patient and therapist contributions followed each other harmoniously throughout therapy and the perceived relevance of their communications. Tracey (1986) reported that among dyads in which the patient terminated prematurely, patients and therapists were less congruent in topic discussion (topics initiated by one participant were not followed by the other). As well, therapists' interventions were perceived as more irrelevant by patients who terminated prematurely compared with patients who completed therapy (Duehn & Proctor, 1977). Collectively, the findings concerning problem agreement suggest that patient-initiated premature termination is much more likely to occur when the therapeutic relationship is fraught with disagreement in regard to the nature of the problem to be worked on and in which manner.

Therapeutic Alliance

The factor that addresses the quality of the relationship between patient and therapist most directly is the therapeutic alliance. Although there are variations in definitions of the therapeutic alliance, there is general agreement that it reflects the collaborative, working relationship between the patient and therapist. The therapeutic alliance is recognized as one of the most crucial ingredients for successful treatment. A weak alliance (particularly early in therapy) reflects a poor affective bond between patient and therapist, a lack of collaboration and mutual involvement in therapy, and disagreement on the tasks and goals of therapy. An increasing number of studies have found that patients who terminate prematurely report a weaker alliance with their therapist compared with patients who continue in therapy (Mohl, Martinez, Ticknor, Huang, & Cordell, 1991; Piper et al., 1999; Tryon & Kane, 1990).

An evaluation of the alliance as early as the first session can be a good predictor of patient-initiated premature termination (Kokotovic & Tracey, 1990). Although it is usually the patients' perceptions of the alliance that differentiate premature terminators from continuers, some studies have found that therapists' perceptions of the alliance also differentiate these groups (Piper et al., 1999). Thus, it appears that a patient's decision to end therapy prematurely is influenced, to some extent, by how well he or she is able to establish and maintain a collaborative working relationship with the therapist.

Other Interactive Factors

In an attempt to achieve a better clinical understanding of the patient–therapist interactions of therapeutic dyads in which the patient terminated prematurely, our research group (Piper et al., 1999) conducted a comprehensive qualitative analysis of the last therapy sessions of 22 patients who terminated prematurely from short-term, individual, interpretive therapy. We believed that the last session might be particularly charged and important to examine given that the patient never returned. A clear pattern, represented by a sequence of nine features, emerged from our analysis. This pattern was particularly consistent and striking for dyads that engaged in a high amount of work with the transference. The nine features are as follows:

1. The patient made his or her thoughts about dropping out clear, usually early in the session.
2. The patient expressed frustration about the therapy sessions. This often involved expectations that were not met and the therapist's repeated focus on painful feelings.
3. The therapist quickly addressed the difficulty by focusing on the patient–therapist relationship and the transference. Links were made to other relationships.
4. The patient resisted the focus on transference and engaged in little dynamic exploration (work). Resistance was often active, for example, verbal disagreement, and sometimes passive (i.e., silence).
5. The therapist persisted with transference interpretations.
6. The patient and therapist argued with each other. They seemed to be engaged in a power struggle. At times the therapist was drawn into being sharp, blunt, sarcastic, insistent, impatient, or condescending.
7. Although most of the interpretations were plausible, the patient responded to the interpretive persistence of the therapist with continued resistance.
8. The session ended with encouragement by the therapist to continue with therapy and a seemingly forced agreement by the patient to do so.
9. The patient never returned.

The patient and therapist appeared to be caught up in an unproductive power struggle that increased the frustration of both. Persistent use of transference interpretations on the therapist's part was not successful in resolving the impasse. At the same time, this strategy was adherent to the guidelines in the therapy manual. Despite considerable clinical experience and success in treating many other patients in interpretive therapy, the therapist was often unable to avoid countertransferential reactions. After the difficult session, the patient never returned.

In the group situation, consideration has to be given to the composition issue. To bring in a patient who is some way "deviant" risks a premature termination. Precisely what constitutes a group patient as deviant is difficult to define. It may be a patient who deviates from the agreed-on work task of the group for any number of reasons; perhaps, for example, he or she cannot tolerate the anxiety, lacks the skills required for the group's work task, or is consumed by personal concerns that are too pressing or too different from those addressed in the group. Such a new member is, of course, in danger of becoming a group scapegoat. Other deviant group patients may enact behavior in the form of destructive interpersonal patterns that replicate in the group those difficulties they have been encountering outside of the group. This replication may lead to a similar outcome in the group—the patient antagonizes others; withdraws following a hostile response from the other members; or experiences feelings of being ignored, ostracized, or overlooked. Group therapists must not only effectively prepare a patient about to enter group, but they must also prepare the group for the patient's arrival. Consideration should also be given to the new patient's fit with the existing group members.

Perspective Divergence

Reis and Brown (1999) suggested that a recurrent theme arising from many of the studies of patient-initiated premature termination is that when perspective divergence occurs in therapy, premature termination becomes more likely. *Perspective divergence* may be defined as a situation in which the patient and the therapist hold differing, incompatible views concerning one or more aspects of treatment, for example, the nature of the patient's difficulty, expected roles of the patient and therapist, or criteria for success. Patients and therapists both approach the therapeutic enterprise with a whole host of expectations, which, if not consistent with each other, are likely to result in a less than optimal experience in therapy and increased risk for premature termination. Reis and Brown claimed that the unfavorable effects of perspective divergence are manifested in negative impressions of the other therapy participants, disagreements, and weak alliances. Each of these can directly influence a patient's willingness to stay in therapy.

Garfield (1994) and Reis and Brown (1999) suggested that perspective divergence also accounts for the association between low socioeconomic status and premature termination. They argued that there are no inherent deficits associated with low socioeconomic status that lead to patient-initiated premature termination. Rather, patients from lower social and economic levels often have different value systems and expectations of treatment compared with middle class therapists. These differences result in perspective divergence. To support their claim, Reis and Brown reported that matching patients and therapists on gender and ethnicity (which presumably reduces perspective divergence) resulted in lower rates of patient-initiated premature termination. Because psychotherapy is a collaborative endeavor, an inability or failure to recognize and acknowledge the perspective of the other persons in the therapeutic situation can lead to a cascade of negative events (e.g., problem disagreement), which may precipitate premature termination.

Group Factors

Certain characteristics of group psychotherapy may also contribute to patient-initiated premature termination. The demands intrinsic to the group setting are many: having to share time and attention with several strangers; being subject to their scrutiny; being invited to disclose highly personal information in a public forum; being exposed to the unsettling feelings and problems of others; and having to negotiate issues of confidentiality, privacy, trust, and boundaries. Several dynamic properties of therapy groups, such as cohesion, group norms and roles, communication structure, social comparison, and developmental stage, may also affect patients' decisions about whether to stay or leave.

Despite a large body of clinical literature on the topic of patient-initiated premature termination from group psychotherapy, there has been a minimal amount of research conducted. Nevertheless, consistencies in the clinical literature suggest that certain group phenomena may be associated with premature termination and deserve further attention.

Interpersonal Feedback

Clinicians frequently remark that highly critical interpersonal feedback from group members about one's personal shortcomings is a potent motivating factor behind the decision to terminate prematurely, particularly in the absence of a cohesive group climate (Roback, 2000). Although it is helpful for a person to learn about the inappropriateness of his or her interpersonal behavior in the context of a safe and supportive group, such feedback can be quite damaging if it is provided in an aggressive manner. This is particularly the case in a group in which there is little solidarity.

Overstimulation

The group experience also submits individuals to a highly charged stimulus situation, which may activate destructive forms of resistance such as premature termination (Rosenthal, 1998). Intense interpersonal feedback, irrational perceptions, misunderstandings, and unabated emotional outbursts may all contribute to overstimulation. Excessive stimulation may undermine ego controls and leave patients with no other choice but to remove themselves from the setting (i.e., terminate prematurely).

Low Cohesion

A low degree of cohesion among group members has also been cited as a major contributing factor to patient-initiated premature termination (Roback & Smith, 1987). Patients in groups that are characterized by low cohesion often feel a lack of support, belonging, and mutual understanding. These factors heighten distress and lessen patients' perceptions of the group as potentially helpful, thus, paving the way to an early exit.

Scapegoating

Scapegoating is another group dynamic that often results in premature termination (Dies & Teleska, 1985). In this case, the group identifies a deviant member and, possibly in an attempt to create unity, pressures that person to conform to group norms or withdraw from the group. This may be consistent with Lothstein's (1978) intriguing, if somewhat cynical, interpretation of patient-initiated premature termination. That is, he contended that the group's early expulsion of certain members may be a necessary group function in its establishment of group boundaries, a sense of togetherness, camaraderie, and cohesion. In this conceptualization of the premature termination phenomenon, the group ritualistically sacrifices its deviants to achieve stability.

Other Group Factors

Studies that have investigated other factors that contribute to premature termination in group psychotherapy have revealed interesting findings that are worthy of consideration. For example, a study conducted by our clinical research group (McCallum, Piper, Ogrodniczuk, & Joyce, 2002) found that patients who terminated prematurely from short-term group psychotherapy for complicated grief could be distinguished from completers on the basis of their level of positive affect experienced during the first session, and by the therapists' ratings of their cohesion to other group members. Specifically, we found that in the very first session, premature terminators reported experiencing significantly less positive affect (pleasure, warmth, acceptance, or optimism) than remainers. The two patient groups did not differ on their level of experienced negative affect. In addition, we found that after the first third of therapy (i.e., after the fourth session), therapists' ratings of patients' positive qualities, personal compatibility, and significance to the group were considerably lower for premature terminators compared with remainers.

The finding concerning positive affect may confirm the obvious—patients who did not feel positive about their experience did not stay. The therapist's cohesion ratings may reflect his or her early realisation that the premature terminators were subdued and detached from the rest of the group. Alternatively, perhaps the therapist (consciously or unconsciously) contributed to the departure of these "unlikeable" patients from the group. This suggests the potency of the therapist's countertransferential feelings in patients' decisions to terminate prematurely. It is possible that the therapist was less likely to engage these patients in the therapeutic process, preferring to let them fade into the background and ultimately drift out of the group.

In a study of short-term group therapy for mood disorders, Oei and Kazmierczak (1997) found that patients who terminated prematurely reported significantly greater difficulty in being able to express themselves in the group compared with remainers. In addition, it was found that premature terminators received significantly lower ratings (by the therapist) for participation in the group after the 1st week compared with remainers. These findings suggest that patients who terminate prematurely feel less able to engage in group activities and that their passivity is recognized early by the therapist. Again, it is possible that the therapist exerted less effort to engage these patients, thus contributing to their early exit from the group.

STRATEGIES FOR PREVENTING PATIENT-INITIATED PREMATURE TERMINATION

Considering the enormity of the literature on the topic and the variety of factors involved in a patient's decision to end therapy prematurely, clinicians find themselves in a difficult situation when trying to determine the best strategy for preventing or minimizing patient-initiated premature terminations. Clearly, because of the multiple factors involved, there is no one strategy that will be equally effective across all types of patients or treatment settings. Rather, multiple strategies may be required to address the many elements involved. In the following sections, we describe several strategies for consideration. These are also listed in Exhibit 7.2. Although these strategies are frequently endorsed in the clinical literature, research that may provide empirical support for their effectiveness has been sorely lacking.

Patient Selection

Patient selection refers to the process of carefully screening and choosing the most appropriate candidates for a particular form of therapy. The argument for this strategy is that with accurate classification and appropriate placements, the number of premature terminations will be reduced. This is a common practice among clinicians and parallels discussion in the literature in regard to the need for suitable patient–treatment matches. It should be noted that although selection may help reduce premature terminations, it also may deprive more difficult patients of a potentially useful treatment. This creates an important ethical dilemma for clinicians.

Clinicians and researchers have identified several characteristics that make patients most suitable for certain forms of psychotherapy. However, suitability is typically considered in reference to optimal outcomes. Rarely has attention been directed at patient–treatment matching for the purpose of minimizing premature termination. Nevertheless, information about what makes a patient successful in a particular form of therapy may be useful for also preventing premature termination. Efforts can be made to facilitate the skills or aptitudes that are associated with success in a certain therapy, which may increase the probability that the patient will remain engaged in treatment. For example, patients with considerable interpersonal difficulties may

EXHIBIT 7.2
Strategies for Preventing or Reducing Patient-Initiated Premature Termination

Patient selection

- Screen and choose the most appropriate candidates for particular forms of therapy.

Treatment negotiation

- Negotiate an agreement on the nature of the patient's problem and the manner in which it should be addressed in therapy.

Time-limited treatment contract

- Implement a time limit on the duration of therapy.

Pretherapy preparation

- Implement procedures prior to the commencement of therapy that ready the patient for working in treatment.

Appointment reminders

- Provide brief reminders of upcoming, scheduled appointments.

Facilitating a therapeutic alliance

- Foster a strong working relationship early in treatment and maintain awareness of the quality of this relationship throughout therapy.

Encouraging affect expression

- Provide a safe environment in which patients can explore both negative and positive feelings.

---

have such maladaptive behaviors that they are unable to remain in or benefit from group psychotherapy. Social skills training may be required for such patients prior to admission to a therapy group. Learning adaptive social skills such as being able to listen, give and receive constructive feedback, and reduce impulsiveness may enable these patients to tolerate the interpersonal demands of group therapy.

Treatment Negotiation

Studies have found that problem disagreements lead to unsuccessful psychotherapy. That is, disagreements in regard to the nature of the patient's problem and the manner in which it should be addressed in therapy often compel patients to make an early exit from treatment. This suggests that treatment planning should be carefully negotiated in the first couple of meetings with patients before formal therapy actually begins. Therapists should be mindful of the patient's perspective regarding the nature of the problem and expectations for how it should be worked on. This will help them develop and agree on a treatment plan that is compatible with both the therapist's and patient's perceptions of illness etiology and strategies for cure, expectations, and personal capacities. Keeping in mind that therapy is a collaborative endeavor, therapists should be open to modifying their perspectives, as they expect patients to modify theirs (Reis & Brown, 1999).

Successful treatment negotiation also involves discussing the motivation for the referral to a particular form of therapy. This is perhaps most important for referral to group therapy. Patients often experience narcissistic injury upon placement in a therapy group. It is important to provide the patient with a clear and acceptable rationale for the referral.

Finally, an integral part of treatment negotiation involves addressing the issue of a patient's involvement in multiple treatments. This typically involves situations where a patient is involved in both an individual and group treatment. When a patient is being treated by another therapist, it is desirable to secure the patient's permission to make contact with the other therapist to share impressions of the patient and to make certain that treatment goals are compatible and mutually reinforcing (Bernard, 1989). Such contact also gives the therapist an opportunity to reassure the other treatment provider that he or she is respectful of what the other is doing. This communication can prevent the development of a competitive relationship between the therapists (sometimes fueled by the patient), which can ultimately undermine both treatments.

Time-Limited Treatment Contracts

The rate of patient-initiated premature termination may be reduced by up to half if a time-limited treatment contract is implemented. Such contracts are typically associated with brief therapies. Some patients simply may be more willing to persist with treatment when they know it will end soon. Other aspects of time-limited psychotherapy, such as setting a focus, the rapid establishment of a collaborative working relationship, and greater therapist activity, could also contribute to a patient's decision to continue in therapy rather than terminate early. Time-limited contracts could also enable the therapist to determine motivation for longer term treatment. In some cases, this may involve multiple negotiations of shorter term contracts on a continuous or intermittent basis, or the agreement to meet specified objectives for a time-limited period (Sledge et al., 1990).

Pretherapy Preparation

Pretherapy preparation is the most frequently discussed strategy for preventing patient-initiated premature termination. *Pretherapy preparation* refers to any procedure that attempts to ready the patient for treatment. Beginning psychotherapy is a challenging task for almost all patients, even those who have had previous experience. Anxiety, uncertainty, and misconceptions are commonplace. Group therapy, compared with the individual therapy situation, is typically associated with greater threats to the patient's sense of control, individuality, understanding, privacy, and safety. For many patients, trusting and relating to others on a personal level represent both presenting problems and required processes in therapy. Because of the challenging tasks of beginning psychotherapy and getting off to a good start, as well as the association between inadequate preparation and premature termination, effective and efficient preparation procedures are strongly recommended.

Many procedures for pretherapy preparation have been described. They involve different activities and stimuli. Some are provided to individual patients and some to groups of patients. Most procedures are relatively brief (an hour or less) and are integrated with routine clinical tasks such as conducting initial assessments and discussing treatment alternatives. Providing information and discussing issues in interviews are often supplemented with written material that the patient can take home. Sometimes audiovisual material is used to convey information and model (demonstrate) typical therapy processes. More elaborate procedures involve the patient participating in experiential tasks that simulate therapy-like experiences. It has become common to use multiple activities and stimuli, which increases the possibility of achieving multiple objectives.

The objectives of pretherapy preparation include providing information about the nature and process of psychotherapy, the roles and obligations of therapist and patient, and difficulties that can arise in the process of treatment. Such information is intended to clarify patients' misconceptions about therapy, reduce incongruence between patients' and therapists' expectations of therapy, and enhance patients' motivation for treatment. Rainer and Campbell (2001) argued that a benefit of the preparation process is the enhanced psychological mindedness of the patient. They indicated that prepared patients also display increased hopefulness and reported a better understanding of the therapy process and their role in it. Furthermore, Rainer and Campbell suggested that prepared patients develop attitudes conducive to involvement in therapy, including comfort with self-disclosure, willingness to discuss problems, and directness with the therapist. Another benefit of the preparation process is the development of a therapeutic alliance with the patient. This is perhaps one of the most important benefits of preparation because it is often the alliance with the therapist that sustains a patient through the difficult period of beginning treatment.

Bernard and Drob (1989), in their discussion of pretherapy preparation for group therapy, pointed out that some therapists believe that explicit preparation should be kept to a minimum so as to encourage the exploration of patients' projections in therapy. Bernard and Drob argued that this position has merit only with those patients who can tolerate and work effectively with this ambiguity. When therapists are working with high-functioning patients interested in examining their experiences in an unstructured and spontaneous fashion, preparation may be limited to an explication of the basic logistics of the treatment.

Appointment Reminders

Most health care providers (e.g., dentists, optometrists, family doctors) use appointment reminders as a low-cost means to ensure that scheduled appointments are attended. Many psychotherapists (typically those working from a psychodynamic perspective), however, have resisted appointment reminders because they wish to emphasize patient responsibility for attendance and because no-shows and cancelations serve as valuable material for interpretation in therapy (Reis & Brown, 1999). It could be argued that it is more important to ensure attendance at sessions than it is to risk premature termination for the sake of interpreting resistant behaviors. For those therapists whose orientation does not preclude appointment reminders, this seems to be an efficient method to reduce patient-initiated premature termination. It will be important for researchers to help determine the effectiveness of this strategy.

Facilitating a Therapeutic Alliance

It is becoming clearer that a strong therapeutic alliance with the patient is critical not only for facilitating a positive outcome but also for keeping the patient engaged in treatment. The alliance is viewed as an essential ingredient of therapy that fosters the patient's trust in the therapist's perspective and acceptance of the treatment goals. Some authors argued that the establishment of a positive alliance must be accomplished within the first three sessions in order for it to have a significant impact on premature termination (Rainer & Campbell, 2001).

There are varied recommendations for how to foster a strong working relationship with the patient. In addition to reaffirming the core conditions of warmth, regard, empathy, and genuineness, most authors recommend that the interpersonal dynamics of the real relationship between patient and therapist be attended to throughout therapy. Prior to or early in treatment, the therapist should focus on establishing agreement on what needs to be accomplished and the procedures that provide the working plan for therapy. Communicating respect for patients' perspectives and interest in working with them will help develop satisfactory levels of collaboration and trust. Later in treatment, the focus will be on dealing with ruptures in the alliance. The therapist should recognize and address here-and-now relationship problems as they occur in therapy. Willingness to work with negative processes should help enhance the alliance. The therapist's willingness to own some responsibility for struggles in the therapeutic relationship validates the patient's experiences and contributes to the perception of therapy as a collaborative endeavor.

Encouraging Affect Expression

Providing a safe atmosphere in which patients can explore, ventilate, and work through negative feelings can help diminish patient-initiated premature termination (Bernard & Drob, 1989). When patients fail to express negative feelings about their experience of being in therapy, the therapist, or the group in the case of group treatment, they often resort to acting them out by leaving therapy.

In group treatments, failure to express negative feelings is often attributable to group norms that preclude such expression. For example, in one of the short-term, dynamically oriented therapy groups for complicated grief that we conducted in our clinic, a patient, Anita, was struggling with the loss of her mother. She had had a poor relationship with her mother for most of her life. Only recently had they begun to reconcile. However, this process was cut short by her mother's death. Anita was consumed by conflicted feelings toward her mother—love, hate, relief, sadness, guilt, and anger. The negative feelings were particularly powerful for Anita, and she often brought them up in group. However, after each time that Anita discussed these feelings, the group would fall into a long, uncomfortable silence. The members would watch Anita struggle alone with her feelings, offering no solace to her. Another female patient, Jill, usually broke the silence. Jill would recollect advice given to her by a favorite aunt, that one should not dwell on painful feelings, but rather find the humor in the situation that led to the hurt. Jill's statements were never directed specifically at Anita but instead were offered to the whole group. It is not surprising that such advice did not resonate with Anita, and it came to be that she seemed more reluctant to feel and discuss painful emotions in the group. When she did, she would apologize to the group.

Sometimes, therapists contribute to such norms by shifting focus away from patients whom they perceive as negative. For example, in another of our complicated grief therapy groups, a male patient, George, struggled to have his feelings recognized by his therapist, and the group. George was a particularly angry person. His difficulties started in the first session when he arrived late, claiming that the therapist failed to retrieve him from the waiting room, where he had been for 30 minutes prior to the beginning of the session. The therapist did not acknowledge George's anger. She merely asked him to have a seat, noting the group had already started. No other member of the group spoke to George until 5 minutes were left in the session. In the next few sessions, George would often voice his displeasure about the therapist's style, which was consistent with the psychodynamic model, that is, passive–receptive and interpretive. George preferred that the therapist offer direct advice and guidance. The therapist would not address George's negative feelings toward her directly, electing instead to return to whatever topic preceded George's interjection. Although it seemed that some of the other group members supported George's appeal for more direction from the therapist, none would verbally acknowledge this. In the fifth session (of the 12-week treatment), George vented furiously toward the therapist about her passivity and her unwillingness to explain why she continued to leave empty chairs in the group when it was clear that the members who once occupied them were not coming back to the group. He got up from his seat, stacked the empty chairs beside the therapist, returned to his seat, and fell silent. Although the therapist did begin to work with George's anger then, it was too late. The session ended shortly after this incident, and George never returned.

Therapists should actively encourage patients to express their doubts and questions about them or the therapy. Understandably, therapists may be reluctant to have negative feelings predominate the early stages of treatment. However, the exploration of such feelings can often dissipate them and contribute to the patient's understanding that all feelings and experiences can be expressed and examined in therapy.

Most authors appear to emphasize the expression of negative affect in therapy. However, a unilateral focus on negative feelings may actually be destructive, particularly in group therapy. Bonanno and Kaltman (1999) have argued that continuous expression of negative affect tends to irritate, frustrate, and alienate others, whereas the expression of positive affect tends to increase contact and support from others. Thus, it may be more prudent to facilitate the expression of both negative and positive affect in psychotherapy in an effort to keep patients engaged in treatment.

CONCLUSION

Many authors consider a carefully negotiated termination to be central to realizing the full benefit of psychotherapy and to maintaining treatment gains. Patient-initiated premature termination is recognized as a significant obstacle to effective treatment. It is usually considered to be a negative event that occurs unnecessarily and is usually avoidable. We have reviewed a considerable number of factors that research or clinical experience has suggested may be related to a patient's decision to terminate therapy prematurely. Although the isolation of individual factors associated with patient-initiated premature termination may be useful in the initial stages of inquiry, it is believed that a more rich understanding will come from the simultaneous consideration of multiple factors. As Koran and Costell (1973) argued,

> the decision to terminate therapy, like the decision to begin it, depends on multiple influences. . . . The more of these factors one can take into

account, presumably the better one should be able to identify patients highly likely to terminate early. (p. 348)

In addition to identifying stronger associations, investigating multiple factors may provide a better understanding of the mechanisms that underlie the phenomenon of patient-initiated premature termination. Understanding these mechanisms and processes will enable clinicians to develop more efficient and effective strategies for keeping patients engaged in treatment and, thus, minimizing patient-initiated premature terminations. We have highlighted several strategies for consideration that may contribute to reducing premature terminations. In chapter 8, we consider terminations of a different sort—those initiated by the therapist.

8

THERAPIST-INITIATED TERMINATION

Therapist-initiated termination of psychotherapy is sometimes referred to as forced termination. Here, the therapist unilaterally makes the decision to end therapy. Similar to patient-initiated termination, there are many reasons for therapist-initiated termination. Perhaps the most common reason is that the therapist's training or clinical rotation has ended, and he or she must leave the institution or the area. This routinely happens to many therapists in training and their patients. Somewhat similar, although much less frequent, is the situation in which a clinic's health care policy forces the cancelation of treatments or entire services. Also quite common in our contemporary mobile society is termination because of a geographical move on the therapist's part or a work or career change. The therapist may need to terminate therapy because of family or other life circumstances such as pregnancy, retirement, or a simple desire to spend more time with his or her children.

Therapists also terminate treatment because of their satisfaction or dissatisfaction with its progress. In the former case, the therapist believes that the objectives of therapy have been achieved and that continuation runs the risk of negative consequences, such as unnecessary dependency on the therapist or treatment. In the latter case, the therapist is dissatisfied with the behavior of the patient, the process of therapy, or the extent of progress in regard to outcome. These impressions may be based on the therapist's realistic assessment of and/or the therapist's countertransference reaction to the treatment situation. *Countertransference* refers to the therapist's subjective displacement of feelings and attitudes toward past persons to the patient.

For example, the therapist reacts with anxiety or anger to the patient's accurate assessment that he or she has accomplished what he or she intended and would like to terminate therapy. The therapist has enjoyed working with the patient and will miss interacting with the patient. He suddenly feels deserted and responds in kind by abruptly ending therapy. Another example is when the therapist finds the patient to be unlikable or difficult. With a reasonable but invalid rationale, the therapist communicates to the patient why therapy should soon end. Rather than seek consultation from a colleague or supervisor in an effort to understand and resolve the countertransference, the therapist unfortunately acts on his or her impulses in these examples. The therapist's reactions are usually a combination of realistic appraisal and countertransference. Consultation can help sort these out.

Despite the large number of reasons for therapist-initiated termination and their varied nature, therapist-initiated termination appears to have a singular meaning for patients: The therapist has put his or her needs ahead of the patient. This fact runs contrary to the initial expectations (agreement, contract) and intentions of both patient and therapist. Although this circumstance may be easier to accept when the therapist has been forced to terminate treatment because of life circumstances that are out of the therapist's control (e.g., serious illness), the impact of the realization that the therapist's needs have come first, nevertheless, remains intense and represents a large impediment to achieving a smooth and satisfactory termination. For this reason, most of the literature suggests that whenever possible, therapist-initiated termination should be avoided.

Compared with the topic of patient-initiated termination, the literature on therapist-initiated termination is sparse. In addition, almost all of the literature concerns individual therapy rather than group therapy or other multiperson therapies such as couple or family.

The remainder of this chapter focuses on four topics: theoretical conceptualizations of therapist-initiated termination; the patient's reactions and therapist's reactions to therapist-initiated termination; and guidelines for managing therapist-initiated termination. Finally, some concluding comments are provided.

THEORETICAL CONCEPTUALIZATIONS

Compared with material regarding consideration of the patient's and therapist's reactions to therapist-initiated termination and practical guidelines for dealing with it, material regarding theoretical conceptualizations of the events in the literature is rather brief. Most authors have a psychodynamic orientation. As suggested previously, almost invariably the announcement to the patient about the termination of treatment is viewed as a highly stressful event (Bostic, Shadid, & Blotcky, 1996) or trauma (Pistole, 1991) that signifies a real loss. The need to mourn the loss is often emphasized in the literature. In Beatrice's (1982–1983) terms, following Langs's (1976), there is a permanent break in the therapeutic framework. The patient is no longer able to use the therapist as a safe container to store pathological contents. The process following the announcement, for those patients who choose to continue until the therapist departs, is frequently compared to the anticipation of the death of an important person in the patient's life or to the anticipation of the patient's own death because of a terminal illness (Parsons, 1982). Some authors (Bostic et al., 1996; Parsons, 1982) have indicated that the patient experiences something similar to the anticipatory stages to death as described by Kübler-Ross (1970), that is, denial, anger, bargaining, depression, and acceptance.

Other authors use concepts from attachment theory and object relations theory to understand the events. Elkind (1996) wrote about the patient's loss of a significant attachment bond. According to Elkind, who cited the work of Bowlby, when attachment bonds are in jeopardy, the patient experiences panic and anxiety. When attachment bonds are severed, the patient is left to mourn the loss. She claims that many therapists underestimate the severity of the patient's reactions and how long it takes the patient to recover. This is because the therapist is also facing a severed attachment. For example, the therapist often does not understand why the patient is unable to make plans to engage in a new therapeutic relationship right away. Elkind argued strongly for the use of a consultant who can help both the patient and the therapist accept and deal with the inevitable severed attachment bonds.

Following Winnicott (1969) and other analytic developmental theorists, Coker (1996) suggested that the therapist serves as a transitional object between the announcement of termination, the departure, and the introduction to the new therapist. If successfully managed, this represents a considerable achievement for the patient. Martinez (1989) described the patient as struggling to hold on to a useful internal image (representation) of the therapist during therapist-initiated termination. She claimed that her own experiences with forced terminations have revealed that nontransference interventions facilitate analytic work and the formation of a usable object by the patient.

Finally, Zahourek and Crawford (1978) used an ego development perspective to portray the patient as experiencing perceptions of being out of control that are similar to those experienced during the separation–individuation phase of early development. If the patient had considerable difficulties passing through this phase during development, he or she would be likely to have considerable difficulties with forced termination of therapy. Developing a constant mental image or memory of the therapist can be very difficult. Ideally, more adaptive defense mechanisms and more effective coping mechanisms can be valuable consequences of successfully working through a forced termination. Again, despite the presence of a number of such conceptualizations, what stands out is their brevity and lack of complexity or elaboration. It is almost as if the various authors required a convenient bridge to take them from the announcement of the termination to a consideration of reactions and guidelines. We consider these topics next.

PATIENT REACTIONS

In regard to patient reactions, authors such as S. Smith (1982–1983) reported a plethora of negative affective states in response to what is consensually viewed as a very stressful event. These negative affective states include abandonment, anger, anxiety, confusion, dejection, despair, detachment, fear, helplessness, loneliness, loss of control, rage, regression, rejection, and sadness. A variety of defensive and essentially regressive behaviors can accompany these affective states. Long, Pendleton, and Winter (1988) and Garcia-Lawson and Lane (1997) pointed out that some patients terminate abruptly in response to the therapist's announcement. Others miss sessions, complain about the treatment conditions and returning symptoms, and criticize the therapist. Some patients miss payments and allege that the therapist does not really care about them (Bostic et al., 1996). In contrast, other patients attempt to preserve a positive image of their therapists by blaming others for the decision to terminate and giving their therapists gifts. Potential replacement therapists are degraded. Both extremely negative reactions and extremely positive reactions indicate a failure to achieve tolerance of ambivalence toward the therapist in what is, indeed, a highly conflicted situation. The stages articulated by Kübler-Ross are often cited as describing the behavioral patterns of many of the patients. Many of the patient's reactions are viewed as transference reactions. They refer to the patient's subjective displacement of feelings and attitudes toward past persons to the therapist.

THERAPIST REACTIONS

A number of authors have indicated that the therapist experiences many of the same negative affective states as the patients do in the context of a forced termination. The negative affect that appears to be predominant in many authors' descriptions is guilt. The therapist feels responsible for the negative feelings and behaviors of the patient. Given that the therapist initiated the termination, this type of affective response is to be expected. However, when coupled with a personal sense of loss and sadness, which is also frequently experienced, the consequence can be very painful and debilitating. The therapist may attempt to accelerate the process of therapy, may increase the medication that is prescribed for the patient, may pressure the patient to continue with another therapist, or may provide inappropriate last words of advice (Weddington & Cavenar, 1979).

As mentioned previously, the concept that is used to understand the essentially irrational reactions of the therapist is countertransference. Because countertransference reactions are so commonly reported, some clinicians have regularly provided consultation to therapists who have initiated terminations. Elkind (1996) described her work in providing such consultation. She attempted to help the therapist take the perspective of the patient. In addition, she attempted to highlight the vulnerabilities of the therapist and to provide much needed support. Nevertheless, the consultant often becomes an ambivalent object. She is both a companion in a time of need and a person who is unable to avert the loss. Sometimes she works with both the therapist and the patient, both of whom she perceives as struggling with the impending termination.

There is no doubt that a sense of disillusionment is present in therapists who repeatedly must initiate terminations. This, of course, is often the fate of trainees. de Bosset and Styrsky (1986) conducted a survey of psychiatric residents at the University of Toronto regarding termination of their individual psychotherapy cases. The majority of residents had mixed feelings about the patients' readiness for termination. In only 16% of the cases did the resident believe that the patient was definitely ready to terminate. Their findings also suggested that the more difficult cases were often those that were terminated earlier. It also appears to be the case that supervision time is more often devoted to cases where mutual decisions between patient and therapist have been made rather than unilateral decisions. Yet, it is probably the latter cases that are in greater need of supervision.

A few articles in the literature make reference to potential positive outcomes associated with therapist-initiated termination. Some authors speak about opportunities to examine and resolve issues related to separation and loss. Garcia-Lawson, Lane, and Koetting (2000) studied patients who had lost their therapists through death. The patients reported an increase in autonomy and internal strength to take responsibility for themselves. The experience helped them deal more effectively with other incidences of separation and loss. In a different context, loss of therapists because of training rotations, Long et al. (1988) reported that the losses provided an excellent opportunity for patients to explore their own dynamics in regard to separation and loss. Similarly, Zahourek and Crawford (1978) reported that forced terminations provide patients with an opportunity to resolve and reexamine past separations and losses over which they had no control.

Other authors speak about opportunities for personal growth. Parsons (1982) described a case in which the therapist initiated termination because of the lack of progress. Although such cases are laden with difficulties, Parsons added that they can be opportunities for personal growth. Pearson (1998) agreed and asserted that it is a good opportunity for the patient to internalize functional aspects of the therapeutic relationship such as support, acceptance, empathy, and respect. McGee (1974) suggested that it can be an important humanizing procedure for therapists. However, these references to positive outcomes tend to be quite brief and rather vague. They appear to be paying lip service to possible but unlikely outcomes.

GUIDELINES

Despite the preponderance of negative outcomes and negative reactions to therapist-initiated termination that have been documented and discussed in the literature from the perspectives of both the patient and the therapist, there has not been much space devoted to how to best handle what are clearly difficult situations. This may be related to an historical difference of opinion, concerning the therapist's use of transference and nontransference interventions. Transference interventions are those therapist statements that address the patient's subjective displacement of feelings and attitudes toward past persons to the therapist. Nontransference interpretations are everything else. On one side, the traditional position is represented by Dewald (1965, 1966), who recommended maintaining an emphasis on interpretation of the transference just as one would with a mutually agreed-on termination. Nontransference interventions are to be deemphasized. On the other side, a more contemporary position is represented by Beatrice (1982–1983), who recommended the careful use of nontransference interventions to acknowledge the reality of the loss (e.g., "As you know, our work together will come to an end before you must make that decision"). Or, the therapist may reassure the patient that the patient's reaction is appropriate given the reality of the therapist's departure (e.g., "In contrast to previous times in your life, you have reacted to the announcement of my departure with calmness and thoughtfulness; that definitely seems like a sign of progress").

Martinez (1989) further refined the use of nontransference interventions by restricting them to three areas of interaction: implicit or explicit acknowledgment of countertransference and counterreaction, provision of information about the reason for termination, and the consideration and implementation of referral for continued therapy. She provided case examples where the use of nontransference interventions appeared to facilitate analytic work. The interventions attempted to maintain the analytic alliance, preserved the patient's capacity to recognize and make use of the transference, and provided avenues for recognizing past traumas and the actual loss

TABLE 8.1
Therapist Guidelines for Handling Therapist-Initiated Termination

Author	Guideline
Bostic et al. (1996) Long, Pendleton, & Winter (1988)	Allow ample time for termination (e.g., 6 months).
Long et al. (1988)	Present the reason for termination. Make a statement about what therapy has meant.
Bostic et al. (1996) Coker (1996)	Allow the patient to make decisions (e.g., set the date, decide whether to be referred to another therapist, choose another therapist).
Mikkelsen & Gutheil (1979)	Use a death metaphor in referring to the process.
Pearson (1998)	Accept and work through your intense feelings. Reflect on each client and imagine how it will be. Maintain physical energy levels through adequate rest, nutrition, and exercise. Seek professional and personal support. Review each client's progress, previous reactions to loss, defenses, and emotional expressiveness. Announce your decision soon after it is made. Tell clients where you are going and why. Allow clients to respond spontaneously. Respond empathically. Assess each client's need to continue counseling. Encourage clients to review their progress and review with them their accomplishments and need for future work. Facilitate the transfer–referral process. Provide a forwarding address. Say goodbye and end the relationship.
Tapper (1994)	Inform the patient about why you are leaving. Provide the names of two physicians to continue the care of the patient. Inform the patient about the risks of not being transferred.

of the analyst. Bostic et al. (1996) arrived at the same conclusion in regard to countertransference. If the patient discerns countertransference, then it should be honestly acknowledged.

A number of practical suggestions that have been provided by various authors are listed in Table 8.1. Bostic et al. (1996) and Long et al. (1988) advocated allowing ample time for termination, for example, 3 to 6 months for deeply invested patients. Long et al. (1988) also suggested presenting the reason for the termination and making a personal statement about what therapy has meant to the therapist. Several authors such as Bostic et al. (1996) and Coker (1996) emphasized the importance of facilitating the autonomy of the patient. For example, the patient can be allowed to set the date for termination, decide whether referral to another therapist for treatment should occur, and choose among more than one possible therapist.

Mikkelsen and Gutheil (1979) have found it useful to use a death meta-phor in referring to the process of therapist-initiated termination. From their perspective, it has helped patients move from the stages of anger to depres-sion as described by Kübler-Ross. Pearson (1998) offered a set of 14 practical guidelines for the therapist, such as informing patients soon after the thera-pist has decided to terminate therapy and providing a forwarding address. Both Elkind (1996) and Pearson (1998) recommended that the therapist seek consultation or support from colleagues. The potential for countertrans-ference and realistically based painful reactions is high. Tapper (1994) has provided a short list of practice guidelines for handling therapist-initiated terminations as advocated by the Canadian Psychiatric Association.

One of the most distressing and final types of therapist-initiated termi-nation is the death of the therapist. Several authors have addressed this topic (Garcia-Lawson & Lane, 1997; Garcia-Lawson et al., 2000; Steiner, 2002). In their survey study, Garcia-Lawson et al. (2000) found that 90% of thera-pists who died had not specified a plan to assist colleagues and patients after their deaths. This appears to be a clear and nearly universal case of denial. Some authors have proposed that therapists construct a professional will that includes important information to assist survivors in dealing with their pa-tients in a helpful and therapeutic manner (Firestein, 1994; Steiner, 2002). Steiner has created a useful guide titled "Preparing Your Clients and Yourself for the Unexpected." It includes explicit instructions for creating a plan as well as sample letters and forms. These instructions include selecting a small set of colleagues to serve as an emergency response team, writing one's prac-tice disposition guidelines, choosing a bridge therapist who serves as a transi-tional figure for a short time during a crisis, and selecting a group of potential therapists for patient referrals. Steiner also emphasized the importance of creating a central file that includes contact information and status summa-ries for each patient. Creating a plan represents a sensible and thoughtful procedure that safeguards the interests of one's clients. It is something that the large group of aging therapists in our society should seriously consider.

CONCLUSION

Although small compared with the literature on patient-initiated ter-mination, the literature on therapist-initiated termination of therapy per-mits several conclusions to be drawn. First, therapist-initiated termination, especially in training situations, may be considerably more prevalent than most therapists assume. Second, there is a general consensus that therapist-initiated termination represents a problematic situation in which therapists have placed their needs before those of their patients. The negative affective states and problematic behaviors on the part of both the patients and the therapists in reaction to therapist-initiated termination often represent transference and countertransference reactions. However, a number of authors have suggested that they also represent reactions to a real loss.

Despite the problematic nature of therapist-initiated termination, guidelines for dealing effectively with the situation have received only brief attention in the literature. It is as if practitioners would prefer to deny the high probability that one will have to face the problem eventually if one has not done so already. (This denial certainly pertains when the cause of termination is the therapist's death. In that particular case, though, there is some useful literature one can turn to in seeking to protect patients' interests.) There is a great need for further research on the causes and effects of therapist-initiated termination and guidance on how to handle its ramifications.

9

THEMES, SUGGESTIONS FOR EMPIRICAL RESEARCH, AND CLINICAL PRINCIPLES

The working hypothesis governing our development of the termination phase model was that the ending of therapy involves certain understandable principles. The main thrust of this book has been to explicate these principles. We also believed that our attempt to synthesize the clinical and research literatures and our own clinical and research experiences could result in a conceptualization that was applicable across a wide spectrum of therapy approaches and orientations. Identifying the variations to the termination phase model associated with different therapy approaches and orientations appears to be a feasible undertaking. We hope that the model can be taken up by clinicians and clinical researchers and extended further in terms of theory, practice, and empirical study. The degree of implementation or transfer of the ideas in this book will ultimately determine the value of our undertaking.

This concluding chapter comprises two main sections. In the first, we revisit the main conceptual elements of the model to capture the prevalent themes of the preceding discussion. Research directions suggested by each of these elements are outlined. In the second section, our perspective returns to the consulting room, where the central clinical principles of the termination are considered.

THE TERMINATION PHASE MODEL: RESEARCH CONSIDERATIONS

The central element of the model is that the termination phase has its own outcomes that must be considered (see chap. 2). The termination outcomes include (a) review and reinforcement and consolidation of the therapy process and the gains made in treatment, (b) resolution of issues in the therapy relationship, and (c) preparedness for maintaining healthy functioning outside of treatment (Kramer, 1990). An important hypothesis that results from this idea is that the quality of the outcomes of the termination has a direct bearing on the quality of the overall outcome of the treatment. We argue that the termination outcomes can be differentiated from the context, focus, and content of the patient's therapy and also from the outcomes of the treatment. The outcomes of termination are also distinguishable from the indicators for termination, that is, the termination criteria (see chap. 2). However, the termination is not a static set of tasks, activities, or issues; it requires considerable tailoring to the specific patient and therapy. The termination process itself will vary as a function of the therapy structure and orientation (see chaps. 4 and 5), and particularly because of the influence of certain characteristics of the patient (see chap. 6).

Therefore, an important early step in implementing a program of research on termination in psychotherapy would be the development of measures of the termination outcomes. Measures of therapy outcome commonly address status on indexes of symptomatology, personality functioning, interpersonal functioning, and personal well-being or self-esteem. Administration of these measures at different time intervals allows for an estimation of patient change. In the case of the measures of termination outcome, however, the issue is whether certain processes have occurred (i.e., reinforcement and consolidation, resolution, and establishment of preparedness) and whether certain goals have been achieved (i.e., therapy gains acknowledged, closure in the therapy relationship, and readiness for life after therapy). Therapist or observer ratings could prove useful for evaluating whether the patient engaged in each of the core termination processes, and patient ratings or assessor evaluations could address goal attainment. Ratings of audiorecorded session material from the termination phase of different therapies may identify material that clarifies the operational definitions of the termination outcomes. Needless to say, a good deal of creativity would be required to develop valid and reliable measures of these constructs. The development of measures of these multidimensional constructs—addressing both processes in the patient and therapy and certain specific goal attainments—will likely prove demanding. However, there are methods that have been developed that represent powerful means of studying these phenomena, for example, measures of internal representations of the therapist (Arnold, Farber, & Geller, 2004; Blatt, Wiseman, Prince-Gibson, & Gatt, 1991; Quintana & Meara, 1990).

The termination phase model also assumes that the boundaries of the termination phase can be recognized, although the demarcations may not always be particularly sharp. In particular, though, we believe that the termination phase is distinguishable from the working phase of therapy. It is important clinically that the transition between these phases be explicitly acknowledged by therapist and patient. Movement into this pretermination transition is determined by the patient's attainment of certain general therapy objectives: relief from distress, mastery of the associated problems, and increased capacity to function independently of the therapist (see chap. 2). Empirically, these general objectives would reflect treatment outcomes at that point in the course of therapy and could be evaluated by frequently used standardized measures of change. Alternatively, process analyses of material from the later therapy sessions could be oriented to identification of the markers of the transition from the working to termination phases. The relationships between these in-treatment outcomes, the indicators of the appropriateness of termination, the termination outcomes, and the overall outcomes of the treatment would be valuable to investigate. An important issue raised by our conceptual model is whether there are causal connections between emergence of the indicators of termination, the success of the termination phase, and the outcome of therapy.

The termination phase itself represents a transition between the work of therapy and going on in life without therapy. As with every patient, every termination is unique and must be tailored to accommodate the particular case and course of treatment. Nonetheless, certain general factors can be identified that will influence the critical importance that the termination carries for a specific therapy case (see chap. 2). The termination phase assumes greater importance the longer the duration of therapy, the greater the severity of the patient's psychopathology (e.g., structural deficits, profound dependency, a history of serious object loss), or the greater the patient's dissatisfaction with the outcomes of the treatment. The termination is also a critical focus when the end point is deliberately established at the outset of therapy (i.e., in the time-limited approaches; see chap. 2) or when the therapist unilaterally determines the ending of therapy (i.e., "forced" terminations; see chap. 8). Termination assumes less importance in the more structured therapies that aim to foster skills acquisition. However, the greater the emphasis on attending to and using the therapeutic alliance—even in a skills-oriented approach—the more critical the termination phase becomes to the success of the therapy.

Research to examine the validity of the influences that determine the importance of the termination phase (i.e., duration, patient severity, and dissatisfaction) is definitely needed. In addition, studies of the relationship between new measures of the termination outcomes and established measures of the therapeutic alliance would likely be illuminating. These studies would be particularly informative when the therapies studied are those we described as structured and skills oriented, in contrast to those with a greater relational and process orientation. The emphasis on the therapeutic alliance, and the degree to which the quality of the alliance figures in the work engaged in by the therapy participants, may reflect the key influence in regard to the importance of the termination phase to the outcome of therapy.

A consistent theme in the literature on termination—from the early 1930s to the present—is that the ending of therapy can stimulate the emergence of issues associated with separation and loss for both patient and therapist (see chap. 3). The range of patient characteristics that can influence the termination process, as considered in chapter 6, generally have a bearing on the patient's capacity to develop and maintain a healthy interpersonal relationship. It is contingent on therapists to flexibly modify their approach to the termination in light of patients' standing on these characteristics. This highlights the central nature of interpersonal transaction in the psychotherapies and fits in well with the importance of the therapeutic alliance in the therapy process and at the termination. In addition to addressing the range of issues experienced by patients at the time of termination, therapists must also be attentive to their own experience and be aware of possible countertransference feelings interfering with the termination process (see chap. 3). The potential for countertransference problems interfering with the termination likely varies as widely across therapists as the variables addressed in chapter 6 vary across patients. Given our own experience with the value of supervision at the time of therapy termination (Joyce, Duncan, Duncan, Kipnes, & Piper, 1996), we have underscored the importance of such consultation throughout this book.

Indicators that a move into terminating therapy is appropriate can also be identified—these indicators parallel the outcomes to be addressed during the termination phase. These indicators represent the criteria for termination and include the following: First, it can be established that the shared goals of therapy have been reasonably fulfilled; second, there is an observable change in the patient–therapist relationship toward fewer distortions and greater maturity; and, third, there is an observable shift in the patient's concerns toward the future and extratherapeutic circumstances and relationships (see chap. 2). Simple measures of these indicators, based on item ratings or content analyses of session material, could be developed and may serve as baseline measures of the termination outcomes, prior to the actual work of the termination phase. As noted previously, a correlational approach evaluating the relationships between these pretermination indicators, the termination outcomes, and the overall outcome of treatment could yield much information of value to the field.

The chapters concerning variations in the termination process and outcomes associated with structural factors (chap. 4), therapy orientations (chap. 5), and patient characteristics (chap. 6) also offer numerous directions for research investigation. The weight of evidence for the impact of these variables is not great—much of our commentary leans toward the speculative—but the framework provided by the termination phase model may inform the design of studies that address the influence of these factors. Suggestions for preventing premature terminations, or patient dropout, were provided in chapter 7. The effectiveness of these strategies can be assessed in studies that use clinical trial designs. More effective retention of the patient in therapy can translate into a greater likelihood of a viable termination phase and, thus, greater opportunities for empirical examination of the termination process.

IMPLEMENTATION OF THE TERMINATION PHASE MODEL IN THE CONSULTING ROOM

In this section, we highlight important clinical principles that emerged in the discussion of the termination phase model (chaps. 2 and 3). These principles can be identified in the literature; however, the model offers an integrated framework for thinking about the termination as a distinct phase of psychotherapy. The clinical principles are discussed in the following text, with a summary listing presented in Exhibit 9.1.

The degree of emotional upheaval that can be expected for the patient during the termination phase can be predicted on the basis of the patient's responses to other separations (e.g., therapist vacations) during the course of therapy. If even brief breaks during therapy served as triggers for intense affective reactions on the part of the patient, the therapist would obviously need to approach the termination phase with caution and care. A key element of this prediction, then, is an appraisal of the intensity of the patient's dependence on the therapist as the time for termination nears. The patient's dependency will be a function of the critical capacities that the patient does not possess and therefore comes to rely on the therapist to provide. These capacities can include a sense of continuity and worth in the sense of self; abilities to experience, manage, and regulate affect or tolerate anxiety; or the ability to maintain equilibrium under conditions of stress. The appraisal of the patient's strengths and deficits should be well developed by late in the therapy and indeed may have represented a primary focus of the treatment, that is, providing opportunities for the patient's development of greater autonomy.

In contrast to the consistently forward movement of the working phase, the termination phase involves moving back and forth between a review of the work accomplished in the past and how this learning will be applied to

General principles

- The degree of affective turmoil that can be expected during the termination phase may be predicted on the basis of the patient's responses to separations (e.g., therapist vacations) during the course of therapy.
- The termination phase involves an oscillation between a review of the work accomplished in the past and how the patient's learning will be applied to the future.
- The therapist also aims to realize two general objectives: first, that the patient achieves a balanced and realistic view of the therapy process and relationship, and second, that the patient is able to internalize some aspect of the therapy experience that is positive and sustaining.

Moving from the working to termination phases

- Therapists are aware of cues that signal the onset of the transition from the working phase to the termination phase. These cues can be reflective of the patient's attainment of the goals of treatment, a shift in the quality of the therapy relationship, or a shift in the patient's current concerns.
- Raising the issue of ending therapy proceeds in two stages: evaluating the patient's readiness to end and working to crystallize the patient's decision to move into the termination phase. Evaluation of the termination criteria offers a means for determining the appropriateness of termination.
- The effort of preparing to initiate the termination phase concludes with the setting of the date for the final session.

The termination phase and outcomes

- During the termination phase, the therapist maintains an awareness that all of the patient's material will make reference, implicit or explicit, to the upcoming ending.
- Reinforcement and consolidation of the treatment process and gains involves a systematic and collaborative review of the course of treatment.
- Resolution of issues in the patient–therapist relationship is likely the focus found most demanding by the participants. The therapist encourages an atmosphere of immediacy in this process, directly addressing the feelings associated with separation, loss, and abandonment.
- The therapist evaluates the patient's preparedness for maintaining healthy functioning. This outcome is assessed in terms of what the patient has successfully internalized of the therapist and the therapeutic process.
- The therapist frames the termination as an opportunity to engage in a healthy separation from a relationship that has usefully served its purpose.

the future. The focus also shifts, from the patient's point of view regarding his or her issues to the patient's experience of the impending separation from and loss of the therapist and therapy. The therapist's focus is thus both pragmatic, regarding the transfer of therapy gains and insights to the patient's functioning outside therapy, and affective, regarding the patient's experience of the impending ending. Beyond addressing the three outcomes of termination, the therapist works to realize two general objectives: first, that the patient develops a balanced, realistic view of the therapy process and relationship, and second, that the patient can internalize elements of the therapy experience that are positive and sustaining. Contrasting the ending of the therapeutic relationship with the endings of past relationships can highlight the positive work accomplished in the course of treatment and during the termination phase. Acknowledging the patient's contribution to the therapy process and to the realization of therapy gains can reinforce the internalization of the therapist's functions, the quality of the therapy relationship, and the working process.

A central premise of the termination phase model is that there is a clear demarcation between the periods of "working" in therapy and of bringing the therapy to a close. The therapist is attentive for cues that signal the time for the transition from the working phase to the termination phase. These cues will reflect the patient's attainment of the treatment goals, a shift in the quality of the therapy relationship, or a change in the patient's current concerns. Active assessment of change in each of these areas by the therapist can clarify the appropriateness of moving toward the termination phase. Reflection and validation of the patient's judgment that the time has come to conclude therapy can also bolster the patient's sense of being able to continue the work after the treatment has been terminated. Clarifying that the time has arrived to end therapy proceeds in two stages: (a) evaluating the patient's readiness to end and (b) working to solidify the patient's decision to enter the termination phase. Evaluation of the termination criteria can help determine the appropriateness of termination. The decision to terminate should ideally rest with the patient; however, the therapist has the responsibility of evaluating the appropriateness of termination at that point in the treatment. A key indicator for the therapist is his or her judgment in regard to the patient's anxiety about the ending, that is, whether this anxiety is tolerable and whether the patient demonstrates having the resources to undergo the process of termination. The therapist must also ensure that this judgment is not contaminated by countertransference feelings about bringing the therapy to a close. Preparation to initiate the termination phase is concluded with establishment of the date for the final session.

During therapy, but particularly during the termination phase, the therapist's attitude toward the patient is characterized by respect, empathy, tolerance, and nonmanipulativeness. During the termination phase, the therapist remains aware that the patient's material will continually be oriented, implicitly or explicitly, to the upcoming ending. The therapist also attends to the quality of the therapeutic relationship in terms of the alliance, the patient's transference, and the real relationship between the parties. The strength of the alliance may indeed be tested during the termination phase, particularly during efforts toward resolution of issues in the patient–therapist relationship. Underscoring the success of the collaboration at different points in the course of therapy can assist the patient to stay with the sometimes painful work during the termination phase.

Transference reactions by the patient during this phase can recall distortions from earlier in therapy or can reflect stimulation of the patient's issues with loss and separation, calling into play the patient's earlier experiences of significant relationships coming to an end. The characteristics of the patient, the therapy approach, and the strength of the working collaboration will influence the degree to which these transference elements are examined. We believe that developing an understanding of the transference themes is a central element of the work toward the second termination outcome. However, the degree to which the patient and therapist address these themes will be determined in part by the therapy approach; that is, transference issues are central to the conduct of dynamically and relationally oriented therapies but relatively deemphasized in therapies that address the development of cognitive or behavioral skills. Transference manifestations are likely to be especially problematic in the case of dependent patients or those dealing with intense attachment fears or primitive object relations. With regard to the real relationship, the therapist can begin to engage more with the patient as an equal; some practitioners may be comfortable using disclosure and observation to inform the patient that the therapy endeavor was valued but must now be brought to a close. These strategies will allow for the development of a more realistic appraisal of the treatment, dissipating any idealized or highly negative views of the process. The therapist continually monitors the degree of the patient's depressive response to the termination and encourages a thorough exploration of ambivalent feelings about the ending. To protect the integrity of the termination process and perhaps also the accomplishments of the treatment as a whole, the therapist attends to the increased possibility of acting out by the patient in response to the imminent close of therapy.

Reinforcement–consolidation of the treatment process and gains represents the first termination outcome and involves a systematic review of the course of treatment by the patient and therapist. The objective is to determine how much of the patient's learning in the therapy sessions has been generalized to his or her life "outside." The review may result in a resurgence of the issues that originally brought the patient into treatment or the presentation of new problems in an effort by the patient (consciously or unconsciously) to extend the therapy relationship. A comparison of the patient's earlier functioning with their status at the close of therapy may also prompt feelings of grief by highlighting how the patient's earlier behaviors were unproductive and wasteful.

Resolution of issues in the patient–therapist relationship represents the second termination outcome and is probably the most demanding task associated with ending therapy. The therapist should encourage an atmosphere of immediacy and the direct examination of the feelings associated with separation, loss, and abandonment. This strategy is particularly important in the case of forced terminations, or terminations unilaterally determined by the therapist. Issues of separation and loss are central to the work on the second termination outcome. Apart from the patient's loss of the person of the therapist (and fellow members in the case of group therapy) and the struggles and gains associated with the course of therapy, the patient is also taking leave of a unique and productive interpersonal process. With some patients, the therapy relationship can represent one of few that the patient experienced as positive during his or her life. Engaging in the mourning of this loss can contribute to the patient's internalization of the therapist's functions, sustaining features of the therapy relationship, or the elements of the therapy process. The patient's affects in regard to the separation from and loss of the therapy and therapist may take a number of forms other than direct verbalization—resistance, defensiveness, or acting-out behaviors (e.g., canceling sessions or coming late). The therapist's task is to continually inquire about the underlying feelings and encourage their articulation by the patient. In the group situation, other patients will frequently join the therapist to implement this task. Frequently, this work will prompt the patient's reexperiencing of earlier losses, which can be used to address parallels and contrasts to the experience of ending the patient–therapist relationship. The patient is also likely to experience the loss of the "old self" as the therapy process moves toward a close. The therapist can underscore the value of applying the same process engaged in during the working phase to these termination experiences.

Addressing the second termination outcome also stimulates feelings associated with separation and loss for the therapist. One should not underestimate either the impact of losing a patient with whom one has worked for some time or the potential for the termination of therapy to stimulate unresolved issues of loss associated with the therapist's history. For the therapist, the importance of supervision to deal with such issues cannot be overstated, as our own experience attests (Joyce et al., 1996).

Work toward the second termination outcome also requires that the patient achieve a realistic appraisal of the limitations of the therapy and dissolution of an idealized view of the process. Negative feelings toward the therapist or the therapy may emerge as the limitations of treatment are clarified, but it is crucial that these feelings and transferences are fully aired prior to the closing session. This examination may also vary considerably for different patients or for different therapy approaches (e.g., long-term supportive therapy). With certain patients, for example, a patient with mild paranoia in a supportive treatment of some duration, negative transferences may be left unaddressed or responded to by the therapist with the reality of the treatment circumstances.

In the face of the imminent end of therapy, therapists' countertransference reactions are more likely if their empathic connection with the patients is poor. Losing a focus on the patients' experience can increase the chance that therapists will be preoccupied with their own sense of loss, a phenomenon that can be determined by multiple influences. In turn, countertransference feelings can interfere with, or even sabotage, the termination process. It is critical that the therapist be aware of and deal with countertransference feelings, both during and between sessions, so that the patient's experience of the termination is not compromised.

Evaluating the patient's preparedness for maintaining healthy functioning represents the third termination outcome. This outcome reflects the degree to which the patient has internalized aspects of the therapist and therapeutic process. Reinforcing the patient's accomplishments during the review of the course of therapy and facilitating the mourning process in the effort to resolve issues in the patient–therapist relationship can increase the likelihood the patient will assimilate aspects of the therapy. In turn, the probability increases that these internalized aspects will serve as resources for dealing with problems in the posttermination period. Three strategies for addressing this termination outcome can be formulated:

- The steps the patient has taken toward health over the course of therapy are acknowledged and reinforced.
- The more subtle transformations in the patient's behavior toward self, the therapist, or others that occur through therapy can be highlighted and underscored.
- The end of therapy is framed realistically as a step toward healthier functioning; it is emphasized that once the therapeutic relationship has ended, the patient's work will continue.

Finally, and perhaps most important, the therapist should refer to the termination as an opportunity to experience a healthy separation from a relationship that has usefully served its purpose. In terms of the patient's experience, then, a well-managed termination will involve engagement in the various tasks associated with this phase of the treatment, attainment of the termination outcomes, and a sense that the therapy relationship has been relinquished yet retained through internalization, rather than experienced as a painful loss that echoes past losses.

CONCLUSION

Our objective for this book is that it would contribute toward the development of a general model of the termination of psychotherapy that would be useful to therapists of different orientations. It is clearly evident that considerable development remains to be accomplished, in both formulating the central conceptual elements of the termination phase model and investigating our assumptions in regard to the termination process and outcomes. We also recognize the limitations of the view of termination we have put forward. For example, we adhere to a psychodynamic orientation in our theorizing about the termination process and outcomes, which may require subsequent translations to the language of other therapy orientations. Furthermore, our discussion was restricted to individual and group modalities of treatment; the nature of the termination of couples or family therapies was not considered.

As a result, the ending of this book does not represent to us a termination of our involvement with the construct but instead the completion of an initial phase of clarification before moving forward. We hope the perspective on the termination of psychotherapy that was described in this book will stimulate new ideas for the reader, and we look forward to contributions from others to further our collective understanding of the termination of psychotherapy.

REFERENCES

Ackerman, S. J., Hilsenroth, M. J., Clemence, A. J., Weatherill, R., & Fowler, J. C. (2000). The effects of social cognition and object representation on psychotherapy continuation. *Bulletin of the Menninger Clinic, 64,* 386–408.

Ainsworth, M. (1964). Patterns of attachment behavior shown by the infant in interaction with his mother. *Merrill-Palmer Quarterly, 10,* 51–58.

American Psychiatric Association. (2000). *Diagnostic and statistical manual of mental disorders* (4th ed., rev.). Washington, DC: Author.

Arnold, E. G., Farber, B. A., & Geller, J. D. (2004). Termination, posttermination, and internalization of therapy and the therapist: Internal representation and psychotherapy outcome. In D. Charman (Ed.), *Core processes in brief psychodynamic psychotherapy: Advancing effective practice* (pp. 289–308). Mahwah, NJ: Erlbaum.

Aronson, T. A. (1989). A critical review of psychotherapeutic treatments of the borderline personality: Historical trends and future directions. *Journal of Nervous and Mental Disease, 177,* 511–527.

Azim, H. F. A., Piper, W. E., Segal, P. M., Nixon, G. W. H., & Duncan, S. (1991). The quality of object relations scale. *Bulletin of the Menninger Clinic, 55,* 323–343.

Baekeland, F., & Lundwall, L. (1975). Dropping out of treatment: A critical review. *Psychological Bulletin, 82,* 738–783.

Balint, M. (1950). On the termination of analysis. *International Journal of Psycho-Analysis, 31,* 196–199.

Bandura, A. (1989). Human agency in social cognitive therapy. *American Psychologist, 44,* 1175–1184.

Barnett, J. E., MacGlashan, S. G., & Clarke, A. J. (2000). Risk management and ethical issues regarding termination and abandonment. In L. Vandecreek & T. L. Jackson (Eds.), *Innovations in clinical practice: A source book* (Vol. 18, pp. 231–245). Sarasota, FL: Professional Resource Exchange.

Bartholomew, K., & Horowitz, L. M. (1991). Attachment styles among young adults: A test of a four-category model. *Journal of Personality and Social Psychology, 61,* 226–244.

Bauer, G. P., & Kobos, J. C. (1987). *Brief psychotherapy: Short-term psychodynamic intervention.* Northvale, NJ: Jason Aronson.

Beatrice, J. (1982–1983). Premature termination: A therapist leaving. *International Journal of Psychoanalytic Psychotherapy, 9,* 313–336.

Beckham, E. E. (1992). Predicting patient dropout in psychotherapy. *Psychotherapy: Theory, Research, Practice, Training, 29,* 177–182.

Bernard, H. S. (1989). Guidelines to minimize premature terminations. *International Journal of Group Psychotherapy, 39,* 523–529.

Bernard, H. S., & Drob, S. L. (1989). Premature termination: A clinical study. *Group*, *13*, 11–22.

Betz, N. E., & Shullman, S. L. (1979). Factors related to client return rate following intake. *Journal of Counseling Psychology*, *26*, 542–545.

Blanck, G., & Blanck, R. (1988). The contribution of ego psychology to understanding the process of termination in psychoanalysis and psychotherapy. *Journal of the American Psychoanalytic Association*, *36*, 961–984.

Blatt, S. J., & Behrends, R. S. (1987). Internalization, separation–individuation, and the nature of therapeutic action. *International Journal of Psychoanalysis*, *68*, 279–297.

Blatt, S. J., Ford, R. Q., Berman, W. H., Jr., Cook, B., Cramer, P., & Robins, C. E. (1994). *Therapeutic change: An object relations perspective*. New York: Plenum Press.

Blatt, S. J., Quinlan, D. M., Pilkonis, P. A., & Shea, T. M. (1995). Impact of perfectionism and need for approval on the brief treatment of depression: The National Institute of Mental Health Treatment of Depression Collaborative Research Program revisited. *Journal of Consulting and Clinical Psychology*, *63*, 125–132.

Blatt, S. J., & Shichman, S. (1983). Two primary configurations of psychopathology. *Psychoanalysis and Contemporary Thought*, *6*, 187–254.

Blatt, S. J., Wein, S., Chevron, E., & Quinlan, D. (1979). Parental representations and depression in normal young adults. *Journal of Abnormal Psychology*, *88*, 388–397.

Blatt, S. J., Wild, C., & Ritzler, B. (1975). Disturbances of object representations in schizophrenia. *Psychoanalysis and Contemporary Science*, *4*, 235–288.

Blatt, S. J., Wiseman, H., Prince-Gibson, E., & Gatt, C. (1991). Object representations and change in clinical functioning. *Psychotherapy: Theory, Research, Practice, Training*, *28*, 273–283.

Blum, H. P. (1987). Analysis terminable and interminable, a half century retrospective. *International Journal of Psychoanalysis*, *68*, 37–48.

Blum, H. P. (1989). The concept of termination and the evolution of psychoanalytic thought. *Journal of the American Psychoanalytic Association*, *37*, 275–295.

Bonanno, G. A., & Kaltman, S. (1999). Toward an integrative perspective on bereavement. *Psychological Bulletin*, *125*, 760–776.

Bordin, E. S. (1979). The generalizability of the psychoanalytic concept of the working alliance. *Psychotherapy: Theory, Research, and Practice*, *16*, 252–260.

Bostic, J. Q., Shadid, L. G., & Blotcky, M. J. (1996). Our time is up: Forced terminations during psychotherapy training. *American Journal of Psychotherapy*, *50*, 347–359.

Bowlby, J. (1970). Disruption of affectional bonds and its effects on behavior. *Journal of Contemporary Psychotherapy*, *2*, 75–86.

Bowlby, J. (1980). By ethology out of psycho-analysis: An experiment in interbreeding. *Animal Behaviour*, *28*, 649–656.

Bowlby, J. (1988). *A secure base: Parent–child attachment and healthy human development*. New York: Basic Books.

Boyer, S. P., & Hoffman, M. A. (1993). Counselor affective reactions to termination: Impact of counselor loss history and perceived client sensitivity to loss. *Journal of Counseling Psychology, 40,* 271–277.

Brogan, M. M., Prochaska, J. O., & Prochaska, J. M. (1999). Predicting termination and continuation status in psychotherapy using the transtheoretical model. *Psychotherapy: Theory, Research, Practice, Training, 36,* 105–113.

Buchele, B. J. (2000). Group psychotherapy for survivors of sexual and physical abuse. In R. H. Klein & V. L. Scherman (Eds.), *Group psychotherapy for psychological trauma* (pp. 170–187). New York: Guilford Press.

Budman, S. H. (1990). The myth of termination in brief therapy: Or, it ain't over till it's over. In J. K. Zeig & S. G. Gilligan (Eds.), *Brief therapy: Myths, methods, and metaphors* (pp. 206–218). New York: Brunner/Mazel.

Budman, S. H., & Gurman, A. S. (1988). *Theory and practice of brief psychotherapy*. New York: Guilford Press.

Bugental, J. F. T., & Sterling, M. M. (1995). Existential–humanistic psychotherapy: New perspectives. In A. S. Gurman & S. B. Messer (Eds.), *Essential psychotherapies: Theory and practice* (pp. 226–303). New York: Guilford Press.

Butler, S. F., & Strupp, H. H. (1993). Effects of training experienced dynamic therapists to use a psychotherapy manual. In N. E. Miller, L. Luborsky, J. P. Barber, & J. P. Docherty (Eds.), *Psychodynamic treatment research: A handbook for clinical practice* (pp. 191–210). New York: Basic Books.

Caligor, L., Fieldsteel, N. D., & Brok, A. (1993). *Combining individual and group therapy*. New York: Jason Aronson.

Carpenter, P. J., Del Gaudio, A. C., & Morrow, G. R. (1979). Dropouts and terminators from a community mental health center: Their use of other psychiatric services. *Psychiatric Quarterly, 51,* 271–279.

Charman, D. P., & Graham, A. C. (2004). Ending therapy: Processes and outcomes. In D. P. Charman (Ed.), *Core processes in psychodynamic psychotherapy: Advancing effective practice* (pp. 275–288). Mahwah, NJ: Erlbaum.

Clarkin, J. F., & Levy, K. N. (2004). The influence of client variables on psychotherapy. In M. J. Lambert (Ed.), *Bergin and Garfield's handbook of psychotherapy and behavior change* (5th ed., pp. 194–226). New York: Wiley.

Clarkin, J. F., Marziali, E., & Munroe-Blum, H. (1991). Group and family treatments for borderline personality disorder. *Hospital and Community Psychiatry, 42,* 1038–1043.

Clemental-Jones, C., Malan, D., & Trauer, T. (1990). A retrospective follow-up of 84 clients treated with individual psychoanalytic psychotherapy: Outcome and predictive factors. *British Journal of Psychotherapy, 6,* 363–376.

Coker, M. (1996). Ending where the client is: A psychodynamic approach to forced terminations. In J. Edward & J. B. Sanville (Eds.), *Fostering healing and growth: A psychoanalytic social work approach* (pp. 353–371). Northvale, NJ: Jason Aronson.

Conte, H. R., & Ratto, R. (1997). Self-report measures of psychological mindedness. In M. McCallum & W. E. Piper (Eds.), *Psychological mindedness: A contemporary understanding* (pp. 1–26). Mahwah, NJ: Erlbaum.

Crits-Christoph, P., & Connolly Gibbons, M. B. (2002). Relational interpretations. In J. C. Norcross (Ed.), *Psychotherapy relationships that work: Therapist contributions and responsiveness to patients* (pp. 285–300). New York: Oxford University Press.

Cummings, N. (1990). Brief intermittent psychotherapy throughout the life cycle. In J. K. Zeig & S. G. Gilligan (Eds.), *Brief therapy: Myths, methods, and metaphors* (pp. 169–184). New York: Brunner/Mazel.

Davanloo, H. (1978). *Basic principles and techniques in short-term dynamic psychotherapy.* New York: Spectrum.

Davanloo, H. (1979). Techniques of short-term dynamic psychotherapy. *Psychiatric Clinics of North America, 2,* 11–21.

de Bosset, F., & Styrsky, E. (1986). Termination in individual psychotherapy: A survey of residents' experience. *Canadian Journal of Psychiatry, 31,* 636–642.

Derisley, J., & Reynolds, S. (2000). The transtheoretical stages of change as a predictor of premature termination, attendance, and alliance in psychotherapy. *British Journal of Clinical Psychology, 39,* 371–382.

Dewald, P. (1965). Reactions to the forced termination of therapy. *Psychiatric Quarterly, 39,* 102–126.

Dewald, P. (1966). Forced termination of psychoanalysis. *Bulletin of the Menninger Clinic, 30,* 98–110.

Dewald, P. A. (1980). Forced termination of psychotherapy: The annually recurrent trauma. *Psychiatric Opinion, 17,* 13–15.

Dewald, P. A. (1982). The clinical importance of the termination phase. *Psychoanalytic Inquiry, 2,* 441–461.

Dewald, P. A. (1994). Principles of supportive therapy. *American Journal of Psychotherapy, 48,* 505–518.

Diamond, D., Clarkin, J., Levine, H., Levy, K., Foelsch, P., & Yeomans, F. (1999). Attachment theory and borderline personality disorder: A preliminary report. *Psychoanalytic Inquiry, 19,* 831–884.

Dies, R., & Teleska, P. (1985). Negative outcome in group psychotherapy. In D. Mays & C. Frank (Eds.), *Negative outcome in psychotherapy* (pp. 118–142). New York: Springer Publishing Company.

Diguer, L., Barber, J. P., & Luborsky, L. (1993). Three concomitants: Personality disorders, psychiatric severity, and outcome of dynamic psychotherapy for major depression. *American Journal of Psychiatry, 150,* 1246–1248.

Donoghue, K. (1994). The impact of the termination of brief psychotherapy, and its implications for counselling practice. *Counselling Psychology Review, 9,* 9–12.

Dozier, M. (1990). Attachment organization and treatment use for adults with serious psychopathological disorders. *Development and Psychopathology, 2,* 47–60.

Duehn, W. D., & Proctor, E. K. (1977). Initial clinical interaction and premature discontinuance in treatment. *American Journal of Psychiatry, 47*, 284–290.

Eames, V., & Roth, A. (2000). Patient attachment orientation and the early working alliance—A study of patient and therapist reports of alliance quality and ruptures. *Psychotherapy Research, 10*, 421–434.

Edelson, A. (1963). *The termination of intensive psychotherapy.* Springfield, IL: Charles C Thomas.

Ekstein, R. (1965). Working through and termination of analysis. *Journal of the American Psychoanalytic Association, 13*, 57–78.

Elkin, I., Shea, T., Watkins, J. T., Imber, S. D., Sotsky, S. M., Collins, J. F., et al. (1989). National Institute of Mental Health treatment of depression collaborative research program. *Archives of General Psychiatry, 46*, 971–982.

Elkind, S. N. (1996). The consultant's role when the analyst terminates therapy. *American Journal of Psychoanalysis, 55*, 331–346.

Elliott, R., Watson, J. C., Goldman, R. N., & Greenberg, L. S. (2004). *Learning emotion-focused therapy: The process-experiential approach to change.* Washington, DC: American Psychological Association.

Epperson, D. L. (1981). Counselor gender and early premature terminations from counseling: A replication and extension. *Journal of Counseling Psychology, 28*, 349–356.

Epperson, D. L., Bushway, D. J., & Warman, R. E. (1983). Client self-terminations after one counseling session: Effects of problem recognition, counselor gender, and counselor experience. *Journal of Counseling Psychology, 30*, 307–315.

Fenigstein, A., Scheier, M. F., & Buss, A. H. (1975). Public and private self-consciousness: Assessment and theory. *Journal of Consulting and Clinical Psychology, 43*, 522–527.

Ferenczi, S. (1955). The problem of the termination of psychoanalysis. In M. Balint (Ed.), *Final contributions to the problems and methods of psychoanalysis* (pp. 77–86). New York: Basic Books. (Original work published 1927)

Ferraro, F. (1995). Trauma and termination. *International Journal of Psycho-Analysis, 76*, 51–65.

Fieldsteel, N. D. (1990). The termination phase of combined therapy. *Group, 14*, 27–32.

Fieldsteel, N. D. (1996). The process of termination in long-term psychoanalytic group therapy. *International Journal of Group Psychotherapy, 46*, 25–39.

Firetein, S. K. (1969). Problems of termination in the analysis of adults [Panel report]. *Journal of the American Psychoanalytic Association, 17*, 222–237.

Firestein, S. K. (1974). Termination of psychoanalysis of adults: A review of the literature. *Journal of the American Psychoanalytic Association, 22*, 873–894.

Firestein, S. K. (1978). *Termination in psychoanalysis.* New York: International Universities Press.

Firestein, S. K. (1982). Termination of psychoanalysis: Theoretical, clinical and pedagogic considerations. *Psychoanalytic Inquiry, 2*, 473–497.

Firestein, S. K. (1994). On thinking the unthinkable: Making a professional will. *The American Psychoanalyst, 27,* 16.

Fisher, D. B. (1994). Health care reform based on an empowerment model of recovery by people with psychiatric disabilities. *Hospital and Community Psychiatry, 45,* 913–915.

Fleming, J., & Benedek, T. (1966). *Psychoanalytic supervision.* New York: Grune & Stratton.

Fonagy, P., Leigh, T., Steele, M., Steele, H., Kennedy, R., Mattoon, G., et al. (1996). The relation of attachment status, psychiatric classification, and response to psychotherapy. *Journal of Consulting and Clinical Psychology, 64,* 22–31.

Fonagy, P., & Target, M. (1997). Attachment and reflective function: Their role in self-organization. *Development and Psychopathology, 9,* 679–700.

Fortune, A. E. (1987). Grief only? Client and social worker reactions to termination. *Clinical Social Work Journal, 15,* 159–171.

Frank, G. (1999). Termination revisited. *Psychoanalytic Psychology, 16,* 119–129.

Frank, J. D. (1971). Therapeutic factors in psychotherapy. *American Journal of Psychotherapy, 25,* 350–361.

Frayn, D. H. (1992). Assessment factors associated with premature psychotherapy termination. *American Journal of Psychotherapy, 46,* 250–261.

Freeman, A., & Reinecke, M. A. (1995). Cognitive therapy. In A. S. Gurman & S. B. Messer (Eds.), *Essential psychotherapies: Theory and practice* (pp. 182–225). New York: Guilford Press.

Freud, S. (1964a). Analysis terminable and interminable. In J. Strachey (Ed. & Trans.), *Complete psychological works of Sigmund Freud* (Vol. 23, pp. 216–253). London: Hogarth Press. (Original work published 1937)

Freud, S. (1964b). On beginning the treatment (further recommendations on the technique of psycho-analysis I). In J. Strachey (Ed. & Trans.), *Complete psychological works of Sigmund Freud* (Vol. 12, pp. 121–144). London: Hogarth Press. (Original work published 1913)

Frick, W. B. (1999). Flight into health: A new interpretation. *Journal of Humanistic Psychology, 39,* 58–81.

Garcia-Lawson, K. A., & Lane, R. C. (1997). Thoughts on termination: Practical considerations. *Psychoanalytic Psychology, 14,* 239–257.

Garcia-Lawson, K. A., Lane, R. C., & Koetting, M. G. (2000). Sudden death of the therapist: The effects on the patient. *Journal of Contemporary Psychotherapy, 30,* 85–103.

Gardiner, M. (1971). *The wolfman.* New York: Basic Books.

Garfield, S. L. (1986). Research on client variables in psychotherapy. In S. L. Garfield & A. E. Bergin (Eds.), *Handbook of psychotherapy and behavior change* (3rd ed., pp. 213–256). New York: Wiley.

Garfield, S. L. (1994). Research on client variables in psychotherapy. In A. E. Bergin & S. L. Garfield (Eds.), *Handbook of psychotherapy and behavior change* (4th ed., pp. 190–228). New York: Wiley.

Gaskill, H. S. (1980). The closing phase of the psychoanalytic treatment of adults and the goals of psychoanalysis: The myth of perfectibility. *International Journal of Psychoanalysis, 61,* 11–24.

Geller, J. D. (1987). The process of psychotherapy: Separation and the complex interplay among empathy, insight, and internalization. In J. Bloom-Fesbach, S. Bloom-Fesbach, & Associates (Eds.), *The psychology of separation and loss: Perspectives on development, life transitions, and clinical practice* (pp. 459–514). San Francisco: Jossey-Bass.

Geller, J. D., & Farber, B. A. (1993). Factors influencing the process of internalization in psychotherapy. *Psychotherapy Research, 3,* 166–180.

Glick, R. A. (1987). Forced terminations. *Journal of the American Academy of Psychoanalysis, 15,* 449–463.

Glover, E. (1955). *The technique of psychoanalysis.* New York: International Universities Press.

Gold, S. (1996). Termination: The end of the bagel run. *Australian Journal of Psychotherapy, 15,* 80–99.

Goldfried, M. R. (2002). A cognitive–behavioural perspective on termination. *Journal of Psychotherapy Integration, 12,* 364–372.

Golland, J. H. (1997). Not an endgame: Termination in psychoanalysis. *Psychoanalytic Psychology, 14,* 259–270.

Gomes-Schwartz, B. (1978). Effective ingredients in psychotherapy: Prediction of outcome from process variables. *Journal of Consulting and Clinical Psychology, 46,* 1023–1035.

Greenberg, L. S. (2002). Termination of experiential therapy. *Journal of Psychotherapy Integration, 12,* 358–363.

Greenson, R. R. (1992). Problems of termination. In A. E. Sugarman, R. A. Nemiroff, & D. P. Greenson (Eds.), *The technique and practice of psychoanalysis: Vol. II. A memorial volume to Ralph R. Greenson* (pp. 341–342; Ralph R. Greenson Memorial Library Monograph No. 1). San Diego, CA: San Diego Psychoanalytic Society and Institute.

Grinberg, L. (1980). The closing phase of the psychoanalytic treatment of adults and the goals of psychoanalysis: "The search for truth about one's self." *International Journal of Psycho-Analysis, 61,* 25–37.

Groves, J. E., & Newman, A. E. (1992). Terminating psychotherapy: Calling it quits. In J. S. Rutan (Ed.), *Psychotherapy for the 1990s* (pp. 339–358). New York: Guilford Press.

Hardy, G. E., Stiles, W. B., Barkham, M., & Startup, M. (1998). Therapist responsiveness to client interpersonal styles during time-limited treatments for depression. *Journal of Consulting and Clinical Psychology, 66,* 304–312.

Harp, H. T. (1994). Empowerment of mental health consumers in vocational rehabilitation. *Psychosocial Rehabilitation Journal, 17,* 83–89.

Hayes, S. C., Follette, W. C., & Follette, V. M. (1995). Behavior therapy: A contextual approach. In A. S. Gurman & S. B. Messer (Eds.), *Essential psychotherapies: Theory and practice* (pp. 128–181). New York: Guilford Press.

Henry, W. P., Strupp, H. H., Butler, S. F., Schact, T. E., & Binder, J. L. (1993). Effects of training in time-limited dynamic psychotherapy: Changes in therapist behavior. *Journal of Consulting and Clinical Psychology, 61*, 434–440.

Hilsenroth, M. J., Handler, L., Toman, K. M., & Padawer, J. R. (1995). Rorschach and MMPI–2 indices of early psychotherapy termination. *Journal of Consulting and Clinical Psychology, 63*, 956–965.

Hilsenroth, M. J., Holdwick, D. J., Jr., Castlebury, F. D., & Blais, M. A. (1998). The effects of DSM–IV cluster B personality disorder symptoms on the termination and continuation of psychotherapy. *Psychotherapy: Theory, Research, Practice, Training, 35*, 163–176.

Høglend, P. (1993a). Suitability for brief dynamic psychotherapy: Psychodynamic variables as predictors of outcome. *Acta Psychiatrica Scandinavica, 88*, 104–110.

Høglend, P. (1993b). Transference interpretations and long-term change after dynamic psychotherapy of brief to moderate length. *American Journal of Psychotherapy, 47*, 494–507.

Horner, M. S., & Diamond, D. (1996). Object relations development and psychotherapy dropout in borderline outpatients. *Psychoanalytic Psychology, 13*, 205–223.

Horowitz, M. J., Marmar, C. R., Weiss, D., DeWitt, K. N., & Rosenbaum, R. (1984). Brief psychotherapy of bereavement reactions: The relationship of process to outcome. *Archives of General Psychiatry, 41*, 438–448.

Hoyt, M. F. (1979). Aspects of termination in a time-limited brief psychotherapy. *Psychiatry, 42*, 208–219.

Hunt, H. C., & Andrews, G. (1992). Drop-out rate as a performance indicator in psychotherapy. *Acta Psychiatrica Scandinavica, 85*, 275–278.

Huprich, S., & Greenberg, R. (2003). Advances in the assessment of object relations in the 1990s. *Clinical Psychology Review, 23*, 665–698.

Hurn, H. (1971). Toward a paradigm of the terminal phase. *Journal of the American Psychoanalytic Association, 19*, 332–348.

Hynan, D. J. (1990). Client reasons and experiences in treatment that influence termination of psychotherapy. *Journal of Clinical Psychology, 46*, 891–895.

Jenkins, S. J., Fuqua, D. R., & Blum, C. R. (1986). Factors related to duration of counseling in a university counseling center. *Psychological Reports, 58*, 467–472.

Joyce, A. S., Duncan, S. C., Duncan, A., Kipnes, D., & Piper, W. E. (1996). Limiting time-unlimited group psychotherapy. *International Journal of Group Psychotherapy, 46*, 61–79.

Joyce, A. S., & McCallum, M. (2004). Assessing patient capacities for therapy: Psychological mindedness and quality of object relations. In D. Charman (Ed.), *Core processes in brief psychodynamic psychotherapy: Advancing effective practice* (pp. 69–100). Mahwah, NJ: Erlbaum.

Kauff, P. F. (1977). The termination process: Its relationship to the separation–individuation phase of development. *International Journal of Group Psychotherapy, 27*, 3–18.

Kernberg, O. (1984). *Severe personality disorders: Psychotherapeutic strategies*. New Haven, CT: Yale University Press.

Kernberg, O. F., Burstein, E., Coyne, L., Applebaum, A., Horowitz, L., & Voth, H. (1972). Psychotherapy and psychoanalysis: Final report of the Menninger Foundation's psychotherapy research project. *Bulletin of the Menninger Clinic, 36*, 1–275.

Klein, R. H. (1979). A model for distinguishing supportive from insight-oriented psychotherapy groups. In G. Lawrence (Ed.), *Exploring individual and organizational boundaries: A Tavistock open systems approach* (pp. 135–151). London: Wiley.

Klein, R. H. (1996). Introduction to the Special Section on termination and group therapy. *International Journal of Group Psychotherapy, 46*, 1–4.

Klein, R. H., & Carroll, R. (1986). Patient sociodemographic characteristics and attendance patterns in outpatient group therapy: I. An overview. *International Journal of Group Psychotherapy, 36*, 115–132.

Klein, R. H., Hunter, D. E. K., & Brown, S.-L. (1986). Long-term inpatient group psychotherapy: The ward group. *International Journal of Group Psychotherapy, 36*, 361–380.

Klein, R. H., & Kugel, B. (1981). Inpatient group psychotherapy from a systems perspective: Reflections through a glass darkly. *International Journal of Group Psychotherapy, 31*, 311–328.

Klein, R. H., & Schermer, V. L. (2000). Introduction and overview: Creating a healing matrix. In R. H. Klein & V. L. Schermer (Eds.), *Group psychotherapy for psychological trauma* (pp. 3–46). New York: Guilford Press.

Klerman, G. L., Weissman, M. M., Rounsaville, B. J., & Chevron E. S. (1984). *Interpersonal psychotherapy of depression*. New York: Basic Books.

Kokotovic, A. M., & Tracey, T. J. (1990). Working alliance in the early phase of counseling. *Journal of Counseling Psychology, 37*, 16–21.

Koran, L., & Costell, R. (1973). Early terminators from group psychotherapy. *International Journal of Group Psychotherapy, 23*, 346–359.

Kramer, S. A. (1986). The termination process in open-ended psychotherapy: Guidelines for clinical practice. *Psychotherapy: Theory, Research, Practice, Training, 23*, 526–531.

Kramer, S. A. (1990). *Positive endings in psychotherapy: Bringing meaningful closure to therapeutic relationships*. San Francisco: Jossey-Bass.

Kübler-Ross, E. (1970). *On death and dying*. London: Tavistock.

Kumpfer, K. L. (1999). Factors and processes contributing to resilience: The resilience framework. In M. D. Glantz & J. L. Johnson (Eds.), *Resilience and development—positive life adaptations: Longitudinal research in the social and behavioral sciences* (pp. 179–224). New York: Kluwer Academic/Plenum Publishers.

Kupers, T. A. (1988). *Ending therapy: The meaning of termination*. New York: New York University Press.

Lamb, D. H. (1985). A time-frame model of termination in psychotherapy. *Psychotherapy: Theory, Research, Practice, Training, 22*, 604–609.

Lambert, M. J. (1992). Psychotherapy outcome research: Implications for integrative and eclectic therapists. In J. C. Norcross & M. R. Goldfried (Eds.), *Handbook of psychotherapy integration* (pp. 94–129). New York: Basic Books.

Langs, R. (1976). *The bipersonal field*. New York: Jason Aronson.

Lanning, W., & Carey, J. (1987). Systematic termination in counseling. *Counselor Education & Supervision, 27*, 168–173.

Levinson, H. L. (1977). Termination of psychotherapy: Some salient issues. *Social Casework, 58*, 480–489.

Levinson, P., McMurray, L., Podell, P., & Weiner, H. (1978). Causes for the premature interruption of psychotherapy by private practice patients. *American Journal of Psychiatry, 135*, 826–830.

Levy, J. (1986). The working through process during the termination of analysis. *Current Issues in Psychoanalytic Practice, 3*, 121–148.

Liegner, E. J. (1986). The question of termination in modern psychoanalysis. *Modern Psychoanalysis, 11*, 5–18.

Lindy, J. D., & Wilson, J. P. (2001). Respecting the trauma membrane: Above all, do no harm. In J. P. Wilson, M. J. Friedman, & J. D. Lindy (Eds.), *Treating psychological trauma and PTSD* (pp. 432–445). New York: Guilford Press.

Lipton, S. (1961). The last hour. *Journal of the American Psychoanalytic Association, 9*, 325–330.

Loewald, H. W. (1988). Termination analyzable and unanalyzable. *Psychoanalytic Study of the Child, 43*, 155–166.

Long, K., Pendleton, L., & Winter, B. (1988). Effects of therapist termination on group process. *International Journal of Group Psychotherapy, 38*, 211–222.

Lothstein, L. M. (1978). The group psychotherapy dropout phenomenon revisited. *American Journal of Psychiatry, 135*, 1492–1495.

Luborsky, L. (1984). *Principles of psychoanalytic psychotherapy: A manual for supportive-expressive treatment*. New York: Basic Books.

Luborsky, L., & Crits-Cristoph, P. (1997). *Understanding transference: The core conflictual relationship theme method* (2nd ed.). Washington, DC: American Psychological Association.

Luborsky, L., Mintz, J., Auerbach, A., Christoph, P., Bachrach, H., Todd, T., et al. (1980). Predicting the outcome of psychotherapy: Findings of the Penn Psychotherapy Project. *Archives of General Psychiatry, 37*, 471–481.

Maar, V. (1989). Attempts at grasping the self during the termination phase of group-analytic psychotherapy. *Group Analysis, 22*, 99–104.

MacKenzie, K. R. (1996). Time-limited group psychotherapy. *International Journal of Group Psychotherapy, 46*, 41–60.

MacKenzie, K. R. (1997). Termination. In K. R. MacKenzie (Ed.), *Time-managed group psychotherapy: Effective clinical applications* (pp. 231–250). Washington, DC: American Psychiatric Press.

MacNair, R. R., & Corazzini, J. G. (1994). Client factors influencing group therapy dropout. *Psychotherapy: Theory, Research, Practice, Training, 31*, 352–362.

Magnavita, J. J. (1994). Premature termination of short-term dynamic psychotherapy. *International Journal of Short-Term Psychotherapy, 9*, 213–228.

Maholick, L. T., & Turner, D. W. (1979). Termination: That difficult farewell. *American Journal of Psychotherapy, 33*, 583–591.

Malan, D. H. (1963). *A study of brief psychotherapy.* New York: Plenum Press.

Malan, D. H. (1976). *The frontier of brief psychotherapy: An example of the convergence of research and clinical practice.* New York: Plenum Press.

Malan, D. H. (1979). *Individual psychotherapy and the science of psychodynamics.* London: Butterworth-Heineman.

Mander, G. (2000). Beginnings, endings and outcome: A comparison of methods and goals. *Psychodynamic Counselling, 6*, 301–317.

Mann, J. (1973). *Time-limited psychotherapy.* Cambridge, MA: Harvard University Press.

Mann, J., & Goldman, R. (1982). *A casebook in time-limited psychotherapy.* New York: McGraw-Hill.

Marini, Z., & Case, R. (1994). The development of abstract reasoning about the physical and social world. *Child Development, 65*, 147–159.

Martin, E. S., & Schurtman, R. (1985). Termination anxiety as it affects the therapist. *Psychotherapy: Theory, Research, Practice, Training, 22*, 92–96.

Martinez, D. (1989). Pains and gains: A study of forced terminations. *Journal of the American Psychoanalytic Association, 37*, 89–115.

Marx, J. A., & Gelso, C. J. (1987). Termination of individual counseling in a university counseling center. *Journal of Counseling Psychology, 34*, 3–9.

Mathews, B. (1989). Terminating therapy: Implications for the private practitioner. *Psychotherapy in Private Practice, 7*, 29–39.

McCallum, M., & Piper, W. E. (1990a). A controlled study of effectiveness and patient suitability for short-term group psychotherapy. *International Journal of Group Psychotherapy, 40*, 431–452.

McCallum, M., & Piper, W. E. (1990b). The psychological mindedness assessment procedure. *Psychological Assessment: A Journal of Consulting and Clinical Psychology, 2*, 412–418.

McCallum, M., & Piper, W. E. (1997a). Integration of psychological mindedness and related concepts. In M. McCallum & W. E. Piper (Eds.), *Psychological mindedness: A contemporary understanding* (pp. 237–258). Mahwah, NJ: Erlbaum.

McCallum, M., & Piper, W. E. (1997b). The psychological mindedness assessment procedure. In M. McCallum & W. E. Piper (Eds.), *Psychological mindedness: A contemporary understanding* (pp. 27–58). Mahwah, NJ: Erlbaum.

McCallum, M., Piper, W. E., Ogrodniczuk, J. S., & Joyce, A. S. (2002). Early process and dropping out from short-term group therapy for complicated grief. *Group Dynamics, 6*, 243–254.

McCallum, M., Piper, W. E., & O'Kelly, J. G. (1997). Predicting patient benefit from a group oriented evening treatment program. *International Journal of Group Psychotherapy, 47*, 291–314.

McGee, T. F. (1974). Therapist termination in group psychotherapy. *International Journal of Group Psychotherapy, 24*, 3–12.

Meyer, B., Pilkonis, P. A., Proietti, J. M., Heape, C. L., & Egan, M. (2001). Adult attachment styles, personality disorders, and response to treatment. *Journal of Personality Disorders, 15*, 371–389.

Mikkelsen, E. J., & Gutheil, T. G. (1979). Stages of forced termination: Uses of the death metaphor. *Psychiatric Quarterly, 51*, 15–27.

Miller, M. M., Courtois, C. A., Pelham, J. P., Riddle, P. E., Spiegel, S. B., Gelso, C. J., & Johnson, D. H. (1983). The process of time-limited therapy. In C. J. Gelso & D. H. Johnson (Eds.), *Exploration in time-limited counseling and psychotherapy*. New York: Teachers College Press.

Misch, D. A. (2000). Basic strategies of dynamic supportive therapy. *Journal of Psychotherapy Practice and Research, 9*, 173–189.

Mohl, P. C., Martinez, D., Ticknor, C., Huang, M., & Cordell, L. (1991). Early dropouts from psychotherapy. *Journal of Nervous and Mental Disease, 179*, 478–481.

Moras, K., & Strupp, H. (1982). Pretherapy interpersonal relations, client's alliance, and outcome in brief therapy. *Archives of General Psychiatry, 39*, 405–409.

Mozgai, A. (1985). Termination of psychotherapy: Potential problems for patient and therapist. *Carrier Foundation Letter, 111*, 1–4.

Murdin, L. (2000). *How much is enough? Endings in psychotherapy and counselling*. New York: Routledge.

Nelson, W. M., III, & Politano, P. M. (1993). The goal is to say "goodbye" and have the treatment effects generalize and maintain: A cognitive–behavioural view of termination. *Journal of Cognitive Psychotherapy: An International Quarterly, 7*, 251–263.

Novick, J. (1982). Termination: Themes and issues. *Psychoanalytic Inquiry, 2*, 329–365.

Novick, J. (1988). The timing of termination. *International Review of Psycho-Analysis, 15*, 307–318.

Noy-Sharav, D. (1998). Who is afraid of STDP? Termination in STDP and the therapist's personality. *Psychotherapy: Theory, Research, Practice, Training, 35*, 69–77.

Oei, T. P. S., & Kazmierczak, T. (1997). Factors associated with dropout in a group cognitive behaviour therapy for mood disorders. *Behaviour Therapy and Research, 11*, 1025–1030.

Ogrodniczuk, J. S., Piper, W. E., & Joyce, A. S. (2005). The negative effect of alexithymia on the outcome of group therapy for complicated grief: What role might the therapist play? *Comprehensive Psychiatry, 46*, 206–213.

Ogrodniczuk, J. S., Piper, W. E., Joyce, A. S., & McCallum, M. (1999). Transference interpretations in short-term dynamic psychotherapy. *Journal of Nervous and Mental Disease, 187*, 572–579.

O'Malley, S. S., Suh, C. S., & Strupp, H. H. (1983). The Vanderbilt Psychotherapy Process Scale: A report on the scale development and a process-outcome study. *Journal of Consulting and Clinical Psychology, 51*, 581–586.

Palombo, J. (1982). The psychology of the self and the termination of treatment. *Clinical Social Work Journal, 10*, 15–27.

Park, L. C., Imboden, J. B., Park, T. J., Hulse, S. H., & Unger, H. T. (1992). Giftedness and psychological abuse in borderline personality disorder: Their relevance to genesis and treatment. *Journal of Personality Disorders, 6*, 226–240.

Parsons, M. (1982). Imposed termination of psychotherapy and its relation to death and mourning. *British Journal of Medical Psychology, 55*, 35–40.

Pearson, Q. M. (1998). Termination before counseling has ended: Counseling implications and strategies for counselor relocation. *Journal of Mental Health Counseling, 20*, 1955–1963.

Pedder, J. R. (1988). Termination reconsidered. *International Journal of Psycho-Analysis, 69*, 495–505.

Pekarik, G. (1992). Relationship of client's reasons for dropping out of treatment to outcome and satisfaction. *Journal of Clinical Psychology, 48*, 91–98.

Persons, J. B., Burns, D. D., & Perloff, J. M. (1988). Predictors of dropout and outcome in cognitive therapy for depression in a private practice setting. *Cognitive Therapy and Research, 12*, 557–575.

Peternel, F. (1991). The ending of a psychotherapy group. *Group Analysis, 24*, 159–169.

Pfeffer, A. (1963). Analysis terminable and interminable—twenty-five years later [Panel report]. *Journal of the American Psychoanalytic Association, 11*, 131–142.

Pinkerton, R. S., & Rockwell, W. J. K. (1990). Termination in brief psychotherapy: The case for an eclectic approach. *Psychotherapy: Theory, Research, Practice, Training, 27*, 362–365.

Pinsker, H. (1997). *A primer of supportive psychotherapy.* Hillsdale, NJ: The Analytic Press.

Piper, W. E., Azim, H. F. A., Joyce, A. S., & McCallum, M. (1991). Transference interpretations, therapeutic alliance, and outcome in short-term individual psychotherapy. *Archives of General Psychiatry, 48*, 946–953.

Piper, W. E., Azim, H. F. A., Joyce, A. S., McCallum, M., Nixon, G. W. H., & Segal, P. S. (1991). Quality of object relations vs. interpersonal functioning as predictors of therapeutic alliance and psychotherapy outcome. *Journal of Nervous and Mental Disease, 179*, 432–438.

Piper, W. E., Azim, H. F. A., McCallum, M., & Joyce, A. S. (1990). Patient suitability and outcome in short-term individual psychotherapy. *Journal of Consulting and Clinical Psychology, 58*, 475–481.

Piper, W. E., de Carufel, F. L., & Szkrumelak, N. (1985). Patient predictors of process and outcome in short-term individual psychotherapy. *Journal of Nervous and Mental Disease, 173*, 726–733.

Piper, W. E., & Duncan, S. C. (1999). Object relations theory and short-term dynamic psychotherapy: Findings from the Quality of Object Relations scale. *Clinical Psychology Review, 19*, 669–685.

Piper, W. E., Joyce, A. S., Azim, H. F. A., & Rosie, J. S. (1994). Patient characteristics and success in day treatment. *Journal of Nervous and Mental Disease, 182*, 381–386.

Piper, W. E., Joyce, A. S., McCallum, M., & Azim, H. F. A. (1998). Interpretive and supportive forms of psychotherapy and patient personality variables. *Journal of Consulting and Clinical Psychology, 66*, 558–567.

Piper, W. E., Joyce, A. S., McCallum, M., Azim, H. F. A., & Ogrodniczuk, J. S. (2002). *Interpretive and supportive psychotherapies: Matching therapy and patient personality*. Washington, DC: American Psychological Association.

Piper, W. E., McCallum, M., & Azim, H. F. A. (1992). *Adaptation to loss through short-term group psychotherapy*. New York: Guilford Press.

Piper, W. E., McCallum, M., & Joyce, A. S. (1996). *Manual for assessment of quality of object relations*. Unpublished manuscript.

Piper, W. E., McCallum, M., Joyce, A. S., Rosie, J. S., & Ogrodniczuk, J. S. (2001). Patient personality and time-limited group psychotherapy for complicated grief. *International Journal of Group Psychotherapy, 51*, 525–552.

Piper, W. E., Ogrodniczuk, J. S., Joyce, A. S., McCallum, M., Rosie, J. S., O'Kelly, J. G., & Steinberg, P. I. (1999). Prediction of dropping out in time-limited, interpretive individual psychotherapy. *Psychotherapy: Theory, Research, Practice, Training, 36*, 114–122.

Piper, W. E., Rosie, J. S., Azim, H. F. A., & Joyce, A. S. (1993). A randomized trial of psychiatric day treatment. *Hospital and Community Psychiatry, 44*, 757–763.

Pipes, R. B., & Davenport, D. S. (1999). *Introduction to psychotherapy: Common clinical wisdom* (2nd ed., pp. 328–342). Boston: Allyn and Bacon.

Pistole, M. C. (1991). Termination: Analytic reflections on client contact after counsellor relocation. *Journal of Counseling and Development, 69*, 337–340.

Prochaska, J., & DiClemente, C. (1982). Transtheoretical therapy: Toward a more integrative model of change. *Psychotherapy: Theory, Research, Practice, Training, 19*, 276–288.

Prochaska, J., & DiClemente, C. (1984). *The transtheoretical approach: Crossing the traditional boundaries of therapy*. Homewood, IL: Dow Jones Irwin.

Prochaska, J., & DiClemente, C. (1992). Stages of change in the modification of problem behaviors. In M. Hersen, R. M. Eisler, & P. M. Miller (Eds.), *Progress in behavior modification* (Vol. 28, pp. 184–214). Syracuse, IL: Syracuse Publication.

Prochaska, J., Norcross, J., & DiClemente, C. (1994). *Changing for the good*. New York: Morrow.

Quintana, S. M. (1993). Toward an expanded and updated conceptualization of termination: Implications for short-term, individual psychotherapy. *Professional Psychology: Research and Practice, 24*, 426–432.

Quintana, S. M., & Holahan, W. (1992). Termination in short-term counseling: Comparison of successful and unsuccessful cases. *Journal of Counseling Psychology, 39*, 299–305.

Quintana, S. M., & Meara, N. M. (1990). Internalization of therapeutic relationships. *Journal of Counseling Psychology, 37*, 123–130.

Quintar, B. (2001). Termination phase. *Journal of Psychotherapy in Independent Practice, 2*, 43–60.

Rainer, J. P., & Campbell, L. F. (2001). Premature termination in psychotherapy: Identification and intervention. *Journal of Psychotherapy in Independent Practice, 2*, 19–41.

Rangell, L. (1966). An overview of the ending of an analysis. In R. E. Litman (Ed.), *Psychoanalysis in the Americas* (pp. 141–165). New York: International Universities Press.

Reid, W. H. (1980). *Basic intensive psychotherapy*. New York: Brunner/Mazel.

Reis, B. F., & Brown, L. G. (1999). Reducing psychotherapy dropouts: Maximizing perspective convergence in the psychotherapy dyad. *Psychotherapy: Theory, Research, Practice, Training, 36*, 123–136.

Rice, C. A. (1996). Premature termination of group therapy: A clinical perspective. *International Journal of Group Psychotherapy, 46*, 5–23.

Roback, H. B. (2000). Adverse outcomes in group psychotherapy: Risk factors, prevention, and research directions. *Journal of Psychotherapy Practice and Research, 9*, 113–122.

Roback, H. B., & Smith, M. (1987). Patient attrition in dynamically oriented treatment groups. *American Journal of Psychiatry, 144*, 426–431.

Robbins, W. S. (1975). Termination: Problems and techniques [Panel report]. *Journal of the American Psychoanalytic Association, 23*, 166–176.

Rockland, L. H. (1989). *Supportive therapy: A psychodynamic approach*. New York: Basic Books.

Rockland, L. H. (1992). *Supportive therapy for borderline patients: A psychodynamic approach*. New York: Guilford Press.

Rosenthal, L. (1998). Clinical observations on premature termination in group analysis. *Modern Psychoanalysis, 23*, 145–157.

Ruderman, E. G. (1999). The patient, the analyst, the termination phase: Transference and countertransference considerations. In J. Edward & E. Rose (Eds.), *The social work psychoanalyst's casebook: Clinical voices in honor of Jean Sanville* (pp. 185–202). Los Angeles: Institute of Contemporary Psychoanalysis.

Rutan, J. S., & Stone, W. N. (2001). Termination in group psychotherapy. In J. S. Rutan & W. N. Stone (Eds.), *Psychodynamic group psychotherapy* (3rd ed., pp. 332–354). New York: Guilford Press.

Safran, J. D., & Segal, L. S. (1990). *Interpersonal process in cognitive therapy*. New York: Basic Books.

Sansone, R. A., Fine, M. A., & Dennis, A. B. (1991). Treatment impressions and termination experiences with borderline patients. *American Journal of Psychotherapy, 45*, 173–180.

Satterfield, W. A., & Lyddon, W. J. (1998). Client attachment and the working alliance. *Counseling Psychology Quarterly, 11*, 407–415.

Schafer, R. (1973). The termination of brief psychoanalytic psychotherapy. *International Journal of Psychoanalytic Psychotherapy, 2*, 135–148.

Schafer, R. (2002). Experiencing termination: Authentic and false depressive positions. *Psychoanalytic Psychology, 19*, 235–253.

Schermer, V., & Klein, R. (1996). Termination in group psychotherapy from the perspectives of contemporary object relations theory and self psychology. *International Journal of Group Psychotherapy, 46*, 99–116.

Schubert, J. (2000). Give sorrow words: Mourning at termination of psychoanalysis. *Scandinavian Psychoanalytic Review, 23*, 105–117.

Scogin, F., Belon, H., & Malone, M. (1986). Mental health services in a rural clinic: A retrospective study of length of stay and premature termination in psychotherapy. *Journal of Rural Community Psychology, 7*, 35–44.

Shane, M., & Shane, E. (1984). The end phase of analysis: Indicators, functions, and tasks of termination. *Journal of the American Psychoanalytic Association, 32*, 739–772.

Shapiro, E. L., & Ginzberg, R. (2002). Parting gifts: Termination rituals in group therapy. *International Journal of Group Psychotherapy, 52*, 319–336.

Shea, T. M., Widiger, T. A., & Klein, M. H. (1992). Comorbidity of personality disorders and depression: Implications for treatment. *Journal of Consulting and Clinical Psychology, 60*, 857–868.

Shechter, R. A. (1993). Termination fantasy: Transference and countertransference in the ending phase of treatment. *Issues in Psychoanalytic Psychology, 15*, 146–157.

Sifneos, P. E. (1972). *Short-term psychotherapy and emotional crisis.* Cambridge, MA: Harvard University Press.

Sifneos, P. E. (1979). *Short-term psychotherapy: Evaluation and technique.* New York: Plenum Press.

Skodol, A. E., Buckley, P., & Charles, E. (1983). Is there a characteristic pattern to the treatment history of clinic outpatients with borderline personality? *Journal of Nervous and Mental Disease, 171*, 405–410.

Sledge, W. H., Moras, K., Hartley, D., & Levine, M. (1990). Effect of time-limited psychotherapy on patient dropout rates. *American Journal of Psychiatry, 147*, 1341–1347.

Smith, K. J., Subich, L. M., & Kalodner, C. (1995). The transtheoretical model's stages and processes of change and their relation to premature termination. *Journal of Counseling Psychology, 42*, 34–39.

Smith, S. (1982–1983). Interrupted treatment and forced terminations. *International Journal of Psychoanalytic Psychotherapy, 9*, 337–352.

Smith, T. E., Koenigsberg, H. W., Yeomans, F. E., Clarkin, J. F., & Selzer, M. A. (1995). Predictors of dropout in psychodynamic psychotherapy for borderline personality disorder. *Journal of Psychotherapy Practice and Research, 4*, 205–213.

Stein, H., Fonagy, P., Ferguson, K. S., & Wisman, M. (2000). Lives through time: An ideographic approach to the study of resilience. *Bulletin of the Menninger Clinic, 64*, 281–305.

Steiner, A. (2002). *Preparing your clients and yourself for the unexpected: Therapist illness, retirement, and death.* Retrieved October 20, 2003, from http://psychotherapistresources.com/current/cgi/framemaker.cgi?mainframe=articles&subframe=absence

Stevenson, J., & Meares, R. (1992). An outcome study of psychotherapy for patients with borderline personality disorder. *American Journal of Psychiatry, 149*, 358–362.

Stewart, H. (1972). Six-months, fixed-term, once weekly psychotherapy: A report on 20 cases with follow-ups. *British Journal of Psychiatry, 121*, 425–435.

Stone, W. N. (2005). Saying goodbye: Exploring attachments as a therapist leaves a group of chronically ill persons. *International Journal of Group Psychotherapy, 55*, 281–303.

Strupp, H. H., & Binder, J. L. (1984). *Psychotherapy in a new key: A guide to time-limited dynamic psychotherapy.* New York: Basic Books.

Tapper, C. M. (1994). Unilateral termination of treatment by a psychiatrist. Guidelines of the Canadian Psychiatric Association. *Canadian Journal of Psychiatry, 39*, 2–7.

Taube, C. A., Goldman, H. H., Burns, B. J., & Kessler, L. G. (1988). High users of outpatient mental health services: I. Definition and characteristics. *American Journal of Psychiatry, 145*, 19–24.

Taylor, G. J. (1984). Alexithymia: Concept, measurement, and implications for treatment. *American Journal of Psychiatry, 141*, 725–732.

Ticho, E. A. (1972). Termination of psychoanalysis: Treatment goals, life goals. *Psychoanalytic Quarterly, 41*, 315–333.

Tolpin, M. (2002). Doing psychoanalysis of normal development: Forward edge transferences. In A. Goldberg (Ed.), *Progress in self psychology: Postmodern self psychology* (Vol. 18, pp. 167–190). Hillsdale, NJ: Analytic Press.

Tracey, T. J. (1986). Interactional correlates of premature termination. *Journal of Consulting and Clinical Psychology, 54*, 784–788.

Tracey, T. J. (1988). Relationship of responsibility attribution congruence to psychotherapy outcome. *Journal of Social and Clinical Psychology, 7*, 131–146.

Tryon, G. S., & Kane, A. S. (1990). The helping alliance and premature termination. *Counseling Psychology Quarterly, 5*, 233–238.

Tyson, P. (1996). Termination of psychoanalysis and psychotherapy. In E. E. Nersessian & R. G. Kopff Jr. (Eds.), *Textbook of psychoanalysis* (pp. 501–524). Washington, DC: American Psychiatric Association.

Usher, S. F. (1999). *Introduction to psychodynamic psychotherapy technique*. New York: International Universities Press.

Viorst, J. (1982). Experiences of loss at the end of analysis: The analyst's response to termination. *Psychoanalytic Inquiry, 2*, 399–418.

Waldinger, R., & Gunderson, J. G. (1984). Completed psychotherapies with borderline patients. *American Journal of Psychotherapy, 38*, 190–202.

Ward, D. E. (1984). Termination of individual counseling: Concepts and strategies. *Journal of Counseling and Development, 63*, 21–25.

Weber, J. J., Bachrach, H. M., & Solomon, M. (1985). Factors associated with the outcome of psychoanalysis: Report of the Columbia Psychoanalytic Center Research Project: II. *International Review of Psycho-Analysis, 12*, 127–141.

Weddington, W. W., Jr., & Cavenar, J. O., Jr. (1979). Termination initiated by the therapist: A countertransference storm. *American Journal of Psychiatry, 136*, 1302–1305.

Weiner, I. B. (1975). *Principles of psychotherapy*. New York: Wiley.

Weissman, M. M., Markowitz, J. C., & Klerman, G. L. (2000). *Comprehensive guide to interpersonal therapy*. New York: Basic Books.

Werbart, A. (1997). Separation, termination process and long-term outcome in psychotherapy with severely disturbed patients. *Bulletin of the Menninger Clinic, 61*, 16–43.

Werman, D. S. (1984). *The practice of supportive psychotherapy*. New York: Brunner/Mazel.

Westen, D. (1991). Social cognition and object relations. *Psychological Bulletin, 109*, 429–455.

Wierzbicki, M., & Pekarik, G. (1993). A meta-analysis of psychotherapy dropout. *Professional Psychology: Research and Practice, 24*, 190–195.

Wilfley, D. E., MacKenzie, K. R., Welch, R. R., Ayres, V. E., & Weissman, M. M. (2000). *Interpersonal psychotherapy for group*. New York: Basic Books.

Winnicott, D. W. (1969). *Playing and reality*. New York: Basic Books.

Wolberg, L. S. (1980). *Handbook of short-term psychotherapy*. New York: Thieme-Stratton.

Yeomans, F. E., Clarkin, J. E., & Kernberg, O. F. (2002). *A primer of transference focused psychotherapy for the borderline patient*. Northvale, NJ: Jason Aronson.

Yeomans, F. E., Selzer, M., & Clarkin, J. (1993). Studying the treatment contract in intensive psychotherapy with borderline patients. *Psychiatry, 56*, 254–263.

Zahourek, R. P., & Crawford, C. M. (1978). Forced termination of psychotherapy. *Perspectives in Psychiatric Care, 16*, 193–199.

Zinkin, L. (1994). All's well that ends well. Or is it? *Group Analysis, 27*, 15–24.

AUTHOR INDEX

Klein, M. H., 125
Klein, R., ix, 6, 20, 21, 60, 135
Klerman, G. L., 82, 85, 92
Kobos, J. C., 15, 16, 101
Koenigsberg, H. W., 114
Koetting, M. G., 161
Kokotovic, A. M., 144
Koran, L., 155
Kramer, S. A., x, 6, 7, 12, 25, 27, 28, 32, 47, 50, 52, 53, 55, 60, 67, 69, 74, 75, 168
Kubler-Ross, E., 159
Kugel, B., 21
Kumpfer, K. L., 115
Kupers, T. A., x, 6, 11–13, 15, 20, 27, 29, 66, 67, 73

Lamb, D. H., 25, 33, 62, 64
Lambert, M. J., 109
Lane, R. C., 6, 24, 27, 62, 63, 68, 76, 160, 161, 164
Langs, R., 159
Lanning, W., 46, 58, 59, 61, 63
Levine, M., 136
Levinson, H. L., 55, 58, 60, 64, 65, 70, 74
Levinson, P., 27
Levy, J., 46, 51, 73
Levy, K. N., 109, 110, 121, 125, 126
Liegner, E. J., 45, 48, 69, 111, 125
Lindy, J. D., 125
Lipton, S., 46, 58
Loewald, H. W., 41, 42, 50, 62, 63
Long, K., 160, 161, 163
Lothstein, L. M., 143, 148
Luborsky, L., 15, 115, 119, 125, 143
Lundwall, L., 135, 142
Lyddon, W. J., 121

Maar, V., 69
MacGlashan, S. G., 27
MacKenzie, K. R., 18, 82, 103
MacNair, R. R., 138, 140
Magnavita, J. J., 141
Maholick, L. T., 24, 38, 48
Malan, D., 118
Malan, D. H., 15–17, 24
Malone, M., 141
Mander, G., 53
Mann, J., 15, 17, 35, 71, 100, 101
Marini, Z., 115
Markowitz, J. C., 85
Marmar, C. R., 120

Martin, E. S., 5, 24, 69
Martinez, D., 144, 159, 162
Marx, J. A., 17, 38, 54, 63
Marziali, E., 127
Mathews, B., 70
McCallum, M., ix, x, 103–105, 115, 116, 118–120, 141, 148
McGee, T. F., 162
McMurray, L., 27
Meara, N. M., 28, 72, 169
Meyer, B., 121
Mikkelsen, E. J., 163, 164
Miller, M. M., 17, 19
Misch, D. A., 86
Mohl, P. C., 144
Moras, K., 111, 118, 135
Morrow, G. R., 134
Mozgai, A., 24
Munroe-Blum, H., 127
Murdin, L., 50, 51, 54, 58, 61, 63, 64, 76

Nelson, W. M., III, 85, 86, 90, 94, 101
Newman, A. E., 113, 114
Nixon, G. W. H., 105
Norcross, J., 137
Novick, J., 29, 73
Noy-Sharav, D., 16, 71, 100

Oei, T. P. S., 148
Ogrodniczuk, J. S., ix, 104, 116, 120, 141, 143, 148
O'Kelly, J. G., 116
O'Malley, S. S., 112

Padawer, J. R., 139
Palombo, J., 18, 19, 24, 32
Park, L. C., 115
Park, T. J., 115
Parsons, M., 159, 162
Pearson, Q. M., 162–164
Pedder, J. R., 30
Pekarik, G., 134–137
Pendleton, L., 160
Perloff, J. M., 136
Persons, J. B., 136
Peternel, F., 27
Pfeffer, A., 6, 30
Pilkonis, P. A., 114, 121
Pinkerton, R. S., 18, 19
Pinsker, H., 86, 87, 94
Piper, W. E., ix–xi, 20, 103–105, 115, 116, 119–120, 141, 143, 144, 148, 170

Weatherill, R., 139
Weber, J. J., 115
Weddington, W. W., Jr., 68, 161
Wein, S., 117
Weiner, H., 27
Weiner, I. B., 32
Weiss, D., 120
Weissman, M. M., 82, 85, 88
Welch, R. R., 82
Werbart, A., 67
Werman, D. S., 82, 90, 94
Westen, D., 119
Widiger, T. A., 125
Wierzbicki, M., 135–137

Wild, C., 117
Wilfley, D. E., 82, 85, 88, 92
Wilson, J. P., 125
Winnicott, D. W., 159
Winter, B., 160
Wiseman, H., 117, 169
Wisman, M., 115
Wolberg, L. S., 16, 38

Yeomans, F. E., 114, 129, 130

Zahourek, R. P., 159, 161
Zinkin, L., 9

SUBJECT INDEX

Internalization process, 28–29, 47, 71–73, 126

International Journal of Psycho-Analysis, 13, 30

Interpersonal feedback, 147

Interpersonal functioning, 139–140

Interpersonal style, 118–120

Interpersonal therapy, 82
    preparedness for maintaining healthy functioning in, 92, 93
    reinforcement/consolidation of therapy in, 83–85
    resolution of therapeutic relationship issues in, 88, 89

Introjective configuration, anaclitic vs., 117–118

Invitation to return to therapy, 74

Issues stimulated by termination, 25

Journal of the American Psychoanalytic Association, 30

Klein, R., 60

Kobos, J. C., 16

Koran, L., 155–156

Kramer, S. A., 47, 53, 69

Kübler-Ross, E, 159, 160, 164

Kupers, T. A., 29, 66–67

Late working phase, 42, 44–47
    autonomy/dependency issues in, 42, 44
    balanced appraisal during, 47
    changes in therapy process/relationship during, 45–46
    characteristics of, 44–45
    internalization during, 47
    summing-up process during, 46
    therapist's conduct of termination, principles for, 46–47

Levinson, H. L., 70

Liegner, E. J., 45–46, 69–70, 125, 129

Lindy, J. D., 125

Lipton, S., 46

Loewald, H. W., 50

Long-term therapy, 98

Loss. *See also* Separation and loss
    and grief. *See* Complicated grief
    termination as, 37–38
    of therapy enterprise/therapy relationship, 27

Low cohesion, 147

Low socioeconomic status, 146

MacGlashan, S. G., 27

MacKenzie, K. R., 103

Maholick, L. T., 48

Malan, D. H., 16, 17

Mann, James, 15, 100–101

Marx, J. A., 54

Mastery of problems, 23

Maternal transference, 65–66

Measures of termination outcomes, 168–169

Menninger Psychotherapy Project, 115

Mistrust, 113–114

Motivation, 111–112

Mourning, 62–63, 159

Murdin, L., 54

National Institute of Mental Health, 136

Natural emergence of termination, 23–24

Negotiation, treatment, 150–151

Neurotic patterns, 53–54

New issues, introduction of, 58

Noncompliance, 142

Nontransference interventions, 162

Object loss, 25, 37

Oedipal wishes, 66

Open-ended psychotherapy, 19–20

Open groups, 99

Orientations of therapy, 81–96
    and preparedness for maintaining healthy functioning, 91–95
    and reinforcement/consolidation of therapy, 83–87
    and resolution of issues in therapeutic relationship, 87–91

Outcomes of termination, 26–30, 54–74, 168
    countertransference issues, 68–71
    criteria for termination vs., 30–33
    forced-termination issues, 60–61
    internalization process, 28–29
    measures of, 168–169
    objectives/session content/process/strategies for, 56–57
    preparedness for maintaining healthy functioning, 57, 71–73
    reinforcement/consolidation, 27, 55, 56, 58–59
    resolution of issues in therapeutic relationship, 27–28, 56–57, 59–60
    separation/loss issues, 61–64

Transference, 27, 28, 65–68
    decreased distortions in, 32
    patterns of, 66–67
Transference interventions, 162
Transfer issue, 58
Transformation, termination as, 38–39
Transtheoretical model of change, 112
Trauma disorders, 124–125
Treatment approach factors in termination,
    35–36
Treatment negotiation, 150–151
Treatment outcomes, 29, 30
Tripartite analysis, 14
Turner, D. W., 48

Understandable elements of termination, 22

Voyeurism, 70

Wait-list length, 141–142
Ward, D. E., 48–60
Wills, professional, 164
Wilson, J. P., 125
Wolberg, L. S., 16

Yeomans, F. E., 130

Zinkin, L., 9

ABOUT THE AUTHORS

Anthony S. Joyce, PhD, is professor and coordinator of the Psychotherapy Research and Evaluation Unit in the Department of Psychiatry at the University of Alberta in Edmonton, Alberta, Canada. An advocate of the scientist–practitioner model for psychologists, he also functions as a clinician in the department's outpatient service. His research interests include clarifying the process of change in individual and group psychotherapy and developing effective treatments for patients with personality disorders. He contributes regularly to the psychotherapy literature and has coauthored two previous books.

William E. Piper, PhD, is professor, head of the Division of Behavioural Science, and director of the psychotherapy program in the Department of Psychiatry at the University of British Columbia in Vancouver, British Columbia, Canada. His primary research interests include process and outcome investigations for both individual and group psychotherapies. He has been the recipient of many research grants and has published over 160 journal articles and book chapters as well as 4 previous books. He is a past editor of the *International Journal of Group Psychotherapy*.

John S. Ogrodniczuk, PhD, is assistant professor and associate director (research) of the psychotherapy program in the Department of Psychiatry at the University of British Columbia in Vancouver, British Columbia, Canada. His research interests include the relationships among patient characteristics, therapy process patterns believed to mediate change, and multidimensional outcomes. His research has involved a variety of psychotherapies and patient populations, and he has received support as a New Investigator by the Canadian Institutes of Health Research. He is also a recipient of the

Outstanding Early Career Achievement Award presented by the Society for Psychotherapy Research.

Robert H. Klein, PhD, is clinical associate professor of psychiatry at the Yale School of Medicine in New Haven, Connecticut. He is a fellow of the American Psychological Association, past president of the American Group Psychotherapy Association (AGPA), and a life fellow of AGPA. Following 9/11, he served as the cochair of the AGPA Disaster Outreach Task Force. A recognized expert in the area of group psychotherapy, he lectures, consults, and supervises both nationally and internationally. He is the author of numerous publications and a coeditor of *Group Psychotherapy for Psychological Trauma* and *Handbook of Contemporary Group Psychotherapy*. Dr. Klein maintains a private clinical practice with offices in Westport and Milford, Connecticut.